"While reading your personal story, my heart soared with yours on that mountain top. I worried when Rick was sick. My memory raced back with yours as you mourned the loss of your friends and your place among your peers. I cried with you on those nights you cried yourself to sleep. My foot twitched with yours while you were sitting on that couch. My breath was held with all those students while waiting for your mentor to comment on your mission. You **do** make people feel it. You do make them taste, see, and smell it. You make it so real."

—Merijane Bench, mother of six

"The night I sat down to begin reading your introductory chapters, it was already 10:30 p.m. I thought I would at least get started with it—at the most spend half an hour. Quite unexpectedly it 'grabbed' me and at 1:00 a.m. I finished it. When I went to bed I was alert and in deep thought. It led me to believe that if I follow these steps I will in fact have success in fulfilling my mission. Your stories portray real life difficulties and struggles with The Path and how you overcame them—showing the reader just what a mentor/mentee relationship looks and feels like. It is like seeing video clips of your experiences."

—Angela Baker, mother of seven

THE Student Whisperer

INSPIRING ⌐ GENIUS

Oliver DeMille

Tiffany Earl

www.TJEdOnline.com

An Education to Match Our Mission

Published March 1, 2011 by TJEdOnline
in the United States of America.

ISBN 978-0-9830996-1-1

Contents

Introduction 6

Book One

1 Mentors 20
2 Beginnings 49
3 Depth 73
4 Life 118
5 Freedom 149

Book Two

6 Student Whispering. 168
7 Seven Mentors. 180
8 Trail Blazers. 185
9 The Path 193
10 Whispering I: A Whispering Language Lesson 215
11 Whispering II: The Whisperer's Dance 226
12 Whispering III: Seven Questions 247
13 Whispering IV: Inspiring Archetypes 258
14 Getting the Most from Your Mentors 265
15 The Art of Mentoring. 271
16 Spirals. 281

Appendices

I: Student Whispering Questions 290
II: A Student Whisperer's Guide 292
III: The Student Whisperer's Creed. 293
Endnotes. 295
About the Authors 300

Introduction

by Oliver DeMille

I stood in line for lunch at a large conference in Virginia where I had been a speaker earlier in the day. As I waited, I found myself conversing with a gentlemen and his wife. She let me know that he had come under duress—that she had been trying to get him to come hear me speak for several years. She had been trying to convince him to support the idea of Leadership Education for their children for even longer. As I recall, the man (an executive at a major international firm) had resisted because he felt that their schools were doing a fine job—and he was busy with his career and other community and family responsibilities.

"But as I listened to you today," he said, "I saw what my wife has been trying to tell me. Our children have so much potential, and with just a few minor adjustments we can help them do so much better in school and career preparation."

I wondered if he realized how "*not*-minor" some of the adjustments might be, but I didn't contradict him. I asked, "What is your first step going to be?"

He warmed up to the conversation even more at this point, saying, "Actually, I was hoping to get a chance to visit with you. Would it be okay if I gave you a suggestion? It's just an observation that I think might help those who attend your speeches."

"I'd love it," I said as I pulled out some note cards and a pen to capture the moment.

"Well," he said, "In my work my main role includes helping business leaders clarify their core strategic advantage, and focus on those few things that make everything else flourish." He explained more about how he did this.

"Yes..." I jotted down the ideas in my notebook: *Core competency, strategic advantage, and critical catalysts—the things that make everything else flourish...*

"It seems to me that great education, what you call Leadership Education, all hinges on one thing," he paused. "If the mentor is inspiring—really inspiring—it all works. If not, it doesn't."

"That's right," I said, "In fact, that's actually true in all education because..." I stopped, because I could see that he hadn't finished making his point.

"So my suggestion is this: If you really want to help all these people adopt quality leadership education, you need to find a way to teach us all *how to inspire*. If we become inspiring mentors, this will work.

"But if we aren't inspiring mentors, *nothing* else will work—no matter how closely we follow the guidelines of quality education, and no matter how hard we try. Inspiring is the critical element of great education and all successful learning."

The Lineage of Mentors

Aristotle and Alexander the Great. Bach and Mozart. Wythe and Jefferson. The great narrative of history and the pinnacles of human achievement can be chronicled through a lineage of mentors and their protégées. Great mentoring has been around for a very, very long time, but it is too often practiced only by the few—those truly great teachers and leaders who, either by innate gift or long experience, know how to get the very best out of others and help each of us achieve our highest potential. We have reached a point in history where every student needs such parents and teachers. We need help to become such leaders and to catch and pass on a vision of greatness and a cause worth living for.

We can't pass on vision without mentoring. We can tell stories, and a few people might listen. We can take bold actions, and some people might admire us, or even try to follow our example. But to really pass on vision we must mentor protégés over a period of time.

Are you destined to be a mentor? Do you have a vision that matters?

Not all of your students will catch your vision, and a few people you don't personally mentor *will* catch your vision, but if you're not actively mentoring over a long period of time, your vision probably won't get passed on. If your vision is important, you need a mentor—and you need to *be a mentor.*

This book is designed to help you become a *great* mentor—a true Student Whisperer and leader at the highest level. It will also help you work effectively with such mentors as you pursue your goals and life mission. This book is part deep teaching of the vital principles of great Leadership Education, part self-help workshop, part example through parables, and part exploration of the great ideas that make mentoring and quality learning most effective at all ages.

What, Exactly, is a Student Whisperer?

Defining great mentoring sometimes feels like trying to tell someone what salt tastes like, or how love feels. It is not easily articulated or explained to people who haven't encountered it, but we know it when we experience it.

The story of our mentors is the story of our lives; and the lineage of the mentors is the story of our generation—even our civilization. Fortunately, somewhere along the line, virtually all of us have experienced great mentoring—a time when we fell deeply in love with learning, or felt highly inspired to exceed ourselves or do hard things. Think of a time you had such an experience: Perhaps a person inspired you, or an event, a movie, a story, a piece of music, or something else. It can come in many forms. That feeling, that experience of wanting to change, to be better, to...*whatever* it was you felt—is what Student Whispering is all about.

Neither by Force Nor Chance

Perhaps silver bells and cockleshells worked for contrary Miss Mary, but master gardeners do not "make" their gardens grow. And yet it is clearly not by chance or accident that they succeed. They understand the principles that govern their success, and they know their role in the process. Whether explicitly or intuitively, they understand natural law and they orchestrate circumstances to cooperate with it for an optimal crop.

While it is possible to "cheat" Mother Nature in order to achieve a more uniform and marketable harvest, it just so happens that vegetables cultivated in an environment of pesticides, herbicides, chemical fertilizers, preservatives and lengthy storage in unnatural conditions usually don't taste as good or have the same nutritional density as those lovingly raised by the master gardener in rich soil. Those superficially "beautiful" vegetables with such a long shelf life and lovely, predictable shape and color are often not even able to reproduce. One might ponder long to consider all the layers of meaning in such a comparison.

Like a master gardener, a great mentor knows how to set the stage for transformational experiences—as often as they are needed. She knows how to create the environment where such feelings and experiences are frequent, how to use such experiences to help us discover and improve ourselves, and even how to repeat and reinforce such feelings so that our motivation and efforts are sustained. A great mentor cares—and she is effective.

Three Levels of Mentoring

Students set out to learn by listening, studying, memorizing, applying and by utilizing these and other techniques to acquire and use knowledge profitably in their lives. Indeed, learning is a pre-level of mentoring that must never end. When a person learns well how to learn, she is capable of benefiting from mentors, and of becoming a mentor. There are at least three levels of mentoring, the first of which is **Teaching**. At this first level of mentoring, the teacher simply instructs students on how to use learning techniques to learn. When a person knows how to effectively help others obtain and retain knowledge, she is a teacher.

At a second level, **Mentors** go a step deeper. Like teachers, they help students learn—but they also help students connect themselves with the knowledge they obtain. Mentors help students see:

- Why they are learning
- How it relates and correlates
- How it can be used in the real world

Mentors don't just pass on knowledge and skills. They help students discover their life's mission and their inner genius, and then fully prepare for these.

Indeed, mentoring is much more than teaching. Teachers or professors transfer knowledge and skills. Mentors help students build knowledge, skills, purpose, self-discovery, self-mastery and impact on the world. Teaching, as defined here, is the process of facilitating student literacy and helping students meet pre-established standards. In addition to these important things, mentoring helps students personalize the knowledge and skills and use it to benefit self, others and the world.

As a third level of mentoring, **Student Whispering** does all of these things and more. Student Whisperers consistently mentor at an inspired level. They know how to invite in the spark of inspiration whenever it is needed, because they know how to deeply understand each student and help him discover things he doesn't even know about himself. They know how to ask questions and help others have experiences that bring floods of insight, motivation and inspiration.

Above all, Student Whisperers are experts at empowering others. Instead of taking students where the experts think they should go, Student Whisperers help empower mentees to know where they should go from the mentee's own understanding. They help bring out the leadership and genius in everyone they touch. They know the questions to ask of themselves, and of their mentees (which we will cover in great depth in coming chapters), to instigate meaningful progress.

While many Student Whisperers do these things naturally through instinct and intuition, others learn to do them by asking the right questions and taking the right actions. Neither type is superior, and each has its advantages and weaknesses.

For example, while the intuitive Student Whisperer can often make effective mentoring seem natural and effortless, she often relies on a "magic" connection that somehow materializes with a mentee. Without further training, she may have no idea how to generate such a connection where it does not metaphysically appear—no matter how much she would like to, and even if the student is her own child. This book will help such a mentor to bridge that gap. Whether you are instinctual or explicitly trained, you will benefit from the lessons here.

In short, the difference between Student and Teacher is that the Teacher helps others learn knowledge and skills. The difference between Teacher and Mentor is that the Mentor helps learners individualize and personalize the knowledge and skills they learn with direct application to one's personal genius, passion and missions in life. Student Whisperers do all that Teachers and Mentors do, and add the following dimensions: frequent sparks of inspiration, the ability to lead innovatively, the skill of taking wise risk, and the habit of tenacious implementation. This is leadership.

Inspiration

Student Whisperers innovate, with every student and in each situation. They don't settle for anything less than truly great educational experiences. They aspire for every study session, every class, each project and every day to be characterized by epiphany, tenacious progress, and deeply transformational learning. They want learning to be multi-faceted, profound and moving. They want study periods to take place in the energy of vibrant quality.

They believe that learning is inherently great, and that each learning experience should feel and be great. They shun the rote, institutionalized, average and mediocre. They believe in quality, excellence and passion. They know hard work is vital to success, and they also know that time spent in hard work is exponentially more effective when done in the flow of inspiration. Rather than, "Don't work hard; work smart," they teach and exemplify, "Work smart *hard*."

The greatest teachers and mentors are therefore opponents of systemization, over-structured curricula and many objective measures created by experts—these things systematically shut down energy, passion and excellence. It is true that discipline is vital to progress and excellence. There is a huge difference between flat, uninspired discipline that bores the creative mind, shuts down the heart-connection and consistently puts glaze on student eyes, and deep, passionately inspired rigor. The student in the latter circumstance continues to do the hard things even *when* they are hard—not just in order to measure up, but because he is truly in love with studying and zealous about the goals he means to accomplish through his efforts.

Skeptics may fear that this method might lead to chaos, inconsistency or indulgence. This of course belies the skeptic's core values of order, uniformity, and standardized requirements. They doubt that many students will really love learning, or that those who do love it will be disciplined to do the really hard work. Certainly there are some students who will fail in these ways—but some fail in *all* models of education. Yet, how can we suppose that a deep personal commitment and high level of inspiration will lead to *diminished* achievement on the part of the student? Indeed, we have personally witnessed this level of dedication and its amazing outcomes in thousands of students—of all ages.

As we have stated here and elsewhere: when a student is given the opportunity to gain an education, the ultimate responsibility for success or failure rests with him, and it is the role and obligation of the adults in his life to provide the best possible opportunity to gain that education.

Any rational consideration of the models of education must conclude that effective mentoring is *not* the factor that heightens the risk of failure. Any analysis of the data on bureaucratic/compulsory models leads us to challenge the assumption that the conveyor belt is an effective mitigation against the risk of failure. The fact is that where there is great mentoring, students are *less likely* to fail and *more likely* to get truly excited and do the hard work of achieving true excellence.

Find a great Student Whisperer who transcends the system by giving consistently personalized and inspired guidance, and you will find increased activity of students truly excelling and a significant number of them doing literally world-class work.

The thing that is often missing in education is greatness! Greatness is easily recognizable, but it often eludes empirical measurement and rote policy. Greatness is the natural result of personalized, interactive quality with passion, discipline and inspired leadership. This is entirely learnable and duplicable, but it is nearly always sabotaged by too much systemization and institutionalism. Education needs greatness, and Student Whisperers are the experts on inspiring and bringing personal, powerful greatness to each student's learning.

The Highest Level: Student Whispering

Student Whispering, the highest and greatest level of mentoring, includes three central things:

First, Student Whisperers know the voices that speak to the mind of each student. One thing we will cover in much more detail later is that each student struggles with the voices that propose to guide his education. For example, nearly every student frequently hears, among other voices, the voice of self-doubt from the Inner Critic. Student Whisperers are familiar with these voices. They know how to help students discern them, tune out the wrong voices and focus on the voices that facilitate true growth and success.

Second, Student Whisperers know how youth and adults typically respond to each voice, as well as many non-typical responses. They know how to Whisper because they know the other voices that are Whispering. More, they think about these constantly and know how to read student behavior and perceive which voices are winning the student's inner battle.

Third, Student Whisperers know the language of Whispering and how to communicate directly and effectively with students. Very few people have learned this language or use it to communicate with youth—or with others, for that matter. Student Whisperers use this language every day, and because of this they cut out unproductive and unnecessary trial and error and help students focus on what really matters to move more quickly and effectively toward superb learning.

For example, the authors have both experienced students who decide the key to their education is to demand numerous one-on-one meetings with their mentor. We have also worked with those who prefer to be entirely self-contained and seldom interact with their mentor in any meaningful way. While typical mentors may decide to just work with the student's preferences in such cases, Student Whisperers go deeper. Student Whisperers spend literally hours pondering, writing and brainstorming what such students most need from their mentor.

Sometimes the result is that Student Whisperers help the "meeting, meeting, meeting" students become a bit more independent while they ask the self-focused learners to meet more frequently. This can leave the "meeting, meeting" student feeling ignored and the self-absorbed student feeling pushed. Often this is exactly what they need to feel, and over time their weaknesses are addressed and their strengths expanded accordingly.

In other words, being mentored by a Student Whisperer is not always comfortable, but it is profound and effective. Student Whisperers don't always tip their hand by showing the student exactly how they are mentoring, but they do spend significant time thinking and planning for each student or protégée and then implementing the plans to help each mentee truly succeed.

This may sound counter-intuitive, or even abstract, to non-Whisperers—which is one reason there are fewer great mentors than we need. Student Whisperers are paying attention to things most people ignore, and asking questions most people never consider. As a result, they are aware of things going on with students that others don't see.

Indeed, parents could become Student Whisperers in order to better understand their children. The same is true of every spouse, employer, friend, employee, citizen and leader. Human beings communicate so many things that aren't understood by others, and the point of Student Whispering is to explicitly attend to these communications.

In this book, readers will learn how to more effectively and consistently think, hear, speak and act like Student Whisperers. Student Whisperers are needed today, perhaps more than ever before. Every great education is influenced by at least one truly great Student Whisperer. The future of education—and of human achievement, prosperity and happiness—depends on having more of them.

Two Books in One

This book is specially designed and organized with a dual purpose:

1. To help readers experience and recognize what it feels like to be greatly mentored

2. To concurrently outline the principles of great mentoring and help readers turn them into personal skills and even habits

The first part of this book (**Book One**, covering Chapters 1-5) is told as a personal narrative, and immerses readers in a series of life events as a student learns from her mentors and grows in the process. We hope readers *feel* what it is like to experience working with committed and demanding mentors as they go through Book One.

The second part (**Book Two**, comprising Chapters 6-16) contains information that is vital to becoming a great mentor (and to working with great mentors), and guides the reader through several exercises that help turn the concepts and principles of great mentoring into personal skills and strengths.

The authors have worked together (first in a Mentor-Mentee relationship, and later as colleagues) for nearly two decades—as many of the stories in Book One show. Oliver used the methods taught here in mentoring Tiffany and many other people, and Tiffany has applied and expanded on the same principles and methods in her mentoring through LEMI (The Leadership Education Mentoring Institute) for well over a decade.

Over the course of these many years, we have learned what works (and what usually doesn't) through direct mentoring, and vicariously through mentor-protégées. This book imparts what we have come to understand of truly great mentoring—what we call Student Whispering:

Chapters 6-9 provide foundational information valuable for all mentors and those who are mentored.

Chapters 10-13 help readers throw off past biases about teaching and establish a transformational foundation for great mentoring. Topics include:

- The two major balances (first between the Manager and the Artist, and second between the Warrior and the Healer)

- The various voices nearly all students listen to, and how to speak the language of each most effectively

- Seven key questions Student Whisperers ask about each mentee[1]

- How archetypes are central to great education and Student Whispering, and how to apply this knowledge as a mentor

Chapters 14-16 deal with further transformation. This includes workshops on:

- How to get the most from *your* mentors

- How to become a great mentor

- How to plan your strategy of becoming a Student Whisperer so that it encompasses life as a place of learning...and more

Special Thanks

We want to thank our respective spouses, Rachel DeMille and Rick Earl, for their deep involvement in and support for this book. Writing is a challenging endeavor, and our spouses and children have put up with a great deal as we've worked on this project. Beyond the role of spouse and partner, Rachel DeMille has read every word of this book multiple times and provided more suggestions, ideas and changes than we could ever count. This book would not exist without her efforts and expertise in Leadership Education. Many others have helped with this work, especially numerous readers and seminar participants who made suggestions and recommended changes, and we deeply appreciate their contributions.

We also thank our many mentors over the years who have taught, scolded, shared, instructed, demanded, pushed, laughed and even wept with us. We have gained so much from the on-going dance of mentors and the mentored. We feel so humbled and blessed to have worked with truly great Student Whisperers in our lives.

Finally, we want to thank you, the reader, for your interest in learning, improving and becoming a Student Whisperer. Whoever you are: we were thinking of you individually and warmly when we wrote this.

The Student Whisperer

This book is dedicated to you. We hope you can feel how much we really mean this.

The world truly needs more Student Whisperers, and we are convinced that many who have great life missions can learn a great deal from the material in this book. It has been an educational experience and a labor of love for us to go through the many dozens of versions that brought us to this point. We hope it will help you in your own labors of love to truly make the world better. It is why we are all here, after all.

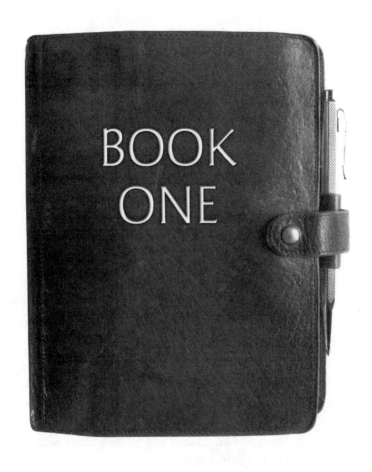

BOOK
ONE

❝ Press on.
Nothing in the world can take the
place of persistence. ❞

–CALVIN COOLIDGE

Mentors

by Tiffany Earl

I sat on the colonial-style sofa in the lounge nervously wiggling my foot. *Why am I nervous?* I thought. *I've known Oliver for years! He's my friend and my teacher. So why am I nervous?* I couldn't fool myself, though. I knew why I was nervous. This was my first formal non-academic mentor meeting.

I knew clearly how this could change my life. I knew what a difference mentors make. Take Isaac Newton, for example—the genius, Isaac Newton. Newton had been in and out of school until he was eighteen. There were times he left school to help with the farm, but he'd end up hiding so he could read and fill notebooks with his inventions, models and calculations.

By age eighteen he was at Trinity College—discouraged with his studies, friends and learning environment, and on the verge of giving up formal schooling forever and going home. The roadblock just seemed too big. He had tried over and over, without success, and this time felt like all the others.

Then he met Isaac Barrow—an eminent mathematician, philosopher and Greek scholar. Barrow recognized Isaac's capabilities and started mentoring him. Almost overnight Isaac Newton changed. Instead of being lackadaisical, he became an eager student who delved into Copernican theories, the writings of Galileo, the works of Kepler,

The Student Whisperer

and the science of optics. Newton got on The Path and went on to give the world a deeper understanding of physics, invent a branch of calculus, and bring greater light and knowledge to the world around him.

I knew his story, as well as the stories of Thomas Jefferson and his mentor George Wythe, George Washington and his mentor Colonel Fairfax, and numerous modern business mentor stories like Andrew Carnegie, Sam Walton, Buckminster Fuller, Dexter Yeager, and Robert Kiyosaki. I knew that successful people get on The Path—which means that they start by getting a great mentor.

I wasn't kidding myself. I *knew* the power of a mentor, but it wasn't just that. I had high hopes. Being a stay-at-home mom who was working on my Masters and building a business wasn't necessarily the normal "mentee" stereotype. Nevertheless, I knew I needed a mentor, and I knew he was the one.

He knew me too. He'd seen my work, my dedication, my strengths and weaknesses; but how would he deal with my situation?

So here I sat, nervously waiting for my first formal mentor meeting.

I thought back to the past few weeks, to the events that had brought me here. The more I thought about it, the more I realized I had been preparing for this meeting for several years.

I looked up from the pile of bills and held back my tears. I had given up getting angry weeks ago—now I was getting emotional. The choking feeling I felt oozing its way up my throat made me feel sick inside. I clicked off the screen and leaned back in my chair.

"Rick, we are barely making it this month. In fact, there are some purchases we are going to have to put on hold."

My husband had run his own business for most of our marriage; and like most everything else, we shared the load.

I re-worked the numbers. I looked over our business strategy. At the time, we had two main clients who bought our manufactured kits wholesale. I looked over our marketing plan. I studied our product line. I read through the business structure. I looked over everything. *What are we doing wrong?* I was grasping for straws.

Should we put more emphasis on retail sales and improve our presence on the web? Should we raise our prices a little, both wholesale and retail? Or would that drive our buyers to our competitors? Should we pay our employees less, or lay off some of them? Should we create a new product? Should we buy the new rock-breaking machinery so we wouldn't have to break everything by hand? Should we network with some other businesses so we can move more product? Should we hire a better salesman?

Should we quit?

I had asked about fifty "should-we's" when I finally let out a huge sigh and shut the books. It was past midnight and any more efforts at solving our business crises would have to wait until morning.

Or so I thought.

I tossed and turned, and at 3:30 I finally got out of bed. I walked over to my dresser, fumbled around in the dark until I found my journal, and quietly exited my bedroom.

I found my way to the den, flipped the light on, sat in the easy chair, and leafed through my journal...

Rick and I both believe we have a personal mission in life. Rick is an inventor at heart. He has what I call the '101 Ways To Do Anything' talent. He loves the process of figuring out how to do something in more economical and technological ways.

I flipped a few pages and kept reading,

I've finally determined that even though Rick and I share our major goals and commitments about life, and even though we love each other dearly and support each other in all worthy endeavors, there are some things I feel extremely passionate about that aren't his mission. They are my mission, and I must do them.

I smiled as I read that, thinking about the time he rigged a copper-pipe water heater around our wood-burning stove to save on electricity costs. He'd forgotten to account for the pressure of steam and finally took it down after it blew a hole through my hutch. Yes, we didn't necessarily have the same gifts and talents, but we both had something to give.

I flipped some more pages and resumed reading,

In some ways I'm just like everybody else. I care what my friends think of me, I enjoy a really nice restaurant, and I think about what happens in the world.

In other ways, I'm not so similar. I must reach the youth. They have so much potential—and yet too few live up to it. They become disillusioned as they hit the "realities" of life. So many people in their later years still talk about high school or college as "the best years of their life." How tragic. People don't live their dreams because they just don't know how.

In another place I wrote:

I always believed my teachers when they told us we could do anything we put our minds to. I believed my parents when they told me I had a purpose in life.

I kept flipping pages and reading:

There are some things I just KNOW—some things I desire so strongly that I can't keep myself from pursuing their course. There are even things that are as good as done even though I haven't begun them yet. I will help people know how to be happy, how to choose their dreams, how to accomplish their missions.

I paused here and pondered, then looked back down. It was good to remember. I read on.

I know that the kind of education I get is crucial to me accomplishing my personal mission . . . I know that I need to build a successful business in order to reach the people I feel called to reach . . . I know youth will sit up as I speak, and be changed . . . I know people will read and be changed, and make choices that will make all the difference . . .

I stopped. I couldn't go on. I knew all these things. They seemed so close, yet so far away. How was I going to accomplish them when Rick and I couldn't even get his business to produce a healthy income for our family?

I closed my journal, and as I did I thought about Abraham Lincoln. I thought about how he'd spent all night on his knees the night before he signed the Emancipation Proclamation. *He had a work to do,* I thought. I wonder how he felt when his business partner defaulted and Lincoln had to spend years repaying both halves of their business loan.

If he could overcome such challenges, so could I.

I thought of Robert Morris and how he financed the Revolutionary War at a critical moment in America's history, and how he spent the end of his life in debtor's prison instead of on a rich man's lane.

This is bigger than me, I thought. This isn't just about machinery, products, payroll, marketing and suppliers. This is part of the formula to help me accomplish my mission.

I opened my journal again and wrote:

No matter the roadblocks, I will succeed! I will do whatever it takes to accomplish my personal mission. I will make the necessary decisions, engage the right people. I will write, I will speak, I will work with the youth, I will make the business successful.

We loaded our small son into the pickup and headed up to Three Peaks. About eight miles in on the dirt road was an old mine on the mountainside—perfect for gathering lodestone, or magnetite. I loved "gathering days." I rarely went with Rick anymore, but every once in a while I'd pack a picnic lunch and Rick would bring Jacob and me along.

Today I had something specific in mind. Today I wanted to get out of the house, away from the desk and telephone, out of the normal routine. I wanted to work *on* the business, *on* our lives, *on* the big picture.

Today I wanted some answers, and the beautiful hills behind Three Peaks would be perfect.

The Student Whisperer

Rick took a five gallon bucket in his left hand, a piece of string with a paper clip tied to one end hanging out of his mouth, and a two-pronged pitch fork and shovel in his right hand. He headed up the mountainside.

We'd driven as far as we could with the truck and it wasn't more than a mile to the top.

Little Jacob grabbed his plastic shovel and bucket and followed his daddy. We gathered magnetite, Rick testing its strength with the paperclip. I asked Rick if he'd keep an eye on Jacob for a while. He would.

I headed energetically to the top of the hill. By the time I made it, I was gasping. I leaned over with my legs bent and my hands on my knees, breathing deeply.

It was beautiful at the summit and I sat down on a big white rock. I gazed around me. I could see down the mountainside where we'd parked the truck and I could see another mountain to the north of me. The truck looked small from here. *This is what I needed—to put life in perspective.* The clouds were bright and billowy. The ones to the south were dark gray storm clouds, but where I stood the sky was bright blue with a few fluffy white clouds.

I was here to clarify my vision and to decide some things. Somehow the outdoors and mountains can put things into perspective. The air is cleaner, the world is clearer, and God feels nearer.

I had one important question on my mind, and it was time I made a decision. I knew about The Path of All Success. For the past four years I had immersed myself in the classics in several fields and The Path was laced throughout each of them. It didn't matter if I was reading Plato, Confucius or Galileo, or listening to Mozart. It didn't matter if it was economics I was studying, or business law, or Shake-speare. In all of them, The Path was clear.

I knew what choice lay in front of me. Either way, I was at a crossroad and it was time to follow Frost's example and take "the road less traveled."

But could I do it? Because I *had* immersed myself in the classics—

walking the streets of France with Cosette and Jean Valjean, seeing the landscape of Russia with Prince Andre and Peter, sitting in the corner of the top floor of the library with Reuben and Danny's father—I knew it wasn't easy. Hamlet had to decide whether to ignore the ghost or test its origin. Once he made his choice, it didn't mean the rest was easy.

I knew this. I knew this choice was vital, but it didn't make easy what lay ahead.

I thought back to the many people who had made this choice and succeeded on The Path. *What gave them the strength to make this choice?* I wondered.

What gave Gandhi the strength? What gave Churchill the strength? What gave Eric Liddell the strength? What gave Socrates the strength? The list went on and on in my mind—and all at once I knew. Or to be more specific, I *remembered.*

I remembered what gave them the strength: It was the personal conviction that they each had a mission to fulfill. It was The Call. It was having a vision of what was expected of them, believing that they had a personal mission, and desiring to be chosen.

The Call. Ah, yes: *The Call.*

It would be really nice if I could tell you that an angel or something came to me, like Joan of Arc—but that didn't happen. What did happen is that as I sat there on the top of the hill looking out on the sweeping southwestern vista, I felt something. It wasn't the first time I felt it, nor the last. But it was *different* somehow. Different because intertwined with the feeling of having an important work to do was something else: a decision. The decision to pay whatever price was needed to accomplish my dream.

The Call came to me like I suppose it comes to a lot of people, packaged in the form of desire—desire to accomplish something really important . . . my unique contribution. The Call is recognizable as a sense of direction, the urge to commit to a course of action—be it as small as starting a fall garden or as great as organizing a school system in rural Africa.

The Student Whisperer

I sat on the white rock and took a deep, cleansing breath. To get back on The Path was going to take some time. I had felt The Call years ago, but I kept hitting roadblocks—and every time I made the wrong choice, I either tried to work things out myself or I picked the wrong mentors to help. So I was always stuck in The Path of Mediocrity. I knew better, but here I was. *Again.*

I took another deep breath. "Okay," I said aloud, "this time I'll do it right. I'll make this Vital Choice correctly. I'll get the right mentor."

But it won't be easy, I thought. *I've tried easy—and it doesn't work! I'm going to do this* right. *I'm going to go back in my mind to the beginning, back to the first time I felt The Call. Then I'm going to go through each time I came to a Roadblock and felt The Call, and I'm going re-experience them again, here, now. Then I'm going to look at the future honestly and make a different choice.*

I closed my eyes and let my mind float back to the first time I felt it—the time The Call came when I was thirteen years old...

It was a rough time for me. It had been about two months since I lost several of my friends. I was searching for meaning in life, and I was questioning what it was that I really believed. I was trying to decide if Mom and Dad were on my side.

I slammed the door shut and threw my backpack onto the sofa. Mom looked up in surprise. I stalked off to my bedroom and slammed that door too. My mom never was one to be stumped over the literal. True, I'd broken rules on three accounts. I slammed the door, I didn't put my backpack in its proper place, and I wasn't very cordial. She knew this, but she also knew something deeper. She knew I was mad. But even more than that, she knew the anger was only covering up something deeper—*hurt*, maybe. She'd find out. She always did.

She came into my room and plopped on the bed beside me. She thought better than to lecture me about the doors and the backpack. She put her hand on my back and said, "Rough day?"

I just wanted her to go away—but only partly. If I *really* didn't want her to know I was hurt, I wouldn't have slammed the doors. "Mom, it's the kids at school. They put another letter in my locker today. Now Tracy isn't even speaking to me. I just don't get it. What did I do wrong?"

I was almost in tears. The past two months hadn't been easy. In fact, they were the hardest of my life to that point. I didn't know it then, but I had another four months to go before I stopped crying myself to sleep at night.

Mom only knew part of the story, but it really didn't matter. She knew that somehow someone had lied about me and that the once "popular" Tiffany was now not only a loner, but, according to everybody else, accused of things that pain me to think of and that no decent person would even say. I'd lost all my friends one by one; but it was losing my best friend Tracy that hurt the worst.

"Mom, it just doesn't make sense. Someone put that mean letter in my locker today, and I don't even know who it is!"

Mom was silent. She kept rubbing my back.

"Why are people doing this? I never did anything to them! Besides, I didn't even do the things they are accusing me of."

My mom could see the crinkled up letter I was holding in my hands.

"What if you *were* guilty of those things they accuse you of?" she asked quietly.

"What do you mean, Mom? I'm not!"

"But what if you *were*? Should they treat you this way then?"

I thought for a moment. *What if I had done all the things they were gossiping about? What if I were what they said I was?*

"Mom, even if I were guilty, it doesn't excuse the way they are treating me. There's no reason to treat people this way."

I hadn't told her, but I had to take the long way home because the neighborhood boys hid behind the fence by the shortcut and threw snowballs at me when I went that way. I had two bruises—they had good aim. No; no one should be treated this way.

I became reflective and remembered the people I'd brushed off, ignored or simply never made an effort to befriend—all because of pre-judgments. I choked back a sob, "Could I have hurt others and made them feel this way?"

Mom left the room, and as she did I let down. I cried for my pain, and for anyone else who had felt this way—alienated, falsely condemned, lonely, confused, hurt, and afraid; but deeper than it all I felt something, something strong and real, something that would never leave. It was fuzzy—I couldn't quite get a grasp on it; but I knew that somehow the world could be better, and that I would be involved in making a difference.

It was four months later that I went to a weeklong seminar at a big university in our state. There were literally hundreds of speakers and topics to choose from, ranging from fencing lessons to what to do on a blind date.

I picked my schedule, and my brother, who was two years older, traipsed around the campus with me for a week. It was the conglomeration of speakers that changed my life.

I found my bearings. I remembered who I was. I started letting go of the bitterness of being lonely and began hoping I could be happy again. I learned that my happiness didn't depend solely on my friends, or lack thereof.

I started applying the lessons they taught. The most important lesson was the decision to read my Core Book. Everybody needs a Core Book. Mine happened to be scripture.

Years later I sat on the big white rock, remembering the faces of the speakers.

I remembered looking around me—I was in a huge gym. There must have been over 500 people in the audience. I kept looking into people's eyes, wondering if the same thing was happening to them. A feeling swelled up within me, and I knew that one day I would do what these men and women did. One day I would work with the youth, and one day I would be a public speaker.

I sat on the white rock thinking, *I haven't done it yet. I'm not making a difference. I work with the youth at church, but not the way I know I will one day. How am I going to reach my dream?*

The Call had been so real. How could I just go on not living it? I mean, I tried to follow The Call, but things never seemed to work out like I expected. I opened my eyes. The clouds were still white and fluffy, and a warm breeze had started. I stood up, stretched, and then sat down again on the white rock.

Mom had taught me since I was young to be picky about my teachers. She'd always helped me get into the classes I wanted, and I often picked them because of the teacher's reputation. I usually picked the hardest, often "most hated" teacher. They were the ones with the highest expectations, standards, and work ethic. I knew that teachers made a huge difference.

I sat for a long, long time—mentally going through the times I'd tried to get on The Path, the roadblocks I'd overcome, the times I'd failed. When the sun was far to the west I realized that Rick would be ready to leave soon. "Just a few more minutes," I said to myself.

I finally asked myself what I should do to get back on The Path; but I already knew. I'd been feeling it for hours. With every memory it kept coming back. I knew the next step on The Path. When you hit the Roadblock, stop and ponder; follow the inspiration. This time it was: *get the right mentor.*

I know, I know. I told my mind. *I know what I must do. If I am to accomplish all I feel called to accomplish, I must make the choice to get the right mentor. My personal mission requires it. The success of our business requires it. My happiness depends upon it.*

It was clear. Everything was clear. It was time and I knew it. I needed a mentor to help me fulfill my mission, the right mentor, a great mentor—the one who had been mentoring me through the liberal arts for four years, the one who just happened to have already walked The Path I was contemplating.

I'll do it, I thought. I breathed in the wonderful mountain air, stretched my arms toward the sky and stood up. Heart full of determination, eyes full of dreams, and a smile on my face, I descended the mountain.

The Student Whisperer

I tucked the kids in at 8:30, "Okay you guys. Goodnight; I love you." I shut the door quietly and tiptoed into the living room.

I pushed the button and the screen lit up, and the computer made its familiar noises of booting up.

PowerPoint was fun to learn. It really wasn't too hard, and the templates in it helped me to clarify my business proposal. I stayed up each night until Rick got home around 11 pm and then I slipped into bed exhausted.

Two months later, laptop computer with the PowerPoint presentation in hand, I entered Oliver's office with a proposal...

The answer was *"no."*

I couldn't believe it. I knew my plan was solid. I knew it was needed. Why "no"?

Along with the "no" came an assignment. *What's that about?* I thought. *He says "no" to mentoring me and then sends me on a project!* But I wanted a mentor, wanted **this** mentor, so I did the project. It entailed nothing less than setting up a private school for teenagers. In addition, I started youth conferences and created a leadership program for youth. I did the projects I knew needed doing, and I did them well. I just wished I had a mentor to help.

About three months later Oliver called me. "You need a mentor," he said. I agreed. *What a great idea!* We set an appointment.

Oliver came out to the foyer, smiled and invited me into his office. I got off the colonial-style couch and took a deep breath.

When I stepped into Oliver's office he kindly shook my hand, looked in my eyes and invited me to sit down. My eyes quickly glanced around the room. There was a picture of George Washington at Valley Forge on the wall behind him—the one where he kneels in the snow next to his horse. There was a wall lined with books, classics in all fields. There were charcoal sketches of Churchill, Gandhi and Martin Luther King, Jr. in matching frames. There was a window overlooking the entrance to the building.

He got right down to business. "What are your goals, and how can I help you?" My thoughts began to stutter. Should I tell him my huge dreams and goals? Or should I tell him my current situation that I needed help with? I decided the latter and showed him the project I was working on.

He stopped me—which I soon got used to. He didn't want to waste my time and he knew where he wanted to lead me. "Let me tell you how these mentor meetings are going to work, Tiffany." I looked up at him.

"When you leave here today you will have a list of commitments you have made to me. These aren't goals. Goals are something written that you *want* to accomplish. A commitment is much more than that—it's a *promise*. A commitment is a promise that you make to me that says you are going to do something specific.

"When you come back one of two things will have happened: You will have either kept your commitment or not. Let me warn you now. If you don't keep your commitment I will look you in the eye and tell you I am disappointed in you. I may attach consequences. I won't mentor someone who doesn't keep commitments. If you do keep your commitment you will have progressed toward your goals. I will be pleased and so will you, and we will go from there. Understood?"

I gulped a yes.

"You should read *The One Minute Manager* so you'll know how we'll work."

I nodded, quickly scribbled the name of the book in my notebook, and we went on. We began to look at my project. I wanted to build a successful business. I don't remember every detail we went over, but I remember what Oliver taught me.

"Take out a sheet of paper, please." I did. "Draw a circle in the center and write the name of your roadblock." I did. "Now start brainstorming. I want you to brainstorm bubbles all over that paper of what you need to know, learn, feel, understand and do to overcome the roadblock." I began writing. I had a list of twelve categories with up to five sub-categories each brainstormed within just a few minutes.

"Good. Now put them in the order you are going to do them." That was harder. "Now write down your plan for doing them." That wasn't too hard. I would learn about how to use the Internet better from my husband. I would learn about how to publish from a friend who had published.

I quickly made the list. It looked daunting. I knew that if I were a full-time student committing 40-80 hours a week this would take me a year. But I was a mom and business owner who could eke out *maybe* two to three hours a day, and that was if I kept a tight schedule!

I took a deep breath and sighed. I wouldn't let him see the tears I was holding back. I knew what I wanted, and I decided I didn't care how long it took. I also knew I wouldn't be coming to these formal mentor meetings twice a month like his full-time people were.

He asked me what the constraint was, the one thing that blocked all the others. We spent time on that, then on how to fix it, and I made my commitment. We both wrote it down on our formal mentor record and I left. I knew better than to commit to a time frame. I knew myself well enough to know that my family came first, and that I couldn't guess the time frame at this point. I would just get back to him when I'd completed my work.

At my next mentor meeting Oliver could see an area I really needed to work on if I was going to accomplish my many goals.

"Systems," he said.

"Huh?" I looked at him quizzically. I had heard him mention systems before, but I'd never been able to grasp the simple concept. It was now time to learn it.

"A system is simply a choice that has already been made." He looked at me and knew I just didn't get it. He pulled out a legal pad and began to write. "A system is a series of events that have been pre-determined." I still didn't get it.

He backed up. "Okay," he said, "do you smoke?"

"No."

"When did you decide you weren't going to smoke?"

"When I was five and my friend's mother smoked. My mom taught me the consequences of smoking and I decided then that I wouldn't smoke."

"Did anyone ever offer you a cigarette?"

"Yes, of course."

"What did you do?"

"I did what I decided a long time ago. I said, 'No.'"

He nodded. "*That* is a system!"

"It is?"

"Yes, it was a decision already made. You had a system in place. You knew you would say 'no.' You didn't have to spend a lot of energy and time deciding what to do anytime someone offered you a cigarette. You had a system in place and you just followed through. It was easy."

I felt like I was catching on a little. "Tell me another system!" I said.

"How do you do the dishes at your house?"

Ugh! I was embarrassed to tell him the truth, but I swallowed and did it anyway. "I notice we don't have any clean dishes left and so I soak the dirty ones and then wash them."

He laughed. "That's a system by default. The fact that you don't have any clean dishes triggers the need to wash the dishes. Some people use other systems—better ones. I've seen some homes where everyone washes their own dishes and the rest of the kitchen duties are rotated between children. I've also seen some homes where dad and mom do dish duty right after each meal. These are systems. They are choices that are already pre-decided and then fulfilled."

"So what does this mean to me?" I asked sincerely.

"It means that you have to put better systems into your projects. Each area needs systems. You need to determine what they are and build them. You should read a book called *The E-Myth*."

I went home in a stupor, but I got started. I soon learned that my mentor had saved me months of diversions, had helped me skip numerous roadblocks. I began to train my mind to think in terms of systems. I began to see them everywhere—and the lack of them too. I began enjoying the task of seeing the systems that worked well. I soon noticed that most problems occurred where there weren't efficient and well thought-out systems. I became good at not only solving problems (creating systems) but at identifying problems.

I'm not sure when it happened, but at some point most of my roadblocks just melted away. As I studied *The One Minute Manager*, *The Theory of Constraints*, *The E-Myth* and other books and seminars recommended by my mentor to deal with specific problems, the roadblocks became more manageable. Business improved as I made better choices, and things were looking up. I thought everything was going great.

If I had been on my own at this point, I would almost certainly have fallen back onto The Path of Mediocrity, because even though I felt good about things, I was still facing the big roadblock, the major concern that seemed to be at the root of my stifled progress. I wasn't fully back on The Path yet, and my mentor knew it.

"Pick one, Tiffany. Pick one thing. Pick the thing you are going to do, and then do it well. No more 'this and that'. It's time to choose." Oliver didn't usually talk this way. Normally he used lots of questions, eventually getting me to see the obvious; but when he did talk this way, he meant it. It made me think of the "wax on, wax off" lesson from *Karate Kid*[2]. I knew I should just trust him, but it was so hard. I was so invested in all five current projects, and it seemed to *me* they were synergistic.

After we hung up I looked at my list—all five were important. Could he be right? Did I really have to pick only one? Was it about timing? Was it that I needed to do one thing at a time? Was it that there is merit in laser focus?

All of them *were* important. All five things I was working on were related in some form or another. I felt a drive to do them all. Why pick *one*?

This is why the decision to work with The Mentor is so challenging, I thought. *It's not just 'get a mentor and get past roadblocks'. You have to do what the mentor says and trust the mentor's experience. Well, I'm not going to blow it now.*

I'll try it, I thought. *I'll pick one and see what happens.* Truth be told, I knew I needed help. Business was going so much better. It would have been easy to just bask in it, but I knew I wasn't there yet. It wouldn't hurt to trust the mentor.

I wrote down the reasons for doing each of the five projects. I wrote down the impact of each, the financial compensation, the outside pressures, and the time commitment. I listed pros and cons like Benjamin Franklin.

I finally chose the one that had the seemingly greatest impact, a high economic return, and seemed to be a prerequisite for two of the others.

I started working on it. I created a plan of action. For a week I worked like crazy, but still I wasn't happy. One day as I was jumping on my trampoline, the wind blowing in my hair, the empty brown fields surrounding me for miles, I looked up at the tip of the mountain.

"I picked the wrong one, didn't I?" I said aloud.

All right, I won't do it. I'll drop it. I won't pursue that one even though it would bring a huge financial return, fit my schedule as a mom, have a big impact on families, and so on. I won't do it. It's not worth being miserable.

A huge wave of relief washed over me. I jumped for another few minutes, hopped down, and went inside. By the time I made it past the living room I knew what I was going to do.

I was supposed to gather up the kids and head to town for a field trip with our school group, but I'd have to be late. I grabbed my note-pad and pen and started writing as fast as I could.

Without a Mission Mentor I'm sure I would have done what I usually did—get off The Path. I'm glad the Mentor knew what was needed. What my mentor didn't know, what none of us knew, was that the stakes were about to get even higher.

When Rick was acting strangely that morning I just thought he was stressed and needed some time alone. It took me several hours to figure out that something was really wrong.

"Rick, are you coming for breakfast?" I asked. He just looked at me.

"Well, if you aren't eating with us, who do you want to say the prayer?" Once again he just looked at me. I looked right back, expectantly. Finally he stammered, "T-Tiffany."

"Okay," I said and then proceeded to ask a blessing on the food. After the kids were fed I looked in the office to see if Rick wanted me to make something different for him. He was indifferent, which wasn't out of the ordinary. It was the tears in his eyes that were unusual.

Man, I thought, *he must be really bothered by something*, and I went to make him a tuna melt. I brought it back to his office where he was bagging triops eggs for educational kits—and the tears were still there.

It was then that I noticed he didn't have shoes or socks on. *Now, that's just* weird. Never in our years of marriage had I seen him walk around the house barefoot. That was something I did, not him. "Where are your shoes?" I asked. He just shrugged.

I sat next to him on the couch, put my hand on his knee, and asked, "Honey, is something wrong? Do you want to talk about it?"

He just said, "I bag fast."

"What? You're upset about triops?"

"I bag fast...not today though.... I can't...seem to bag them very fast."

"You mean you're upset just because you can't beat yesterday's record?" Rick always timed himself when he bagged triops because it was such a monotonous job and he liked to compete with himself for time.

"I just can't go fast," he stammered.

"Rick, I don't get it. Maybe you have a bad batch of plastic bags again and they just won't open well. Here, give me one and I'll try it."

I reached across him and opened a bag by twisting the top together between my thumb and forefinger. "Nope, that's not it. They work just fine."

"Honey, are you really upset because you can't bag fast? *Why?*"

"My hands—they just won't work."

"What are you talking about? Here, I'll watch you for a minute."

Sure enough, it took him a whole minute to open one bag—instead of two seconds.

"Rick, come with me into the front room." He followed me and we sat down.

"Rick, count backwards from ten to one."

He started, going slowly, and he messed up once, but caught it. He knew his name, he knew his address—but a knot of fear started forming in my stomach.

I remembered how the night before he had walked over to me and all of a sudden his face twitched strangely and he fell over onto the couch. I'd rushed to him, grabbed his face in my hand and said, "Rick, I think you just had a stroke!"

He started laughing at me. He was barely thirty years old! His laughing irritated me so I went in the kitchen and started working. He continued to laugh at me for half an hour. At the time I figured he was laughing because he was embarrassed that he fell over.

During the night he'd acted strange too. He'd found a sleeping bag, laid it on his side of the bed, and slept on top of it.

I also realized now that he was speaking very slowly and his words were slurred.

"Rick," I said, "I think you had a stroke."

He looked at me. He looked at me with complete trust, complete love, complete bewilderment.

The first week was unsettling. The doctor said he would regain most of his faculties, since he was young and generally healthy. When he called our daughter Laura "Stacie" (his sister's name) and our younger son Joseph "Jacob" (our oldest son's name), I just acted as if nothing was wrong and tried to make things seem as normal as possible. After the first week it seemed like 80% of his abilities were back.

After the third week I thought he was recuperated enough to help make a "couple's decision." That was the hardest part—harder than watching him relearn to write his name, relearn to talk on the phone, relearn to do everyday things. The hardest part was making the decisions all alone—financial decisions, Rick's work decisions, household decisions, children decisions . . . all decisions.

At the end of week three I sat him down and said, "Honey, I need your help making a decision."

"Okay," he said.

I then proceeded to tell him all about a little business crisis. I'd just barely begun to explain it and was five minutes into the details when he looked at me and said, "Okay. Is that all?" I knew what it meant. We were done talking. I swallowed hard. "Yep, that's all." He got up and walked away.

I slumped onto the couch and took a deep breath. "Alright, I'll decide."

One morning a while later, I sat on the couch staring out the window. My hands were shaking and I felt like throwing up. I was one month pregnant, and I think the emotional strain was making the morning sickness worse than usual.

Will Rick ever be the same again?[3] I wondered. *Will it ever be like it was before, and like we imagined it would be? Will he ever notice the little things again, or help me like before, or talk to me again like normal, noticing when I needed a hug, a smile, an encouraging word? Will I ever be able to confide in him again? How long will it remain one-sided?*

I felt so abandoned, so alone. I never thought this would happen to me. *These kinds of things happen to other people.* I just stared out the window at the barren ground. I felt so alone. He was here physically, but I couldn't even explain the depth of my pain to him.

There was more to it than simply not having my best friend, my confidante, my husband. Our very livelihood and financial peace were at stake.

During that time I made a decision. If I had to work, I was going to do it on The Path. I wasn't just going to just make a living, get a paycheck and pay the bills. I was going to stay on The Path, achieve The Call, and fulfill that unique vision that is such a part of who I am.

When all of Rick's abilities were normal again, we were able to revisit these choices. He voiced his support of my choice to stay on The Path just as I supported him on The Path of his vision. During those cold, lonely days when it looked like so much depended on me, and all the pressure and well-meaning advice was to just do the "normal thing," I made a choice.

I looked at those around me who were seeking to achieve their dreams. A high percentage of them believed *they had to have more money first.* It didn't seem to matter how much money they had. They just needed "more." One friend wanted to be a more attentive mother, but said she needed her husband to make more money first. Another friend wanted to devote all of his life to service, but said he needed more money first. A close neighbor dreamed of creating a children's school for orphans. She was past retirement age, had carried this dream her whole life, but just knew she needed, *what?* More money first. She'd worked for forty-eight years earning money and her dream remained elusive.

Mary didn't tell Gabriel she needed more money before she had Jesus. Mother Teresa didn't need more money before she spent her life in service.

I knew better than to believe the old "money can buy you anything" lie. I needed a qualified mentor. I needed to make the choice all great people had made in the face of tough challenges. Sitting on my couch, staring at the falling snow out the window, I made a decision. Nothing would get in the way of me fulfilling my unique purpose. *Nothing*.

Hopefully Rick would never have another stroke. Hopefully my family would never be dependent on me to provide; but if they ever were, in case it ever happened, that living would have to be provided with me *on The Path!* And I'd get on The Path anyway, because that's why I was born.

Nothing would get in the way. *Nothing*. I watched the snow falling through the window. It looked cold and barren outside, but I gritted my teeth and enjoyed the feel of the warm tears on my cheeks.

I was moving forward on The Path.

I'd been in several writing workshops with Oliver before—only at the time I hadn't had anything I wanted to publish. Either way I knew how he worked.

For one, he had told me he really thought I had something valuable in this manuscript, and two, he had asked my permission to really take it apart, to go deep. I knew this was code for "tear it to shreds."

So be it.

Like I said, I was ready.

On my way to class my prayer was: *Please let me learn what I need to know in order to write this information and inspire others in this area.*

And as a side note: *Please don't let me cry in front of the class.*

Excitement filled the room as my classmates realized that Oliver would be leading the discussion. He walked in after the traditional prayer, pledge, and Mission Statement.

Two long brown tables were pushed up against each other and all of us pulled our black cushioned chairs up to the long table and looked toward one end where Oliver sat alone.

"All right, today we are critiquing Tiffany's manuscript. I want you all to know that I'm not going to go easy on her. She's given me permission to go deep, so we're not going to hold back. Let's give her great feedback that really helps her improve her writing."

This class of adult professionals wasn't used to this and I saw some of them wince. I sat up straight and leaned forward, eager for this long-awaited lesson.

Oliver took one look at my draft and held up his copy.

"Tell me what you see here." he asked the group.

Silence.

Silence.

"I'll tell you what I see on this first page. It reminds me a lot of something I might have turned in as a term paper when I was a sophomore in high school," he said with tease in his voice.

Gasp! (Not from me. Remember, I knew what I was in for.)

Then he unceremoniously removed the staple that was so carefully positioned in the upper left-hand corner.

"Ben, could you please hand me a paperclip?"

"Do you see this?" He slipped a blank white sheet of paper behind the title page and then held up a second copy of my manuscript for comparison.

Holding the two up, one with the extra paper and paper clip in the upper right corner, and my original version with a staple in it, he said, "Can you see the difference?"

We all looked at the two manuscripts.

They *did* look significantly different.

"What do they each communicate?"

Kim said, "One looks a lot sharper because we can't see the ink of the next page bleeding through."

There were nods of agreement and recognition.

"One communicates 'sophomore' and the other 'professional.'"

"Yeah," agreed Jalyn. "The paper-clipped one looks more professional."

Oliver suggested that while there is nothing inherently better about paper clips than staples, he wanted us to think like *writers* rather than just students, and to consider what we want to communicate, and how best to do it—even before the first words are read.

We discussed which "form" of book would be most effective: should it be an academic work or should it be a trade book for everyone?

Forty minutes later, after we'd discussed the title, font, size, whether or not to put 'by Tiffany Earl', we *finally*... turned... the page!

"Okay, read," said Oliver.

I began on the first paragraph of the introduction, *"It is becoming a craze among some educators to study..."*

"Okay, stop there for a second."

I stopped.

"Why did you put the Introduction before the Table of Contents?"

I didn't have a particular reason, so we discussed using style guides in writing—the pros and cons.

He glanced over the Table of Contents, and asked the class for input. They suggested some minor changes, which I agreed to, and we were back to the Introduction.

"Tiffany, could you please start reading again?"

I began again.

"It is becoming a craze among some educators to..."

"Wait—"

I stopped.

Oliver put his paper down and looked at me.

"Tiffany, why are you writing this?"

"I want to teach the art of mentoring."

"Is it an art?"

"Yes."

"Does that mean you think it can be learned?"

"Yes, but that's not all it means."

"Okay, read on."

". . . for good reason, too."

"Stop."

I stopped.

"Why are you writing this? What is your goal?"

My mind raced back...

I had Oliver's book open in my hands. My heart was racing like I'd been running—only I hadn't. I'd only been reading.

Oh my goodness. This is it! These are the words. These are the words I'd yearned for as a youth. It's all here—the kind of education I'd been getting since starting college, the kind I'd craved since I was young.

It's all here—the words to explain how I've always felt. The things I yearned for.

There were tears streaming down my face. I reached through space and time just like I'd done with Tolstoy . . . Potok . . . Moses . . . Oliver's soul spoke to my soul. It was here. *These were the words.*

I kept reading.

"There are two types of great teachers that consistently motivate student-driven education: Mentors and Classics..."

Wait. Wait! That can't be all. I *know* that can't be all.

I quickly skimmed the pages he had written about mentoring.

The Student Whisperer

No! That can't be all, it just can't! I *knew* he knew more than that. I'd experienced him as a mentor.

Didn't he know that other people yearned for this too? Didn't he know that the twelve pages wouldn't suffice? They would only stir the imagination. The people wouldn't know what he really meant by mentoring. You have to *experience* it!

As I sat there, a familiar feeling washed over me. I could see it clearly. There were different kinds of mentors. Most people didn't know about them all.

Many people have Soul Mentors—those friends who are there through thick and thin, the ups and the downs. The ones who know how to tell you that you look awful or when to force a smile and say you look great. Whatever they choose to call them, people know about Soul Mentors.

Most people also know about Informal Mentors—the teachers who spend a little extra time with you, the drama and sports coaches who spend a lot of extra effort helping you; the scout leader who plants a seed once in a while; the uncle or grandfather who inspires you to try your hand at something new. People know about Informal Mentors.

But how many people know about Formal Mentors? I thought back to how hard it was to submit to a Formal Mentor—*but how worth it!* My strength and will to succeed increased ten times, maybe a hundred times! How many people know about Formal Mentoring? How many parents and teachers know how to be a Formal Mentor?

Then my heart skipped a beat: and what about Mission Mentors? My hand flew to my head! Mission Mentors! Mission Mentors weren't mentioned!

I'd been mentoring others, and knew the constraints on each type of mentoring: Informal, Soul, Formal, Expert, and Mission mentoring.

I got calls all the time from people seeking a mentor:

"I'm 60 years old, back in school, and someone recommended you as a good mentor, can you help me?"

"My daughter is 15. She's really talented in music, but has no desire to branch out, could you mentor her?"

"I'm 30 years old, trying to get a promotion, can you help me?"

"I'm president of my company. It's floundering, and I need some help. Can you arrange a time to meet with me?"

People sensed my clarity on The Path, and wanted the same. They were desperately reaching out for a mentor, not knowing what they were really reaching for.

Yes, being on the other end now made me see the huge need for people to understand the different types of mentoring, the constraints, the elements, the principles, the how, the why, and the when.

There are times for Expert mentors, Soul Mentors, Informal Mentors, Formal Mentors—and especially for Mission Mentors and Parent Mentors.

"Tiffany . . ." I heard Oliver's voice and came back to the present.

"Tiffany, what are you trying to accomplish? What is your goal?"

"My goal? I want to inspire leaders, teachers, parents, professionals and entrepreneurs to become better mentors. I want to teach about Formal Mentors, Informal Mentors, Soul Mentors, Expert Mentors and most importantly, Liberal Arts and Mission Mentors—and the impact each has on us."

I could tell he wasn't finished with me.

"To whom are you writing?"

"Anyone who wants to succeed, who needs mentoring to get ahead on The Path."

"What is it you want your readers to *know* . . . to *feel* . . . to *do*?"

Hmm, I thought to myself, *What do I want my readers to* **know**? *What do I want them to* **feel**?

My mind stretched and my eyes squinted. I reached for the words: "I want my readers to feel mentored. I want them to know which kind of mentor they need and why. I want them to *be* better mentors."

"What does it look like when you're done?" he asked. "Not how does the *book* look . . ." he continued, "How is the world different when the readers have finished your book? How are they transformed? How does the world look, feel, and taste different because of your work?"

He was looking straight at me. The whole class was looking at me. I closed my eyes and tried to picture how it felt to be mentored. I just kept seeing myself before I had a mentor, how hard I worked and how it never seemed to change things. I was in a rut for so long.

With a real mentor, I had to work even harder—but I kept getting better and better results. Sometimes it was really hard to take when a mentor told it to me straight, but I had to admit: I got the results I wanted. It was so much better to be on The Path. Like moving to a whole new climate, the air itself seemed better—more refreshing.

I pictured the people in my seminars, the mosaic of faces—each with a unique story, each wanting a certain fulfillment, and wondering where to get it; willing to do almost anything, but just not knowing what to do. Then I pictured those who had gotten on The Path, the changes in every aspect of their life, the fulfilled dreams they had finally started to achieve. It all started with a feeling—a feeling of what it is like to be working with a great mentor, with a mentor who really knows how to help. I looked up.

"I want them to *feel* mentoring. I want them to know what it feels like to be mentored. It looks hard, and it is; but it's so *wonderful!* I want them to feel it. If they could just feel it, I know more of them would get on The Path and find what they're looking for."

The class nodded. But I knew better—I held my breath while I waited.

Oliver exhaled thoughtfully. He quietly and intently looked at my draft. He just sat there and stared at it. Now the whole class seemed to be holding their breath. Then he looked up. He slowly asked the class, in almost a whisper, "How can Tiffany make the reader *feel* mentored?"

Silence again.

After a moment someone said, "Stories."

Another added, "It's the stories in her manuscript that really reached me."

"Yeah," said another, "it's through her stories that I felt inspired."

"I wish she had elaborated on some of her stories. They really piqued my interest."

"The bad mentors taught me as much as the good ones."

"Yeah, I learned that I'm a great Soul Mentor but a terrible Formal Mentor," one woman said.

One of the businessmen in the room spoke up, "I need a Mission Mentor."

"I've made the Vital Choices wrong at least twenty times," another one said.

Everyone laughed.

It got quiet and everyone looked at Oliver.

The smile left his face and he solemnly looked me right in the eyes.

"Tiffany, you don't need to write an article, monograph, or any kind of scholarly work. Your message isn't academic. Your message is universal, and it's needed by so many people."

"What you need to do," he paused a moment, ". . . is *tell your story*!"

Beginnings

by Tiffany Earl

"Daddy, tell me the story of my pinky finger again."

"Okay, one more story." He had finished the story of Peter Rabbit, which always made me nervous. I couldn't stand it that Peter continually disobeyed his momma and went into Mr. McGregor's garden. Why did he always think he could outsmart Mr. McGregor? Why did he want those onions so badly that he'd sneak under the fence? My tummy would tie in knots whenever Peter was being foolish. I just knew Mr. McGregor was around the corner!

Dad started the next story:

"We were at Grandma Rhoades' house and Robbie and Uncle Merlin were playing hide-and-seek. Tiffany was just a baby, learning how to walk. If she held on to something she could make her way around. All of a sudden we heard a door slam and Tiffany cry. Her pinky had been caught in the hinge part of the door.

"Grandma and Grandpa, and Mom and I, all rushed to see what happened. The top portion of Tiffany's pinky was cut off . . . hanging on by a piece of skin."

"What did you do, Dad? What did you do?" My little sister's eyes were huge.

Robbie answered, "He'll tell you. Be quiet and listen, SILLY."

"When we got to the hospital the doctor said he couldn't save her finger, but I told him to sew it back on anyway. I really felt it would heal. He sewed it on. The hardest part for me was seeing my little girl in pain. I had never hurt so badly in my life. I prayed that God would take the pain away from Tiffany and give it to me."

"Did He Dad? Did He?" It must have been the first time Kami had heard the story.

"No, He didn't. He wouldn't transfer the pain she felt to me. He just reminded me that He loved me and that He loves all of His children, and that how I was feeling, seeing my little girl in so much pain, was in a small way how He felt when He gave the world His Son. I was in the worst pain I had ever felt in my whole life—and it was only my daughter's little finger. I couldn't imagine how Heavenly Father must have felt when He gave the life of His Son. But I believed her finger would heal, and so the doctor sewed it back on."

"Did it Daddy? Did it heal?"

"Take a look for yourself," and he held up my hand for Kami to see.

"Let me see it. Let me see. Let me see." Kami jumped over to my bed and inspected both my pinkies.

"See, Kami, you can hardly tell which one it was. Except this one is a hair shorter and has a little line right here!" Kami looked at both my pinkies and giggled.

"Alright, it's time for bed now." And with that, Mom joined Dad in song and the familiar words lulled us to sleep.

I felt fortunate to be the second oldest. By the time we were all here, there were eight of us—or "two and a half dozen," as my father loved to boast. The way I figured, Kami was supposed to be a boy, but God couldn't do that to her and so it went: Boy, girl, *girl*, girl, boy, girl, boy, girl. Of course, when I was six there were only four of us: Robbie, me, Kami and Angie.

One particular day I'd been a bit too ornery and Dad was mad. I felt the slap of his hand as it whapped my behind. It smarted, but I checked myself in time. Again, Whap! I clenched my teeth and fists and stubbornly held back the tears. Another, Whap! Finally my dad stood me up. I stoutly put my hands to my hips and glared through the slits of my eyes. We stared at each other. My chest was heaving, but I would not cry.

Dad looked at his hand and I saw that it was red. His blue eyes looked back at me. There was something wet on his face.

What's that? Is Daddy crying? His hand is red, and... he's crying. My throat could no longer hold back the flood I'd so resolutely held at bay while being spanked, my dad's tears tore down my dam and I ran to his chest to be enveloped in his arms.

"Oh, Daddy, I'm sorry. I'm sorry. I'm sorry, Daddy. I won't ever hurt you again. I'm sorry I made you cry, Daddy. I love you." I stayed in his arms and I promised myself, over and over, *I won't ever hurt Daddy like this again.* It felt so good to be held.

A little while later I was playing under the table when I heard Daddy talking to Mom.

"Kath, I don't know what would have happened if I didn't break first. I'm afraid she wouldn't have cried no matter how many times I spanked her. I've learned something tonight, Kathy, and I'm glad I've learned it while she's little. It's a soft answer that'll reach her. Humility. That's the voice she hears and follows. It's like the Proverb says, 'a soft answer turneth away wrath, but grievous words stir up anger.' I need to remember this. It's how I'll influence her.

"She's got grit, Kathy. She's got something special inside of her—something strong, but good. She has a will like I've never seen; and yet, if I can reach her heart she'll bend to me."

Mom didn't say anything. She just patted Daddy's back and cleared the dishes. I continued to play quietly with my dolly under the table.

Four kitchens and five years later I walked into the kitchen and my dad motioned for me to sit by him. It was the same old table I had played under in every home we lived in. Dad's scriptures were spread out before him and his yellow legal pad had his scribbled text half way down the page. I don't know why, but my dad never used cursive, and his print was always in capital letters. I take that back. His signature was in cursive, a funny sort of cursive. It was really just a squiggle with a "J" at the beginning, an "A" in the middle, and an "R" near the end. He seemed to be like his handwriting—two extremes. He had an all-or-nothing sort of personality.

Lucky for me he was usually "always" pleased with me. Today he wanted my advice.

I sat down at the table across from him, set both my palms on the table with my elbows out like chicken wings, leaned toward him and said, "Yeah?"

"I'm preparing a lesson for the combined young men and young women this Sunday. There will be about 150 youth there. I want to inspire them to stay morally clean and chaste. Any ideas?"

I thought for a moment. "Yeah, if I were you I'd tell the story of Joseph of Egypt. That's a killer. Tell all about how Joseph had every excuse to sleep with Potiphar's wife, but chose to go to prison instead because he remained chaste.

"Then I'd tell the story of David and Bathsheba. I'd clearly draw a parallel between Joseph and David and show the consequences of how David was blessed of the Lord. He had the guidance of the Holy Ghost, the blessings of prosperity upon his seed, and the spirit of prophecy and love. Then I'd show how David became miserable. He couldn't sleep at nights. He killed his best servant to cover up his sins. He was found out in the end, and his posterity paid a heavy price for his sin."

He wrote two words in print on his paper and underlined them: "Joseph" and "David."

I continued, "You might want to add in how both David and Joseph are elect. Both of them knew the commandments of God. Both of them were taught the commandments by parents. Both of them loved the Lord, and both of them wanted to get back to heaven. So why did one fall and not the other?"

I paused there. I tapped my fingers and added: "I think I'd tell them the 'power thing' you taught me once. Tell them about how God gives us powers and depending upon how we use those powers we determine what power He'll give us in the future. Yep, I think you ought to tell them that."

He smiled appreciatively. "Thanks, Tiff. I knew you could help."

I smiled back, got up, walked over to reach myself an apple and headed to my bedroom.

I'm only eleven years old, I thought, *but my dad is already asking me for help on his lessons.* It wasn't until I was fifteen or sixteen that I suspected he might not really *need* my help. *He was just teaching* me.

Whatever the reason, it did several things. It taught me the habit of thinking things through from an end result backwards through the needed steps. It taught me the language of the classics—so much so that I was surprised in college when other people struggled with Shakespeare or Plato; after the Bible they seemed easy. Most importantly, it made me feel my dad's love for me. I knew he respected my understanding and insights, and it made me push myself. It taught me how to question and explore different ways of teaching principles. It was my first introduction to Soul Mentors and Informal Mentors— and how they can mix.

Not only did my dad informally mentor me, but I was fortunate enough to be formally mentored by him as well. I made commitments to him each month, and the next month we met again to analyze how I was doing and review my goals. The goals were academic, as well as personal and spiritual. Somehow these early formal mentor meetings had a big impact on me.

Once a month after our usual Monday evening family get-together, Dad would announce our monthly interviews. I loved these interviews with Dad.

One by one each of us would take a turn and go visit privately with him. I remember several meetings in great detail, but there is one that stands out in my mind.

My dad brought an article about photographic memory to our

meeting. I was intrigued and I blurted out, "Dad, I wish *I* had a photographic memory!"

"Why, honey?"

"Because I spend about 80% of my study time memorizing. With seven hours in school and about four hours of homework, that means that I spend over 8 hours a day memorizing just so I can get good grades. It really wastes my time. What I really want to be doing is *studying*. I want to be reading. I want to be talking to people about what I read. I want to be learning the important stuff, not just dates and names and places and bones and math figures and conjugations.

"If I had a photographic memory then I would be so much further ahead in my goals. Can you imagine how much I would really learn if I could memorize things at a glance—being able to recall what I memorized at a later date?"

My dad was intrigued and spent hours helping me learn about photographic memory. While he tried to diligently help me find out how to develop a photographic memory, I ultimately changed my focus to spend my time deeply understanding and internalizing, instead of memorizing.

Although I didn't learn how to memorize everything I read and saw, I *did* learn that my dad was truly interested in me, and in my dreams and goals.

The alarm went off at 5:00 a.m. I groaned and wished I could go back to sleep, but sleep wasn't what I'd be getting today. Some part of my groggy mind remembered that something was more important to me. I rolled out of bed and when my knees hit the floor I quickly said a prayer, adding, "Please help us to get the move right this time!"

In the dance studio three hours later, after two hours of grueling ballroom dancing, I found myself on my knees again. All eight of us girls were kneeling up. We were in a diagonal formation across the floor. We had each just spun as the music changed from a cha-cha to a waltz. Our partners dipped us and we went on our knees facing the west wall while the men waltzed to the side of us.

In a ripple, Melissa, the best dancer of us all, was the first to fan her left arm above her head in a circle, followed by her right arm. Her left arm stretched gracefully toward the west wall, her body faced the east wall—along with her right arm. In this kneeling position she then gently tilted her head to look toward her left hand and she dipped backward toward the floor. The muscles in her legs were toned and strong, and the first time doing the move was no problem; but this wasn't our first time. It was at least our twentieth, and my legs were feeling it.

On every half count the next girl in line arced her arm above her head exactly as Melissa had, pausing at the end and holding their positions five inches from the floor.

On count "three-and-a-half" I circled my left arm above my head and leaned into position.

"Stop. Stop. Stop. Stop!" said Mr. Wilding, or "Paul," as we called him.

"Do it again on my count—only this time ladies, make sure you take the full count as you fan your arm. And start precisely on your beat. Don't be late!"

Our partners helped us up and we began again on Paul's count.

Melissa was on her knees . . .

"One," (Paul's voice rang out) Melissa's left arm fanning above her head . . .

". . .and," Christy's arm fanned . . .

". . .two," Jaimee's arm began her fan . . .

". . .and," Heidi's arm fanned . . .

"Stop!" boomed Paul, "Let's do it again. Stay on your knees and on my count . . ."

I took a deep breath. My legs were beginning to shake . . .

"Five, six, seven, eight—One!" Melissa's toned (and tanned) arm stretched above her head and gently extended in position as her body leaned gracefully back . . .

". . .and!" Jaimee's arm . . .

". . .two!" Heidi's arm was supposed to fan but didn't . . .

". . .and" Lori's arm fanned and finished before Heidi was half-way through the move . . .

Paul walked over to Heidi and took hold of her left arm. Matter-of-fact-like he said, "On count 'two' your arm should be here." He put her arm into position.

"On count 'two-and' your arm should be here." He moved her arm above her head and toward the east wall.

"On count 'three' you lean into it and lay your body back, like this: Melissa, show her."

Melissa easily glided into position.

"Try it," said Paul to Jaimee, "on my count:

". . .two, " her arm shot out . . .

". . .and," it flowed above her head and pointed toward the east wall . . .

". . .three," she leaned her body back into position . . .

"Good. Again . . ."

". . .two" her arm went into place . . .

". . .and," again executed perfectly . . .

". . .three," she leaned back . . .

"Good. Once more."

"Two. And. Three." She did it.

"Everyone on my count!"

I'd been sitting on the floor, thankful for the rest. I got to my knees and faced the west wall.

"One," Melissa began the ripple . . .

". . .and," Christy moved next . . .

The Student Whisperer

". . .two," Jaimee hit her mark . . .

". . .and," Heidi's arm fanned above her head.

He got to "three-and"; I fanned my arms.

"That was better. Now let's do it to the music."

We got up and our partners spun us across the floor, dip, on our knees, listen close, one-ripple, and-ripple, two-ripple, and...so on until my turn.

Paul pulled his measuring tape out. He measured the angle of our diagonal line and how far apart we were from each other. One of us moved slightly forward, the other slightly back.

"Men, look over your left shoulder down the diagonal. You shouldn't be able to see anyone but the one directly in front of you. Walk around your partner until you are directly behind her. Take her right hand in your right hand, cup your left hand under her left bicep and gently help her up—don't look down. On my mark...."

The details were getting down to the nitty-gritty. The big university ballroom dance competition was in two weeks. We were all feeling the stress: extra dance rehearsals, private lessons for those competing in individual events and, of course, excitement. Our youth team had taken first place several times in a row and this year our rival team, "Buckles and Bows," swore they'd win.

My legs were burning. I thought that if I had to stay on my knees, leaning back, holding in my tummy and bottom for ten more seconds I'd collapse. Of course I didn't; but I felt relieved when rehearsal was over.

Two weeks later I stood in the sectioned-off dressing room in the big university ballroom.

There were flashy costumes hung up all over—the red and black flamenco dress for tonight's *Paso Doble*, the flowing pastel-colored dresses for the Quickstep, the half-skin-colored dresses for the Cha-Cha competitors.

I pulled on my fishnet stockings and stretched my legs once more. I slipped out of my long sweatshirt and into my aqua dress. To the right of me a woman was applying her lipstick and making stretching faces in the mirror. On my left Christy was buckling her dance shoes.

I could hear the blaring music and knew that our turn was two songs away. The music ended. I heard the clapping. Soon the girls from that team streamed into the dressing room.

"Sheesh, that was a mess! I told Jared not to hold me so tight on the lift—I could barely breathe. I'm surprised I could still dance when he put me down!"

"Oh yeah," exclaimed her friend, "my buckle came undone on my shoe and it was a pure miracle I wasn't dancing one-legged!"

They streamed past, in their own world. I exhaled sharply and knew we were only minutes away from show time.

I stretched my lips as I walked toward one end of the dressing room where our partners were waiting outside, "aaay, eeee, aiye, ooooh, ewwww." As I said "ewwww" I pursed my lips as far forward as they'd go.

We lined up. Our breathing was deeper and more rapid than usual. The butterflies in my stomach were annoying. My partner squeezed my hand and said, "You'll do fine, Tiff." I smiled and relaxed a little.

This was my dream. To come to a university like this someday and be on the Ballroom Dance team.

Our team was announced, the trumpets blasted and we cha-cha'd and waltzed our way to First Place.

At the time, I thought it was all about the competition. In retrospect I know that what Paul Wilding taught me had to do with so much more than dancing—things like trusting my mentor, working in a team, how to get more out of myself when I really want to quit, how to support others who are struggling to reach a common goal, aspiring to a standard of excellence; all these and more I learned from him. But soon things were to change. Soon I wouldn't be dancing with the team I loved so much.

The Student Whisperer

Kami had her arms folded across her chest. Her eyes looked dark and her brow was furrowed. She was fourteen and had just made the basketball team for next year at the high school. And now Mom and Dad were talking about moving—again!

It wasn't a big deal to me. Somewhere along the way I'd learned to accept the fact that we moved a lot. We'd moved 16 times by the time I was 16. I liked the opportunity to "start over" as I always had things I wanted to do differently and better.

My mom walked into the room and could feel the contention. Dad had called a family council and we eight kids were about to duke it out. Mom and Dad assessed the situation and sat down.

Dad spoke first, after a quick prayer from ten-year-old Shawn. "Mom and I would like to know how you all feel about moving to St. George."

All at once we exploded.

"No way!" said Kami.

"It's fine with me," I said.

"Where's St. George?" asked Angie.

"Don't be selfish, Kami. This is about being a family. I want to go if that's where Dad's job is," I exerted.

"I'm *not* being selfish. You just don't have anything to stay here for," she retorted.

"That's not true. For one, I have Wendy!" (She is still a close friend to this day even though we ended up moving over 300 miles apart.) "And I have lots of things I'm involved with at school. Don't forget: It's me who's moving at the end of my junior year, not YOU!"

Quietly Mom said, "I have an idea." We stopped arguing and looked at her.

"I want you all to look around."

We all looked at each other. Shawn was in cut-offs. His shirt was dirty from playing outside and his hair tousled. Angie was in jeans and a t-shirt. We just let our eyes roam around the room as we looked at each other.

My mom continued, "Now I want you to trade places with the one next to you." There were an even number of people. Kami and I traded places.

"As you do so, I want you to become that person . . . put yourself in their place . . . pretend you are them."

I sat down on the wooden chair where Kami had been, and she sat on the couch. This was going to be fun. We were all squirming in our seats until we were in each other's normal poses or stances. The little kids started giggling.

Angie put a piece of hair in her mouth the way Sarah usually did. Shawn sat up straight and tall and put his hands quietly upon his lap the way Robbie always sat. Kami and I just looked at each other and tried not to laugh.

"Okay," said Mom, and she looked at *me*. "Kami, how do you feel about moving to St. George?"

I paused and concentrated for a minute . . . "I worked really hard to make the basketball team. Try-outs are over now and if we move to St. George I won't get to play basketball next year. I just don't want to go."

The family was surprised. My mom went on. She looked straight at *Kami* and said, "Tiffany, how do you feel about going?"

"All that I care about is doing what God wants. If Heavenly Father wants us to go then I say 'Let's Go!' I'll go wherever he sends us. I just want to do what's right. So if you and Dad feel like this is right, I say: 'Let's go'."

I looked closely to see if she was mocking me—but no, she meant it. I was shocked. I had no idea that Kami actually *understood* me. We continued around the room and everyone had a turn being someone else and seeing The Move through someone else's eyes.

By the time we were done we were all looking at each other differently. When we did move, seven days later, I felt really bad that Kami had to leave the basketball team, and Kami had a little more courage that things would work out. They did—including Kami playing high school ball.

It was hard saying goodbye to my best friend, Wendy. We'd been friends for almost four years. We didn't start out that way though. At first I almost hated her.

When she moved in I became jealous of her when she hit it off so well with all my friends and teachers. It felt like she replaced me. Our parents wanted us to be friends, though. Her dad wanted her to hang out with me because I got good grades, and my dad liked her because he knew what a caring and loving person her mother was.

Pretty soon we saw the good in each other and arranged our schedules so that we could see each other every day. Her dad may have wanted her to improve her grades and thought she would if she spent time with me, but I admired her because she didn't play "the game". If she wanted to learn something she let her homework slack and just studied what she wanted. I remember the time she stayed up all night to read her favorite book, *Christy*, and didn't learn much at school the next day. Somehow, I admired that; and I admired her integrity and honesty—but most of all, her virtue.

When I was almost seventeen and we were moving, Wendy and I went on a walk around the neighborhood, our familiar stomping grounds, for the last time.

"Let's give each other one piece of advice before you leave, Tiffany," she said. I thought it sounded like a great idea, so we did. I don't remember what I told her, but I do remember her counsel to me. I remember it because it changed me. Wendy and I were not critical of each other, and to have her advice to me be what it was made it pretty important.

"Tiffany, my advice for you is . . . be nicer to Shawn."

My jaw dropped. Shawn was both ten years old and my "little brother." Why should Wendy care?

"What do you mean, Wendy?"

"I mean, you may not know this, but you are very critical of him. Whenever you are with him you boss him around."

"I do?" I really had no idea that I did. Then I thought about it. Almost every time I came home and saw him he was sitting at the computer or TV playing video games. Sure enough, I always told him what a waste of time it was and that he should turn it off and go do something else.

"What he really needs from you is just your love."

I took Wendy's advice seriously and I tried to be a better sister to Shawn.

Sometimes there are those few people in the world that we connect with, that are there for us, and that have influence over us in profoundly quiet ways. Wendy was one of my soul mentors, or for lack of a better word, *friend*; and in Scholar Phase, Soul Mentors are as significant as other mentors—for good or for ill. Not even the miles could separate our love and friendship, but the road to being nicer to my brothers and sisters wasn't easy.

I hefted my heavy JanSport backpack higher up on my shoulder as I let out a groan. I said goodbye to my ride, and as I turned to look at my front door I mentally assessed the situation. As I saw it, I had at least two hours of non-interrupted intense study to do in order to be prepared for tomorrow's exam. I had my readings to finish, vocabulary to memorize, and some memorizing for the essay exam—dates, names, events, facts to prove my point, etc.; and of course I had the biology assignment to do.

Why the trepidation? This was no different from every other Thursday. Why the sigh? Because this Thursday *was* different from every other Thursday. I knew what awaited me in the house. Mom had surgery today and wasn't due home for a week—and she would be bedridden for two weeks after that. My dad was working out of town and I was the oldest girl. My brother Rob was running the fort on his own until I walked through those doors. Rob was out of college for the term and lucky for us, he could help during the day.

Here it goes! I thought as I walked through the front door.

Sarah was the first to meet me. "Tiffany! Tiffany! Watch me! Watch me! I can do a cartwheel! Wanna see?" She grabbed my arm and pulled me into the living room. My backpack fell to the floor where she grabbed me and I grudgingly followed to watch her cartwheel.

After a dozen cartwheels back and forth I started to turn back to the hall where I'd left my work. Sarah called to me, "Did you see that one? Want to watch me do a round-off now, and a back-bend?"

"Maybe later, Sarah. I've got some homework to do." With that I left her beckoning me and sat down in a blue rocking chair next to the piano. I opened my biology book and started reading, "Mitosis: the . . ."

Six-year-old Jonathan jumped on my lap, upsetting my books and papers. "Read to me. Read to me. I want to study with you, Tiffany. Read to me!" I sighed and lifted Jonathan down. "Later, buddy, later. I'm studying my biology right now."

"I want to study biology! Read to me!"

Just then four-year-old Katie came in with her teddy bears. There were crocodile tears in her eyes. "Will you play 'house' with me Tiffy? No one else will!"

I sighed as I put down my book. *Where was Mom? Why was she gone? The kids needed her. Where was Dad? Why was he gone? The kids needed him. Where was Rob? Oh—he was in the kitchen cleaning and cooking. At least I didn't have to take care of that part!*

I plopped my biology book down. I gathered up my papers and put them all in my backpack. My heart was heavy and hurting. I really wanted to just be let alone so I could study for my test and do my homework.

A thought squeezed its way into my mind: *There are tests that are unseen, and no one knows the grades of others.*

What? Like this is some sort of test. The devil/angel-on-your-shoulder skit was playing now. One side said, "The test at school tomorrow is the most important. Your grades are everything! College, scholarships—everything depends on your grades." The other side piped in, "This whole life is a test, Tiffany, and you're on trial right now."

I closed my eyes and leaned back into the chair as Katie set her white teddy bear on my lap. Jonathan took my biology book and climbed up on me. Sarah came into the room and commenced doing cartwheels.

Here were three precious little souls, needing me, needing my attention, needing me to hold them, to listen to them, to watch them, to play with them, to read with them, to love them, to reassure them while their life was a little out-of-kilter for a few days. And there lay a book unread, an assignment unfinished, and a list unmemorized.

I took Jonathan into my lap and for the first time, *put people first.* For the first time it hit me. My education was about one thing: It was about my ability to serve. It was no longer an abstract goal of accomplishment. It was very literal. I made up my mind right then that I would pass the higher test, the unseen test, the *real* test.

I taught Jonathan biology. I played "house" with Katie. I even tried a backbend with Sarah. The next day in fourth period I failed a test for the first time in my life. I can't say that it felt good to fail, but I can say that somehow on that unspectacular day I internalized a much-needed life lesson. It's been clear to me ever since why I seek an education: to be able and willing to serve with greater capacity.

I sat across from my mom and explained my dilemma: I needed more time to study. She looked over my schedule, realizing how heavy my workload was. I had the credits I needed for graduation, but what I wanted was time at school to study. Neither one of us knew how much power we really had—that I could just come home early and study. We never looked at that as an option.

Instead I went to the secretary of the high school the next morning with a plan.

You'll have to talk to the principal about it," she said. Picking up the phone on her desk, she said, "Mr. Brockbank, can you see a student for a moment? Thank you." Looking at me, she smiled and said, "Go on in, Tiffany."

With that I stepped into the principal's office. I explained my plan to him.

"Mr. Brockbank, I have a very heavy load and I don't want my studies to suffer. I have an extra hour that I'd like to take as a study hour instead of filling it with just any class. My old high school allowed us to do this. If we had an Advanced Placement class, we could sign up for a study hour. Can I take a study hour please?" I had two AP classes.

He looked at me from across his desk. He looked over my schedule. He could see the hard classes I was taking. I thought for sure he'd let me.

"Tiffany, I'm sorry, but it's not in our policy. You'll just have to sign up for another class."

"What do you mean it's not in your policy?"

"I mean, we don't make exceptions for just one person. What we have for one, we have for all. We don't have study hour. You will have to choose another class."

"You mean that because there aren't other students who need a study hour that you can't let me take a study hour?"

"It's not in our policy. Good day, Miss Rhoades." He stood and reached out to shake my hand.

It wasn't the first time I'd seen bureaucracy, but it was the first time I felt a deep hatred for how policy can get in the way of serving the mission of the organization. I was mad. I'd played the game long enough to know I wasn't beat. I'd find another way to have a study hour.

In that moment I took a mental note that made me decide what good policy and bad policy were. The number one policy had to be the goal of the institution, even if other policies didn't match it. I was too young to question if maybe business, or money, or politics, or something else, *was* the number one goal of the school, and only secondarily the student's education—and so maybe they followed their policy just fine. I never threatened to leave, so they never had to offer me a better option.

I looked over the available classes once again and did some investigating. I found one that was a no-brainer. The first five minutes were spent recording the next day's school news to be broadcast at the nine o-clock hour and then it was free time for the rest of the hour. There were only four other kids in the class. The teacher was Mr. Andrus, the librarian, and we all really enjoyed being around him for some reason. Even though we never talked about anything very deep or instructive, I really came to sense a deep goodness in him. And he gave me my space.

Perfect, I thought, *I can help with the recording for a few minutes and then study in the library for the rest of the time.* The other four students split up and went their own ways, usually wandering the halls. I just found a little nook in the library and opened my books.

Half the reason I wanted an hour to myself was because I was frustrated that I hadn't signed up for calculus. I'd given up cheating years before, and I just couldn't maintain an "A" in calculus and earn the much-needed scholarship. I actually loved math. I'd just hit a place where my best seemed to be a "B." I was tentative on some of the pre-calculus principles and I didn't dare go on.

I wanted to go at my own pace. My math teacher had said I could come in any time for a coaching session. I started reading the trig book. Nothing was making sense. It was a blur. I could figure out the answers, using the formulas with the sines and cosines, the tangents, all of it, but none of it made sense. I didn't want "answers" without the sense to go with it.

When I went in and asked questions of my math teacher, he just didn't understand my questions. "Why? Why? Why?" was all I could say.

He'd back up and give me the numerical reasoning behind why. What neither of us knew is that I was searching for the qualitative, not the quantitative answer behind each numerical symbol. I was tired of having half the math. I was tired of the observation without the application. I needed something real to grasp onto before any more measurement made sense.

I struggled with my math texts for a few weeks without any breakthroughs and finally focused all my energies on my other studies. I read classics in literature and enjoyed being able to study while being at school.

Graduation time neared, and I dressed up for the Awards Ceremony. The whole student body was there, along with many prestigious state colleges and private universities.

One by one the universities announced the recipients of scholarships to their schools. One by one the honored seniors walked up on stage to receive their certificates and be applauded by the student body.

When it was all over my legs were a little shaky. I wasn't used to wearing a nice dress, my best dress, to school, all decked out in hose and heels. I'd gone up on stage several times. Besides the university scholarships, there were awards from various school organizations: Drama, English, Math, Debate, Sterling Scholar (the scholarship offered by our state to recognize outstanding students), and several more.

As I counted, I realized I'd gone up on stage eleven times to receive my awards and scholarship—far more than the next most honored student. When it was all over and the auditorium emptied, I stayed in my seat to savor the moment as people milled around with hugs, handshakes and well wishes.

After about half an hour I slowly stood and gathered my ribbons, pins, certificates, and awards. I took a last look around the room, and then I slowly walked up the aisle and out of the auditorium. The school was quiet, the lights weren't bright, and I was still in my own world as I rounded a corner and bumped into the librarian, Mr. Andrus.

"Tiffany, hello."

"Hello, Mr. Andrus. How are you?"

"I'm fine. Um, Tiffany, congratulations on all your hard work and scholarships," he said. "I, uh..."

I just waited while he searched for the words. He wasn't overly tall, maybe 5'11". He wasn't skinny or fat. He had thick brownish-blond hair. His eyes had always been kind. I'd always felt beholden to him because I was left to myself in the no-brainer class and could do what I wanted. Now he was stammering, trying to tell me something.

"What is it, Mr. Andrus?" I had no idea that the following year he would be the new principal. He was just the librarian to me.

"I—; Tiffany, I didn't know you were *smart*." I just looked at him. I took a deep breath of happiness. After an evening filled with awards and recognition, his one statement meant so much to me. Ever since I could remember, I'd played the game; and one of the rules of the game was: if you are smart, the teachers like you and treat you better. If you are not smart, you will only be in their way. So, I'd played the game to win. I had ribbons and certificates and scholarships. I had arrived! It was all worth it—every last, hard hour spent memorizing while my friends played.

Now his words gave me a different level of satisfaction, of joy, because it turned out that with him I hadn't had to play the game to win affection and respect. Mr. Andrus had always treated me as kindly as all of my other teachers had, but *he* hadn't played the game. He liked **Me**—whether I was smart or not.

I want to be like you, Mr. Andrus, I thought. *I don't want to judge people on their ability to do well at academics or not. I want to be like you.* The thing is, there was something I knew inside, something other people never guessed: I wasn't really smart.

I learned that in the tenth grade.

I had a geometry test 7th period on Monday afternoon. Usually they were on Fridays. Thursday night right before bed I crammed for half an hour, then at lunch I looked over my notes once more, and by 7th period I would ace the test.

I didn't study on the Sabbath, though. I was taking the counsel of one of my religious leaders and trusting that if we kept the Lord's Day reserved for the Lord and His work, then we would have treasures of wisdom—so I didn't study on Sundays.

The Student Whisperer

There's no such thing as cramming Saturday for a test Monday—that defies the Laws of Cramming; but I wasn't the least bit worried. I'd done this many times before, and I was completely confident in my ability to cram on Monday and ace the test. *No sweat! I was good at this, and my abilities had never failed me.* I would just take the sheet of paper that had the twenty-two theorems and postulates on them (which filled the whole page, single-spaced and typed) to gym Monday morning and memorize it while I jogged around the track.

Only it was different this time. After jogging around the track once, I should have had at least five theorems and postulates memorized. I looked over the first sentence, shut my eyes, and tried to see the words in my mind. I couldn't see them. I opened my eyes, looked down at my paper, shut my eyes again, and tried to repeat the theorem. I couldn't do it.

What's wrong? This is really weird! I slowed down to a walk. I concentrated harder on my paper. I shut my eyes and tried to repeat the theorem. Nothing. Nothing. Nothing. Absolutely nothing. I gasped. I stopped in my tracks.

Class ended and I was shaken. *I'll just have to bring my math paper with me to 2nd period.* I did. I didn't hear a word my teacher lectured about. I just stared at my geometry theorems and couldn't believe that I couldn't memorize them.

This is bad, I thought, *I'm going to have to take them with me to seminary.* As a general rule I didn't take homework to seminary (a scripture-study class with other youth of my faith). I reserved that time for studying scriptures. *But this was an emergency.* If I didn't get above 80% on this test, I would fail Geometry. That was Mr. Hilton's rule. Everyone passed the theorems with 80% or higher or failed the class. End of story.

I brought my paper to seminary. It was the same as before. At the end of class, I knew nothing. Absolutely nothing.

I took my math to English class. Same thing. Nothing.

I skipped lunch and bored into my paper, but the added effort did no good. *This is so weird! I can't even memorize one theorem. Man, this is freaky!* I finally decided to call home.

"Rob, is Mom there? Where is she? Do you have the car? Oh good. I need you to come pick me up. I have a test in two hours and I don't think I'm going to pass. I need you to come pick me up. What? You won't come get me?

"Rob, I'm desperate! I've never asked you to do this before. *Please! Come get me.*"

He refused to check me out of school. I hung up.

I was immediately humbled. I found my way to the only private place in the whole school, the girl's restroom. I went into the stall and, shutting the door, I cried while I prayed, "I didn't know it was *you*. I thought it was me. I didn't know it was a gift. I didn't know that I couldn't even memorize a silly list of sentences all by myself. Please help me. Please help me pass this test. Now I know that I can't even pass a test on my own."

I went to 5th and 6th periods and still tried to study my theorems, but at the end of Spanish class, 6th period, I still couldn't recite even one theorem.

I slowly walked up the stairs to my math class. I dropped the math sheet in the garbage before walking in. I sharpened my pencil and sat at my desk. My mind was blank. I didn't know one theorem. All these years I'd seen myself as *smart*. All these years I'd thought it was me; but now I knew. Now I knew it was God. He was the *real* mentor. Mr. Hilton passed out the papers. The exam began. I put my pencil to the paper and in twenty minutes finished writing. Every theorem was written in its entirety. I turned in my exam and left when class was over.

I was a different person. For the first time in my life I realized that it wasn't me. It was all God.

So when Mr. Andrus looked in my eyes and said, "I didn't know you were smart," it felt like the greatest compliment ever. He liked me, and cared about me for just me. His interest was unconditional—and I knew I wanted to be like him. In my hand I had several awards, all for excellence; but in front of me was someone who was interested in me not for my achievements, but just because I was a human being.

Like my friend Wendy, he was a mentor to me in a way that I really needed at that critical time in my life, even though I didn't realize it—and probably he didn't either. Through his example I saw the connection between being a great teacher and being a great human being. I saw a man whose actions were in line with his Core values. I saw a glimpse of the kind of teacher I might someday be.

My academic decisions didn't come as a surprise to Mom and Dad. They understood my hunger. They understood my desire for knowledge. There were no words to express the fulfillment and deep satisfaction I got from learning.

The first time I knew of someone else who had experienced what I hungered for was when I was fifteen. Only I couldn't talk back and forth with the person; I didn't even know him. I only knew he understood my feelings because it was in his book. The Unexplainable Feeling was in his book.

It was late and everyone else had gone to bed, but I just couldn't put the book down. It was Saturday and I'd been reading *The Chosen* all weekend.

Something was happening inside of me. Danny and Reuben had been forbidden to speak to each other. I was holding back the tears as they crossed each other in the school halls and glimpsed into each other's eyes, searching, longing to speak to one another. My tears were beginning to swell—though none had fallen.

I ached for them to connect with one another. The waterfall came as they sat in class and the Rabbi opened the scriptures before them and asked for explanations of the passage. No one understood the doctrine, the mnemonics or the commentaries as well as Danny and Rueben. Soon the entire class sat in awe listening to the two expound, debate, and finally conclude. Now Reuben understood the silence Danny was raised with.

I sat on my sister's bed, clutching the book, with tears wetting my face for two reasons. First was because of the pain and rejoicing I felt for Danny and Reuben and second, for a purpose not easily defined. Something reached across both space and time, and somehow I knew that Chaim Potok understood me in a way that no one else seemed to. He understood what joy it brings to discuss ideas that can change you.

I couldn't put words to it at the time or, in fact, for years. I yearned to experience greatness, great art, great literature, great ideas, great people . . . and discuss things that really mattered. I didn't know mentors could be in books, could teach and question and challenge and lead across the decades through little marks on the page. I didn't even know about mentors at the time.

I knew it had to do with my education. I knew it had to do with knowledge. There was something I wanted to become, someone I wanted to be. I yearned to become something more than I was. And somehow I knew that the thing that empowered me more than anything else, the thing that helped me change and grow, was in the stories and writings of great people.

Depth

by Tiffany Earl

I had waited all my life for this—or so it seemed. I loved being a student, but high school was so—*complicated*. It was complicated for good reasons, some reasons that I loved—clubs and activities, family responsibilities, social struggles (okay, so I didn't love that one as much). But now I could be the boss of my time. Now that I was away at college I could study as long and hard as I wanted, and I answered to nobody but myself! Well—myself and my mentor. But having a formal academic mentor was the best thing about it! I looked forward to having what Danny and Reuben had: deep discussions with other serious students about the classics, hours and hours of study without the pull of some other thing on that time, and a guide to help me find more in the books—more in me—than I would on my own.

I had kept a journal for many years, so the new student orientation on the first day didn't catch me completely off-guard. We were each given a hardbound book with dates and lined pages. Oliver explained that George Wythe had his students keep a "Commonplace Book" to record their study hours, their thoughts on lectures and readings, and quotes that inspired thought—whether in agreement or rebuttal.

As he went on to explain how to use the book, and what it had meant for Thomas Jefferson, I fanned the pages from right to left and then from left to right and back again. Seeing all those blank pages waiting to be filled with my ponderings and quotes from great thinkers, leaders, and innovators was a little bit daunting. I wondered what it would feel like, years from that moment, to look back on my commonplace book.

Reading the personal journals I had kept from the time I was eleven was always good for a laugh. Sometimes I would shake my head at the way I had seen things at the time. Sometimes I wished I could just give myself a hug and promise my hurting heart, with the benefit of the hindsight, that it would all work out. Sometimes I marveled at the lessons that came in simple ways. Often I was overwhelmed with gratitude at the sense I had that my life had a purpose, and I was not alone.

Now, fanning the pages of a two-inch hardbound book that was mine to fill with my experiences with classics, mentors, peers and personal ponderings, I wondered what tears, struggles, triumphs and transformations would fill those lines.

Excerpts from my first Academic Journal (" commonplace book"):

We've been asked to keep a "commonplace book," or an academic journal of our "a-ha!s," studies, papers, notes, and readings. I think it's a good idea, though I'm sure it *won't* be easy. I'm used to keeping a journal, but rarely have I taken the time to discuss some of my deepest thoughts in writing. I usually just discuss them verbally with friends. This is going to be a challenge. It takes a lot of work to write thoughts down. It's so much easier to just talk. But I'm going to do it.

Whoever said Shakespeare was entertainment? This is such hard work. Okay, it's entertaining too. I'm frustrated with *Macbeth*. Why read about a madman? Why did Shakespeare waste his talent on such evil, such sickness, such insanity? Just listen to Lady Macbeth:

> *"I have given suck, and know*
> How tender 'tis to love the babe that milks me:

I would, while it was smiling in my face,
Have pluck'd my nipple from his boneless gums,
And dash'd the brains out, had I so sworn as you
Have done to this."[4]

Sick! It's just full of sickness. Why did Shakespeare write *Macbeth*? The first Shakespeare play I ever read was *Julius Caesar*, and I loved it. I appreciate how Shakespeare understands why people do the things they do. I also appreciate his honesty in showing us the natural consequences of choices. It's something rare these days—at least in many forms of media it's rare. It's rare to find movies that are worth watching because of the truths they reveal. I know it's possible. It's just a small percentage of what's available.

I've discovered something I feel passionate about. It has to do with the way I judge books, movies, music, etc. Often I ask myself if the book I am reading, the play I am watching or the movie I am seeing is uplifting or degrading—and yet not all movies that I felt were worthy of my time were necessarily "uplifting".

Categorizing what I read as "good," "bad," "evil" and "uplifting" helps me place the value of what I study in its proper perspective. I stay away from evil books, and I shun movies that are *bad*. I just have no use for being lied to and taught that good is evil and evil is good. Except, I've learned that there are two categories of "bad."

There is the lowest category that has evil shown as good and good as evil, with virtually no educational or redeeming value at all—like pornography or sensational, gory movies. There is another category of "bad": philosophers like Marx describe social ills like the wealthy land owners taking advantage of the proletariat, the property-less, and then jump to a conclusion that everyone can live in an "equal things" state by forcing a "no ownership" form. He flat-out believes—or at least teaches—something I think is a lie. He ignores one of human nature's most basic instincts: that when a few get power, they are going to keep it, skim some significant wealth off the top, and not distribute it equally.

Also: if families have no stewardship over something and no ownership in land, their production goes down. Why have hundreds of millions of people accepted Marx's formula for civilization's happiness when he doesn't address many aspects of human nature? These omissions end up making his formula a formula of calling evil "good." These readings, though "bad", are very valuable and educational. It just takes a lot of work to figure out what an author is saying, and if he or she is calling good evil and evil good.

I appreciate authors who tell me the truth. That's why I like Shakespeare so much. He might talk about lying, murder, adultery, etc., but always he *shows* the truth. It's not like a soap opera where someone is portrayed as being really happy committing adultery. You can't convince me that if somebody lies, cheats, and steals, they're not miserable. Popular media so often portray such behaviors with absolutely no reference to the shame, the loss of self-esteem, the paranoia and irrational self-justification. That's such a lie.

I appreciate movies that tell me the truth, too. I watched a movie the other day that bothered me. It seems everyone likes the movie and so I kept asking myself why it bothered me. I've come to the conclusion that I feel lied to by it, so it's just not entertaining to me.

The movie follows a *Robinson Crusoe* or *Emile* motif of being marooned on an island alone (a little different than *The Lord of the Flies* or *The Tempest* plot of groups being stuck on the island. I wonder why islands are such a theme—I mean, even *Ender's Game* and *Sackett's Land* use the motif). I think it had the makings of a great movie. We get to see the man try to survive physically, from building shelter to finding food. We also get to see how he survives mentally and emotionally—which is where I felt the lies.

I believe that ninety-five out of one hundred Americans would have eventually sought God, whatever their affiliated religion or upbringing. I understand how money and the elite can impact Hollywood. I understand that there is a popular philosophy of post-modernism where people don't turn to God anymore. But if someone is stranded on an island for several years, the teachings of their parents and grandparents are eventually going to strike them as an option. Or at least they will appeal to their inner yearning for help, or some sort of rescue—if only on an emotional plane. When I see a story where this option is never explored, never addressed, never explained—even when the character is desperate and reaching for *anything* for help, companionship, comfort, solutions—it feels contrived to me. To put it more bluntly: it seems like a lie.

Shakespeare doesn't lie to me. Shakespeare doesn't do that. Shakespeare is entertaining, but he's *more* than that. I find myself understanding people and situations better because of my exposure to Shakespeare. At least he shows the truth.

For instance, I had a feeling of jealousy creep up last week, and my mind instantly rebuked the feeling with the words, "Down, Iago, fie. Fie." I have no desire to harbor jealousy when I see Iago and his trickery and abuse.

The other day two of my college friends were upset at each other. One was misinformed and treating the other rudely and mean. "She's just being Othello," I thought. Thoughts like that, from Shakespeare, carry the choice to its clear end. The behavior and its consequence are so clear. Shakespeare brings depth to my life. I crave to understand human nature as he did.

But it's not just human nature he reveals, like Brutus's being tempted to listen to Cassius and commit murder. He also uncovers principles and hidden gems of truths. There are layers and layers to Shakespeare. That is what I am waiting for with *Macbeth*. When will I find it? You won't believe how gross it is. It's just sick to get inside the head of such a wicked man. And his wife, I'll call her Jezebel, is so cruel. I'm so frustrated that Shakespeare would waste his time on a Macbeth. There must be a reason. Until I find it, off I go to more hand washing, avarice, witches, hard-heartedness, murder, and madness.

I'm not so mad at Shakespeare anymore. I kept asking myself why such a genius would spend time on Macbeth. I have enough awe for his other works that I figured there had to be a good reason. The first thing that helped make sense of it was the fact that Macbeth was telling a historical story, even though it's considered one of his tragedies. He wrote the play for the descendant royalty of one of the men that Macbeth, or someone, murdered. I can go there. If it's about a real person I could forgive him a little. But that's not the most fascinating "a-ha." I was reading in one of my core classics and came across an idea that struck me. It made me thankful Shakespeare wrote *Macbeth*.

It said that we should study nations, men, laws, kingdoms, countries, etc. It's important to my freedom that I obtain a knowledge of these things, and part of that is the knowledge of men such as Macbeth.

Though it isn't easy or pleasant to understand such evil, there is wisdom in it. I'm thankful that the understanding can come through such a non-threatening way as reading *Macbeth*. I have friends and acquaintances who won't read something if it's sad, or who won't watch something if there's killing. It reminds me of the weak characters in L'Amour's books. Sometimes an Easterner will decide he wants to move out West, where there's rough country, outlaws, others who are dangerous, and sometimes no law. The Easterner who moves West without a rifle and the wherewithal to use it dies by page two.

But the Easterner who knows better, who realizes there are bad men who will stop at nothing to gain a little, and who brings along his rifle, a little common sense and a lot of hard work ends up building communities, ranches, and a family. Actually, some of them die too. Life is hard.

There are people like Macbeth, people who want power and are willing to sell their soul, hurting others, to get it. I feel bad for people who can't live with their own choices and yet continue in such behavior. It makes me think of Gollum. He was miserable, always fighting himself, always wretched.

Those whose hearts are not full of darkness may as well be aware that there are those whose are. I suppose that is why Shakespeare *didn't* waste his time on *Macbeth*. He knew there was wisdom in knowing about all men, even a Macbeth. I would rather learn about the Macbeths and Hitlers of the world and be armed to discern them through a harmless play than to be in a camp in Germany in 1940.

I want to be like Shakespeare and *know* more—more about every-thing. Shakespeare helps me do this because I learn so many truths from him.

I am so glad Shakespeare wrote *Macbeth*. Okay, I know this is a change, but I love *Macbeth*, or *Macduff* as I now call the play. Oliver said the play is named wrong. He never calls the play *Macbeth*, except to people who won't know what he's talking about otherwise. He says it should be called *Macduff*. 'In the play *Macduff* . . ." he says and then he just keeps talking about it. This has really made me think.

"There is a king and two characters," Oliver said. "Macduff is loyal to the king, supports the king, gives his life for the king, and wants the king to have the glory. The other character, Macbeth, wants the glory for himself. He wants to replace the king. Both seek followers. They've been seeking followers for years—ever since the play was first written and even before that. Over and over each generation chooses Mac-beth—he is the hero, the play is named after him, the best actors get his role. Macduff, on the other hand, is unknown. He is uncomely and has nothing to recommend himself to us. He is ignored and rejected. Yet it is he who bears our sorrows, who carries our crosses, who stands for what is right, as we all should. I have no idea if Shakespeare meant it this way, but it is inspired nonetheless. Each generation gets to choose—Macbeth or Macduff. May we choose wisely."

Wow. Oliver got real passionate as he talked to us about this. He said Macbeth is hugely important to our generation, to all genera-tions. Sometimes I'm really humbled when I go to class. Here I read *Macduff* and didn't even see it. How could I be so blind? I sat there in class dumbfounded. The Biblical allusions in Shakespeare aren't subtle after someone points them out to you. The play has taken on a whole new meaning to me. Even Macbeth's ugly character takes on a whole new meaning—he was always so miserable, so full of hatred, so selfish, so devilish. And then there's Macduff. I just need time to think. I'm thankful for a teacher who can bring out so much more in the classics! I'm glad I'm not going it alone.

My first simulation is coming up. The purpose of simulations is to train us in leadership. In fact, more than just leadership—but *statesmanship*. Simulations can help train our emotions! By role-playing we can give ourselves experiences we couldn't otherwise have and by so doing we can be better prepared for future leadership roles. I don't know, I'm a bit nervous. I've discovered that for normal assignments there's always a sense of completion—I know when I'm "done." With simulations, no matter how much research I do, I just don't feel quite prepared. Besides, role-playing just can't be real, can it?

The simulation is over. I'm exhausted. In fact, I'm still shaking. I feel bad for the students who were afraid of public speaking and who are used to getting away with staying in the background—never taking a stand. This was harder on them since nobody could really sit back very long. At least I'm used to speaking in front of others.

It was nothing like I thought it would be. I thought that we would get together at the summit and break up into committees and form a plan to defend the earth. Instead, for the past two weeks, various delegates have been meeting in secret and forming alliances. That's the number one thing I learned: most negotiations take place behind the scenes! I had no idea that was going on. I only met with my own delegation.

Also, never think you know the objective of the other guy. Or in different terms, never think that *they* have the same objective as you.

I blindly believed that the objective was to defend earth. *Wrong.* There were delegates who saw way past that. They cooperated by getting men to join the united armies, but behind the scenes Russia and China created an alliance and laid plans to rule the world.

Luckily Japan knew a little something and threw a kink into their plans—but not until after damage had been done. Two girls were in tears because they felt the rules of the game hadn't been explained

The Student Whisperer

properly, one classmate threw his book on the floor and stomped out, and we were all threatened by a terrorist who slipped into the meeting and wanted to sell out to the aliens who presented the global threat that led to the summit in the first place.

All through the simulation I kept wanting to tell myself, "This isn't real. This is only a test," like channel 8 used to do. But I kept hearing myself think, "Make it real! It's the only way you'll learn."

Besides, the students who *did* break character had to deal with the mentors who seem to have this uncanny way of bringing you right back into it without seeming to. They would say, "Fine, be out of character, but answer me this question: Don't you think Madison would have said that Federalists 2 – 4 apply even if Paper 8 doesn't?" By the time you're finished answering the question, there are a dozen people gathered around debating and the mentor has been gone for twenty minutes!

It was painful to make it real. I felt so vulnerable. Not only was it intellectually difficult to grasp the power plays going on, but it took all I had to stay emotionally in control—especially when the other people, delegates, just plain didn't care about the things the United States valued: a federal democratic republic, freedom, families, liberty.

That was the hardest part: keeping respect for other delegates whom I didn't think deserved respect. After all the debating, subcommittees, and voting took place our resolutions failed miserably. But Oliver said our simulation wasn't a failure just because we couldn't come to a united resolution. He said sometimes "no deal" is a viable option. It may be the best option in certain circumstances. It's part of real life.

Debriefing was the best part. It was hard for some of us to get out of character though. After hours and hours—weeks really—of playing the part, it was hard to let go. We went around the room and shared what we learned.

How can I explain the change in me? It is still so new, and I feel it so strongly. The two girls who cried later in debriefing said they felt like the rug had been pulled out from underneath them. No one had prepared them for the emotional and intellectual rollercoaster they went through. One girl said she was used to being in control, and when she realized she had no control over the way the simulation was going, it scared her. In fact, she wondered what the use of feeling that way was. She just didn't see the benefit of role-playing. Oliver told her to keep at it anyway because it's "wax on, wax off" and she'll eventually figure it out.

I can see the value without waiting. My friend, who has been to several simulations, told me that when they bought a condo they ended up in a pretty intense situation. One man had a majority vote and wanted to vote himself as chair in the association group and was going to triple everyone's association's fees. No one else was able to keep their cool. Grown men were yelling and swearing, their wives were being rude to each other, threats were made. And the only one who kept their cool was my friend. It took some hard work, but he got it resolved and the others all felt ridiculous. He said the only reason he was able to act coolly in a tense situation was because of simulation trainings. I believe him.

That's why I'm willing to go through the simulations, even though they are hard. Plus the simulations are George Wythe's sports, debate, theater and all the other extra curricular activities rolled into one. And students who have been through simulations say that everything under the sun makes its way into simulations. For now I just want to sleep. It feels like ages since I had any sleep.

I wonder what my classmate is going to say on Monday, the one who threw down his book and stomped out. He really missed something. But maybe he learned a lot too. Oliver said that stuff like that is real. He said that the Constitutional Convention in 1787 nearly came to blows on occasions. It makes sense; even grown men at the condo association meeting were yelling and swearing.

This experience was good for me. I know I'll rely on this experience several times in my life. Covey is right. Sometimes "no deal" is an option.

I feel like I have a million things to sort through, like how to negotiate behind the scenes and prior to the actual simulation. Next time I'll be ready. Our next simulation was handed to us in the debriefing, and

I've already set a meeting with my team. On Monday I want to meet with my opponents and start dialoguing.

I need to learn how to figure out my opponents better instead of being so naïve and assuming everyone is like me. And I need to learn Robert's Rules of Order better so that I can get resolutions passed. This next simulation is a business, hostile-takeover negotiation, and I've already got a stack of books to get started.

The mentors said they'll debrief more in a few weeks after our emotions are settled down, but some other students laughed—I guess there's a simulation from more than a year ago that they're still passionate about. I love simulations! They're impossibly hard.

*Excerpts from
my second Academic Journal:*

The more I learn and study, the more I come to recognize how little I know. I try to follow the reasoning of the men and women whose works I'm reading, and to be successful I usually read with a pen in hand. I mark my books all over the place. Once I decipher what they are saying, I judge it. I have to use discernment to differentiate between the author's assumptions and other data. And then I have to think about it and decide if I agree.

So much doesn't make sense. The only thing that keeps me going is the hope that after I have another one or two hundred classics under my belt I can make more connections.

Right now my papers feel so shallow. They consist of, "Plato says this . . . and Locke says that . . . and Calvin says . . ." And then I point out who I think is right. But I have no original thoughts. It's the same as in high school. When will I draw my own connections? When will I have my own observations? When will I have my own solutions to problems I see?

I may not agree with all the conclusions Darwin came up with when he studied life on the Galapagos Islands, but I look up to him because at least he came up with something! At least he made connections. At least he computed. At least he thought! At least he asked questions that nobody else even thought of, and tried to find the answers.

Half the stuff I'm reading I don't agree with. But I feel like I have no ability to show what it is I *do* think, unless I read it somewhere else. For instance, after reading Marx's and Engel's *Communist Manifesto*, I knew I didn't agree that the solution to man's suffering because of inequality was to take everything away and have the state own it. But I can't say *why* I feel that way. It was a relief to read Madison and find that he held firm to the idea that though part of man's misery is caused by the unequal distribution of wealth, the way to solve it was to have the state protect the property of man, not take it. *But why can't I think of things like that?*

The more I read and the more I study, the *more I realize how little I know.* Like I said, the thing that keeps me going is the hope that one day I'll have something to contribute, one day I'll make more connections and be able to solve problems.

Of course, sometimes it is simply a matter of reorganizing the information and seeing it with new eyes, with a fresh view. I think it was Essex Cholmondeley that said, "It was not the subject treated but himself that was the new thing!"

But there's more to it than what I've said. It's a paradox, really, because in truth I have opinions about everything. I read Freud and think, "Of course he couldn't get past the *id*. He gives no credit to the supernatural." How can anyone understand the psychology of man without understanding man's creator? Isn't that the best place to start? I think about how he was so curious and seemed to have the heart of a scientist, wanting to find the truth and search out answers; but how far can one get if there's no God? If there's no God, there's no creation. If there's no creation, there's no us. If there's no us, then how can we think? If we can't think then I couldn't be asking these circular questions. That's where *my* thinking takes me.

My secular classmates say I talk about God too much. Then I tell them they talk about God too little and we all laugh together. It's nice to be able to be myself and allow them to be themselves too. I learn so much from people with different views than mine. It seems the whole world is constantly fighting about different beliefs, but I think we all learn so much more by listening to people who disagree with us and also by sharing our beliefs with them. When we really try to understand each other, we all learn more and get better.

Take Descartes. He wanted to know the truth so he set out on a truth-seeking adventure. He made some rules for himself because he knew he had to start somewhere. He tried to decide on a standard to measure his reasoning and he finally came up with some tests. One test was to use doubt. He said,

"Suppose [an inquirer] had a basket full of apples and, being worried that some of the apples were rotten, wanted to take out the rotten ones to prevent the rot spreading. How would he proceed? Would he not begin by tipping the whole lot out of the basket? And would not the next step be to cast his eye over each apple in turn, and pick up and put back in the basket only those he saw to be sound, leaving the others? In just the same way, those who have never philosophized correctly have various opinions in their minds that they have begun to store up since childhood, and which they therefore have reason to believe may in many cases be false. They then attempt to separate the false beliefs from the others, so as to prevent their contaminating the rest and making the whole lot uncertain. Now the best way they can accomplish this is to reject all their beliefs together in one go, as if they were all uncertain and false. They can then go over each belief in turn and re-adopt only those that they recognize to be true and indubitable."[5]

In truth, just the other day I bought a box of oranges. I didn't want to pay for any rotten ones and so I emptied half the box, searched through them all and picked out the bad ones. There were five bad ones, and easily sorted because they didn't have the fresh orange skin, they were soft, moldy, and grey. I suppose I did examine them all though. I did compare and judge and select. It was easy to find the bad ones by comparing them to the good ones. I didn't have to examine every good one because the bad ones were easy to spot.

But reading philosophers of all sorts, in all branches, makes me question and examine everything I believe. Well, actually not. It helps me identify the "bad ideas" I believe. By going through the exercise of studying what other men believe and how they view the world, it gives me new frames of reference to look at my beliefs. Kind of like how I had to take half the oranges out and move the box around so that I could see all the oranges from a different angle and find the bad ones.

Exposing myself to the classics allows my mind to shift the way I view the world, I get to look at my beliefs from a different angle. Not in a doubting, skeptical sort of way, though. I'm more than happy to throw out mis-beliefs—but in a way that puts my own character, not the ideals, in question. The ideals hold up. It's the extrapolations that I've held on to without examination that I'm cleaning out. In fact, I suppose that's half the reason I am here. Like Paul said, "Love believes all things, hopes all things…"

I don't believe "all things" yet because I don't know "all things" yet. And many things I do know aren't true. But, I just can't follow Descartes' persuasion to test all because I do *know* some things. Christ said, "doubt not, but be believing" and "thou of little faith, wherefore didst thou doubt?" To me, the way to come to truth, to knowledge, to wisdom, is to believe. But, if I cut into a seemingly good orange and it ends up being bad, I don't hang on to it and eat it! Out it goes! As soon as I know its bad, it's gone!

Then there's the idea of forgetting what one once knew. Descartes seems right when he said:

> The mind, then, knowing itself, but still in doubt about all other things, looks around in all directions in order to extend its knowledge further. First of all, it finds within itself ideas of many things; and so long as it merely contemplates these ideas and does not affirm or deny the existence outside itself of anything resembling them, it cannot be mistaken. Next, it finds certain common notions from which it constructs various proofs; [and so long as it attends to the premises from which it deduced them]…it is completely convinced of their truth. But it cannot attend to them all the time; and subsequently, when it happens that it remembers a conclusion without attending

*to the sequence which enables it to be demonstrated, recalling
that it is still ignorant as to whether it may have been created with the kind of nature that makes it go wrong even in
matters which appear most evident, the mind sees that it has
just cause to doubt such conclusions, and that the possession
of certain knowledge [scientiam] will not be possible until it
has come to know the author of its being.*[6]

Men's minds are so feeble. We get an assurance and once the assurance leaves we doubt or we don't doubt. That's the test. After an
assurance comes that something is so, we then have to live in belief
or in doubt. We either act on our belief that it is so, or we don't
because we no longer believe it. Descartes was discussing the age-
old principle of faith. Are we not exhorted to "fight the good fight of
faith"? I must say I disagree with Descartes: to doubt is not the way,
but to believe.

It makes me wonder: *Who am I to disagree with Descartes?* But my
mind won't rest. It next wonders: *How then is the best way to judge,
since judging does take place? By what light do I judge? Judgment
cannot take place in the dark.*

Descartes set out to make a structured way in which he could judge
the things around him. Do I disagree with his structure? If so, what is
my way? How will I know if something is right or true? I know which
way I judge. If the thing leads to that which is good, which is healthy,
which is kind, which is hopeful, which is liberty and life, then I judge
it to be good. But if it leads to misery, to pain, to shackles and slavery,
to evil, to unkindness, I know the thing is bad. Like I said, I suppose
that is why I am studying, to re-examine my misbeliefs, to believe,
and to have a brighter light by which to judge. Descartes missed it by
a little: I think *because of* I Am.

My mind feels like it's being pulled and stretched and molded in directions I never knew existed. My mom always told me that *the more
thoughts we can think, the more freedom we can have.* I took it for
granted when my mom said such things, but I think I'm beginning

to grasp the meaning of that one. It comes down to words. Simple words.

The first year I studied with Oliver I kept a running list of the words he used when I didn't know the definitions. After the lectures I'd look them up. I find that the more words I understand, the more thoughts I can think.

I've been wondering about politics lately. People ask me where I go to school and what I'm studying and I've come to realize I didn't even know the definition of "political science". I tell people I'm studying the liberal arts and political science and they invariably say, "Oh, you're going to be a politician, are you?" I think, "No. Did I say that?" So I looked up the word *politic*: "the science of government..." and the word *politician*, the kind and positive definition being: "one versed in the science of government and the art of governing." I also looked at the word *polity*: "the form or constitution of civil government of a nation or state." Webster's Dictionary was a place to start, but only a start.

The word "polity" stopped me. There was the word *form* again. Why am I so stuck on that word? My understanding of *forms* is that they are the system, the way, or the chosen structure. America's form of government is a democratic republic. There are other words to describe our forms. Some forms are monarchial, others anarchical.

The Founders debated forms. That's what they did. They chose the forms they believed would form a more perfect union, ensure domestic tranquility, establish freedom and promote the general welfare. I think I'm studying political science so I can decide for myself where I agree and if and where I disagree—about forms, I mean. From government forms (like the difference between a monarchy and a democratic republic), to private forms (like heterosexual marriage and homosexual marriage and societies with little marriage), to public forms (like which kinds of schools promote the best education).

Anyway, I think *that* is why I'm studying the liberal arts and political science: To know forms and their inherent consequences. So, to further study political science, I started with Webster and moved on.

The first political scientist is supposedly Hobbes. He's the one credited, anyway. I don't think he was the first political scientist though. That's the problem with studying history. If you're religious, you have to study two histories. If a political scientist is a scientist of a body politic, of civilizations, of peoples, of what makes a group of people come together and form social compacts and contracts, then I think the first political scientists were the writers of the Bible.

The question my mind always has is: if I believe the religious is the more correct of the two, why study the secular? And yet the more I study Hobbes, the more I appreciate Abraham. The more I study Engels the more I appreciate modern religious thinkers. Students from other faiths say the same thing.

Families need to be versed in the science of government and the art of governing. Even families have forms. Different nations throughout the world promote different family forms. Hobbes says Commonwealths are simply an extended family, a larger family. He says that in studying history and looking at how families vie for land, life, and spoils, it is no different than when states do the same thing (though commonwealths take in more territory and have more members).

President Roosevelt was big on families. He felt that the propagation of the race was a duty of all Americans. He wanted to make laws that were favorable to larger families.

Back to my train of thought: I haven't read Noah, but I have read writings of Abraham, and even some of Enoch. Therefore, if I had to date the first political scientist whose writings I've read, it would have to be Enoch. He wanted to know the same things Hobbes did: *What makes a body politic and how can a civilization be successful?*

I can't help but think of Allan Bloom. He goes to great lengths to show that great civilizations have what Oliver calls a national book, a set of writings that they measure their lives by and set up as a standard to measure and judge everything in the culture. According to Bloom, America's books up until the 1960s were the Bible and *The Declaration of Independence*. A sign of the decay of our civilization is that the Bible is no longer our national book. But it is *mine*. And so when I read Hobbes, I can't help but compare him to Abraham, to Moses, to Joseph of Egypt, to Gautama, to the Rig Veda, and to Jesus of Nazareth.

For instance, in *Leviathan*, Hobbes says,

> But man, whose joy consisteth in comparing himself with other men, can relish nothing but what is eminent.

This made me stop and think because it's part of his assumption. Hobbes says that happiness comes from comparing ourselves to our neighbor. Though I agree that many people believe this is where happiness comes from, I believe it's a lie. And inasmuch as we put stock in a lie we won't get what we are seeking—which in this case is happiness.

If happiness came from being ahead of the Joneses, or comparing ourselves to the Joneses, then why seek happiness? Logic tells us that someone will always be ahead of us. And then seeking happiness would be futile except for the one person at the top.

I think happiness comes from aligning our will with God's. Or, in some people's language, with truth and goodness.

If I take this one idea of Hobbes and compare it to the writings found in the Bible, or my other core books, I find Hobbes missing the point, at least on this one assumption: Man is that he might have joy. So what brings that joy? The answers have nothing to do with comparing oneself to his neighbor and everything to do with aligning our wills to God's will.

It's critical to understand the meaning of "will" if we are to take the argument further. If happiness comes from aligning our will to God's will, what is "will"? I was reading a Charlotte Mason Companion the other day and was struck by Mason's definition of "will." She said that "will" implies choosing, and that "will" is teaching through freedom. "The will's function is to choose," she says. In fact, the repeated action of will creates character. Mason also says we keep a child's will weak by constant suggestion, deciding everything for them. Molding will equals *right* thought, *right* ideas, which come from *right* books, *right* pictures, *right* lives.

The use of *right* reminds me of Buddhism and *right* living. So many

The Student Whisperer

traditions teach the importance of aligning our will to God's.

What then, is meant by *will?* What is meant by *will power?* Suzuki has an interesting insight into *will,* and coupled with Charlotte Mason's thought that *will* implies choosing, it makes sense. Suzuki says:

> We simply have to train and educate our ability, that is to say, do the thing over and over again until it feels natural, simple, and easy. That is the secret.

How can we choose something if we have no ability? How can I be free to sit at the piano and play Bach if I haven't done as Suzuki teaches, which is to do the thing over and over again until it feels natural, simple, and easy? Until I do so, I am not free to choose to play Bach and my will is lessened. How can I choose to be self-reliant if I don't know the first thing about gardening? How can I choose to be a good mother if I don't know how to keep order in the home? How can I choose to be a good wife if I don't know how to forgive? What does this have to do with happiness? How can I grow my will? My ability to choose is directly tied to my will.

How can I grow my ability to be happy? Is it by the pursuit of knowledge? Is the Proverb correct, *"Happy is the man that findeth wisdom"?*

Whenever I write in my commonplace book I have more questions than I have answers.

So, I'm a bit miffed. I know I have only picked one paragraph out of Hobbes to talk about. It seems a bit unfair, especially when Hobbes has done so much for the study of political science, and since he has plenty to offer; but it's what I find my mind doing. There's plenty to agree with, so why write about that? It's the portion that misaligns with what I believe to be true that I ponder about and try to rectify in my mind.

This one paragraph though, this one idea of what happiness is, is not exclusive to Hobbes. Nichomachus writes about it too. In *Introduction to Arithmetic* he assumes:

We crave for the goal that is worthy and fitting for man, namely, happiness of life—and this is accomplished by philosophy alone and by nothing else, and philosophy, as I said, means for us desire for wisdom, and wisdom the science of the truth in things.[7]

Is happiness accomplished solely by philosophy, by knowing the truth? I don't think so. Someone can know the truth and still choose to be unhappy. Someone can have the gift of wisdom—Solomon for example—and not choose *right*. Once again, I think happiness comes from *right* living, or aligning our will to God's.

In Star Trek mythology, the Borg assimilates sentient beings it conquers, basically aligning their wills to the collective. Afterwards, individuals have no will of their own. In contrast, the more we align our wills to our creator's, living by celestial principles, the more power and choice and will we have.

The Borg also uses force: "Resistance is futile." God, on the other hand, uses invitation, choice, persuasion, long-suffering, kindness, gentleness, and love. Then, we use our will to align our will to His.

Some people think they lose their will when they align it with God's. But I believe that just the opposite happens. It is interesting to note how many opinions there are concerning "what makes happiness".

Nichomachus says it comes through philosophy, the accumulation of wisdom, truth. Hobbes says it is by comparing oneself to our neighbor—through perception. Ayn Rand has a totally different view. In fact, her view is quite paradoxical, and I don't think she even saw the paradox.

To understand her view, I had to take a good hard look at her life history. By doing that, she finally made sense to me. In her book, *Anthem*, she expresses her philosophy through her character, Equality 7-2521, or Prometheus.

Equality 7-2521 lives in a futuristic society where all individuality has been denied and the men and women live, breed, work, and think *for* the state. Phrases of control are the norm, such as: "We are one in all and all in one," or "There are no men but only the great WE, One, indivisible and forever." These were their mantras. Another was,

> We are nothing. Mankind is all. By the grace of our brothers
> are we allowed our lives. We exist through, by and for our
> brothers who are the State. Amen.

Equality 7-2521 finally rebels against the state and seeks self-knowledge
and awareness. He runs away with the woman he has fallen in love
with and they go into the "Forbidden Forest" and after traveling for
several weeks find the ruins of the "old world"—a home.

In this home Equality 7-2521 finds books that reveal to him the se-
crets of the ages. He learns he is no longer a "We", but an "I". This
very notion frees him mentally from the State he left physically. He
comes to realize that he doesn't live for the state, for the brotherhood, for others, but for *himself*. He comes to believe a new truth, a
truer truth, that he has no obligation to the brotherhood and state,
but only to himself.

He says:

> I stand here on the summit of the mountain. I lift my head
> and I spread my arms. This, my body and spirit, this is the
> end of the quest.

He goes on:

> I need no warrant for being, and no word of the sanction
> upon my being. I am the warrant and the sanction. It is my
> mind which thinks, and the judgment of my mind is the only
> searchlight that can find the truth.

Rand means that part very literally.

She later taught in her non-fiction works that:

> Man's reason is fully competent to know the facts of real-
> ity. Reason, the conceptual faculty, is the faculty that identi-
> fies and integrates the material provided by man's senses.
> Reason is man's only means of acquiring knowledge. Thus
> Objectivism rejects mysticism (any acceptance of faith or
> feeling as a means of knowledge), and it rejects skepticism
> (the claim that certainty or knowledge is impossible).

As Equality 7-2521 continues his soliloquy on free thought he says:

It is my will which chooses, and the choice of my will is the only edict I must respect.

Concerning happiness he says:

...I know what happiness is possible to me on earth. And my happiness is not the means to any end. It is the end. It is its own goal. It is its own purpose.

I do not surrender my treasures, nor do I share them...I guard my treasures: my thought, my will, my freedom...I owe nothing to my brothers...I am neither a foe nor friend to my brothers.

Rand defected from Russia in her twenties. She lived through two revolutions, the second being the imposition of communism. To understand her views I had to look at what she was fighting and what she was saying. She grew up brainwashed and being the property of the state, so to have had the "a-ha" that she was an individual must have been liberating.

But then, I vehemently disagree with her philosophy of happiness; and ironically, apparently so does she. Her character, Equality 7-2521, claims his happiness will come from self-reasoning, not from others, and yet he only becomes truly happy when he has a woman by his side that he loves and that loves him and creates a family with him.

I read many books for many days. Then I called the Golden One, and I told her what I had read and what I had learned. She looked at me and the first words she spoke were: 'I love you.'

And does the book end happily with Equality 7-2521 resting on the statement that he owes "nothing" to his brothers? No, instead Equality 7-2521, now named Prometheus, declares:

I shall call to me all the men and the women whose spirit has not been killed within them and who suffer under the yoke of their brothers. They will follow me and I shall lead them to my fortress.

So it turns out that Ayn Rand's hero actually does feel an obligation to the brotherhood. His first action when he learns anything new is to run share it with his partner, and then he sets out to bond with other men and help them seek their freedom also. Why should he? He is free, and he doesn't need protection. In fact, by seeking out "brothers" he puts his own freedom back into danger. Yet he is not self-sufficient. He needs social interaction.

Prometheus continues:

> Here on this mountain, I and my sons and my chosen friends shall build our new land and our fort.

Notice the word *our*: he cannot do it alone. There is no such thing as alone, he must have his woman, and he must have his brothers.

Ayn Rand rejected the imitation and simultaneously rejected the "real thing." She rejected communism with its "two-headed dragon" of terror and force and all its inherent evils, the indignity it brings upon mankind. And like a person who rejects imitation vanilla as not quite cutting it and at the same time decides to discard all vanilla, Ayn Rand rejects the imitation brotherhood and also throws out the real brotherhood in her writings. But in her heart of hearts she held to the real, though her words denied it. Her whole life was dedicated to mankind, lifting them from the yoke of force, terror, Communism. It's ironic, really.

The sad part is that what most people take from Ayn Rand is her words, which make man the worship of man:

> And now I see the face of god, and I raise this god over the earth, this god whom men have sought since men came into being, this god who will grant them joy and peace and pride.
>
> This god, this one word:
>
> "I."

Her words contradict themselves. Her life contradicts her words. She thought man was an end unto himself, but it seems that her own happiness came from her conviction to serve the real brotherhood.

She never openly wrote that the real difference didn't rest in the "individuality" of the soul, but in another object altogether—in freedom, choice, and will. Maybe she never saw that it was the *forced* brotherhood that was the enemy, not the brotherhood of mankind itself.

The trick is as old as Cain and Abel. The Bible says that Satan lied to Cain, telling him he could have his cake and eat it too, taking all Abel had and becoming victorious. And what was Cain's reply when God asked of him, "Where is thy brother?" Cain's answer was no different than Ayn Rand's: "Am I my brother's keeper?" Rand's philosophy could be called "Cain's edict." It gets one as far as it got him.

That's the paradox: Ayn Rand didn't really believe in her own philosophy. She freely chose to sacrifice and work to seek the brotherhood of mankind, and encouraged them to throw off the yoke of force and communism. But she missed the mark, leading people astray to Cain's edict, for happiness can only come through losing ourselves in goodness.

The more we align our will with natural law, the more will and choice we have. But it cannot be forced upon us. That is the difference. We have the free will to choose.

Ayn Rand's paradox is not limited to her. Orson Scott Card once said that to know a person's true religion isn't to listen to their words, but to look at their life, their behavior, their choices. Men can profess anything and everything, and *they do*. But to really know a man's belief, all we have to do is look deeper. We act according to what we *really* believe. What we *say* we believe is our theology, and what we actually *do* our religion.

A person will seek happiness where they truly believe it is to be found—we each have the free will to choose.

I decided I am all wrong about Hobbes. Or at least, there's plenty I agree with that is worth discussing. He is nothing short of a genius. I read more and now I wonder, where did he come up with his stuff? How much of it is his, and how much borrowed? I was reading John Dewey's *Experience & Education* and noticed his definition of knowledge and education, and now I read Hobbes and realize that Dewey's definition can in part be traced to Hobbes. I disagree so vehemently with parts of Dewey that I just kept pondering his words.

He bashes learning from our elders, from classics, and from the past. Only, he says it in such an intelligent, persuasive manner, that one hardly dares disagree with him. Dewey criticizes the traditional schools of his time. He says:

> *The main purpose or objective is to prepare the young for future responsibilities and for success in life by means of acquisition of organized bodies of information and prepared forms of skill which comprehend the material of instruction.*[8]

I think he is saying that the instruction is through data and facts, maybe stories too, and through acquiring skills. I don't disagree, but I do believe that traditional education was more than just "organized bodies of information and skills." Then he says:

> *Since the subject-matter as well as standards of proper conduct are handed down from the past, the attitude of pupils must, upon the whole, be one of docility, receptivity, and obedience.*

He further belittles the schooling that used the past as a great teacher and said,

> *The traditional scheme is, in essence, one of imposition from above and from outside. It imposes adult standards, subject matter, and methods upon those who are only growing slowly toward maturity.*

Oh, those poor kids who would like to steal what doesn't belong to them, when mother grabs their hand and tells them 'no!' Those wronged youth who want to idle away their day when their father calls them to the field to work, or to the bench to read! Those poor children who have loving parents and teachers impose on them!

> *...Learning here means acquisition of what already is incorporated in books and in the heads of the elders.*

And what is so wrong with that? Granted that Emerson wants

originality, initiative and thinking rather than just copying past thinkers. But even Emerson thinks we should study past thinkers as well as thinking on our own. Dewey seems convinced that good thinking is done in a vacuum.

Hobbes thought highly of the acquisition of what already is incorporated in books and in the heads of elders. And yet (and here's the paradox) though books and elders are revered, a true scientist or seeker of truth will look to natural law, and natural consequences, and obvious truth when it varies from books and elders. They do what we call *thinking!*

This is what Hobbes did. He published a work that was in his own day burned, and fled to another country! But, he wasn't above looking at the past. In fact, that's how he proved the future. Same with Emerson.

Hobbes said,

> *There is a saying much usurped of late, that wisdom is acquired, not by reading of 'books' but of 'men'. Consequently whereunto, those persons, for the most part can give no other proof of being wise, take great delight to shew what they think they have read in men, by uncharitable censures of one another behind their backs.*[9]

He goes on to implore the non-reader to at least *read thyself* and then to read *mankind* for the study of those who govern, but my point is that there is merit in the lore that is handed down. Hobbes knew it.

Why did Dewey disregard it so blithely?

> *Let us say that the kind of external imposition which was so common in the traditional school limited rather than promoted the intellectual and moral development of the young. Just what is the role of the teacher and of books in promoting the educational development of the immature? Admit that traditional education employed as the subject-matter for study of facts and ideas so bound up with the past as to give little help in dealing with the issues of the present and future.*[10]

I thought the whole reason it was bound up with the past *was* to teach how to deal with the present and the future.

Our educational forms are directly tied to our ability to promote liberty in our nation. The founders argued extensively that the nation's education was directly tied to the nation's security. Our educational form changed drastically due to Dewey, and our freedoms have suffered. Oliver gives me more sources to read when I ask him these questions—about how our education is tied to our freedom. Sometimes that is so frustrating. Why doesn't he just tell me the answer?

But then, after I asked numerous times, he smiled and said, "Why don't you just think it all up yourself? Why ask me?" I realized he was using Dewey's method.

When I told him I'd figured it out, he finally gave me *his* answer. "Teachers should do what Dewey said on this point—that is, let the student figure it out on his own. But teachers must also take a stand—not always, not with every question—but teachers must clearly stand for something and on occasion they must take a stand on an issue and clearly defend their reasons. Teaching is all about inspiring, and few things are more inspiring than someone who has clearly thought something through and will openly articulate why.

"Oh, and by the way, there are many places where Dewey is totally wrong, in my opinion. But once in a while he gets something right."

Dewey, Hobbes, Emerson—all have some truth. I need to keep reading. My mentor sent me to Locke, Jefferson and Lewis.

*Excerpts from
my third Academic Journal:*

I've always loved the study of history, but I used to see history as its own subject. Now I realize I can't study any subject, topic, or course in its entirety without its history—whether it is health, mathematics, biology, business, government, music, Shakespeare, or motorcycles. History is inseparable from all sciences and fields. Anyone who tries to separate them does himself a disservice.

Orson Scott Card's idea about history intrigues me. From him I learned that history is simply the stories that have been passed down from generation to generation. Some cultures have their history passed down through oral tradition only, and some combine the oral tradition with the written tradition. Either way, the knowledge, lore, traditions, views, experience, and wisdom are passed down through stories. Russell Kirk shows the importance of history and its stories in our morals and mores.

Many of my favorite studies recently have centered on biographies. What's been happening to me as I read the original works and biographies of the great men and women throughout history, or the classics, is the Transfer of Soul. I can't read a classic without getting to know the author, and the more I know the background of the author the more I understand his work, and the more I feel I understand him and all he stood for. A piece of history, *his story*, is transferred to me. And what is story without soul?

The ability to think like a scientist has been transferred to me via the scientists I have been studying. I actually look at the world differently. I see patterns where before I saw only blur. I see meaning where before I saw only the superfluous. I see color and shades where before I saw black and white. I ask questions with greater reverence because I know the power behind the answers. I *care* more. I *hope* more. I *want* more. I look deeper at who's who in the world. I ask *who* mentored them. How did this knowledge pass down to them and then to me?

I listed some of the profound, guiding principles handed down to me by my mentors, by which I guide my life, and I started tracing the influences that impacted my mentors. I was not surprised by the coincidence that two of the major mentors in my life were mentored by the same man. I traced his mentor to a mentor who mentored three authors that I have read extensively. And so from that mentor, I am being mentored because I bought some of his books. I can't wait to see who *his* mentor was! All of this I have learned from studying the biographies of scientists.

This is such a powerful concept—Oliver calls it the Genealogy of Thought. I'll relate a case in point to illustrate what I mean by it all, why history is interconnected with all subjects, and why it infers a transfer of soul.

Suzuki continues to impact education in a huge way by breaking the traditional bounds of eastern and western culture and carrying his "talent education" to many, many nations on the earth. He tells the following story:

> It was the small Tolstoy's Diary. I casually took it down from the shelf and opened it at random. My eyes fell on the following words: "To deceive oneself is worse than to deceive others." These harsh words pierced me to the core. It was a tremendous shock. I began to tremble with fear and could scarcely control myself. I bought the little book and rushed home. I devoured its contents. I read and reread that book so much that in the end it fell apart. What a marvelous man Tolstoy must have been! My admiration for him led me to immerse myself in all his writings.[11]

Here's the key part:

> Tolstoy provided the staff of life on which I nurtured my soul. Tolstoy said that one should not deceive oneself and that the voice of conscience is the voice of God. I determined to live according to these ideas.

What Suzuki shows here is the transfer of soul from Tolstoy to himself. What is amazing is that it goes from Suzuki to me. But Suzuki doesn't stop there. There are two more of his stories that further the point.

One of his teachers, Professor Klingler, introduced him to this concept. Suzuki says:

> What he taught me was not so much technique as the real essence of music. For instance, if we were working on a Handel sonata, he would earnestly explain to me what great religious feeling Handel must have been filled with when he wrote it, and then he would play it for me. He would look for the roots underlying a man and his art and lead me to them.[12]

Klingler was the one who taught this same concept, of the history and transfer of soul, to Suzuki. And once again, I am learning it from Suzuki. And it will be passed on from me to my future students. Stories tell it all. They're how we pass it on!

Finally, listen to what Suzuki says about Mozart!

> *It was Mozart who taught me to know perfect love, truth, goodness, and beauty. And I now deeply feel as if I were under direct orders from Mozart, and he left me a legacy; in his place I am to further the happiness of all children.[13]*

The thought Suzuki expresses here is captivating beyond words. It is the true purpose of history. At least, it is what I am experiencing in the smallest degree as my character grows, refines, molds, and changes because of the history I am encountering through the classics.

Suzuki was listening to the Klingler Quartet playing Mozart's Clarinet Quintet when he experienced the following:

> *That evening I seemed to be gradually drawn into Mozart's spirit, and, finally I was not conscious of anything else, not even of my own being, I became so immersed...An indescribable, sublime, ecstatic joy had taken hold of my soul. I had been given a glimpse of Mozart's high spiritual world. What I never cease to marvel at in Mozart's music is his superhuman love. It is a great tenderness and love felt only by the soul. And this love takes cognizance of man's deep sorrow... birth and death...the evanescence and loneliness of life...the all-pervasive sadness. This sadness Mozart expressed not only with the minor scale but with the major scale as well, in the midst of his deep love. For man both life and death are the inescapable business of nature. There is in Mozart's music a clear vision of this inevitability.[14]*

Can you see what he learned from Mozart? Mozart's understanding of man, of nature, of life, transferred to Suzuki, and from Suzuki to me. I crave now to listen to Mozart, and to Handel, and to Beethoven as Suzuki did. Look at the transfer of Professor Klingler's soul: he taught Suzuki to look at the man, not just the music.

Klingler's history alone makes this story even *more* remarkable. He was the only professor at the Berlin Music Academy who stood up to Hitler's mandate that the statue of the great late nineteenth century German violinist Joseph Joachim, a Jew, be removed.

"You shall not destroy it," he declared. And for his courage he was expelled from the music academy. Klingler had such moral strength; and he passed it on to Suzuki!

And from Tolstoy, Suzuki charted the course of the rest of his life. *That is what history does to man.* If we but open our eyes to understand it, if we but open our ears to hear it, if we but open our hearts to feel it... *his* story, *her* story, *their* story, *our* story, the earth's story, all of it, is the catalyst which changes us, inspires us, teaches us, and gives us hope for the future. If we have eyes to see, we can see patterns—patterns in people, in governments, in choices, patterns that reveal the cycles of the future.

I cannot study anything under the sun, in the earth, or in the heavens and hope to arrive at light and truth without its *history*.

I was working on a big project, reading the various biographies of Abraham Lincoln, and I had questions. In fact, the more questions I had, the more frustrated I became. It's too bad too, because I knew right at the first question what I needed to do. But I kept reading and reading and getting more and more frustrated. Finally I couldn't stand it anymore. I knew I needed to call Andrew Allison.

It had been several years since I'd seen him. He was a close friend of the family when I was in junior high and high school. One year for Christmas I'd asked for a specific book because he had piqued my interest. It was the first biography of a statesman that I had ever read, and I am studying now to become a statesman, in part, because of the impact that book had on me.

Andrew Allison is about six feet tall and on the slim side. When he sits he almost always crosses one leg over the other. He usually wears a black suit, white shirt, and an inconspicuous tie. His shoes are black penny loafers. His hands are thin and long and can easily grasp his large Bible, which he always brought to our house.

Andrew Allison himself has written biographies of three of America's Founding Fathers, including *The Real Thomas Jefferson*. I decided when I was thirteen that I wanted to know what Andrew Allison knew. I wanted to understand government the way he understood it, and I wanted to be able to think and write with as much influence as he did.

When I hit the roadblock in my studies of Abraham Lincoln for the *third* time, inside I knew he was the one to call. My assignment was to do original research and write a year-end thesis paper. I was considering writing a biography and I needed direction—but I needed a lot more than that, too.

After half an hour of conversation I looked down and had four pages of notes. Our conversation went something like this:

"Let me see if I have this right," I said. "Writing a biography is like writing an arrangement of music?"

"That's right Tiffany, you have your stories all picked out. You notice the themes and character traits you want to pull out, you begin to see patterns. And your job is to bridge them together with narrative."

I took a deep breath. "So what I do is read and read and read other biographies on Abraham Lincoln, his own correspondences, letters, documents, speeches, journals, and I start to get a feel for the themes of his life. I start to gather my stories. I start to experience the flavor of him. And then it's like a piece of music. My job is to make it flow."

"Yes," he said. "Remember, there's no such thing as complete objectivity. It just isn't human. Any biography you read will have the 'bent' of the author. Pick the biographies you read wisely. Get a feel for the author by reading the cover and part of the text. Ask questions like, 'Is the author trying to degrade or ruin the man? Is he harping on only one tune?'

"Soon you will see recurring themes in Lincoln's life. Bridging the stories with the narrative is a piece of art. I can hardly explain what happens. It goes beyond yourself as you compile and compose."

As he spoke I began to understand the process.

"It's like a symphony. You hear the trumpets, and then the trumpets die down and the piccolo picks up the refrain and drifts in and out."

"You let his stories tell about himself. You simply bridge the stories with narrative, a little interjection here or there: 'though Abraham Lincoln appears to have been melancholy he also had his humorous side.' Then show them his humorous side by telling another story."

Lincoln's passion, his intellect, the way he saw the world around him, have begun to shape my thoughts, the way I think, and the way I study. I feel a special connection to Abraham Lincoln. For some reason I resonate with the burden he carried, the pain he felt, the trials he had as he tried to keep our country united and strong. I love studying him. It's strange—I feel so close to the statesmen I study in depth. I feel this way about George Washington, about Ezra Taft Benson, and about Gandhi. I wonder what other statesmen I will grow to love over time.

I have identified a weakness in me I want to purge. It came as a feeling of frustration. Something was missing in my life—but what? It was there, real but fuzzy. Then as I studied literature it began to make sense, and finally I have a specific name for it.

My great-grandmother has it. Her daughter, my grandmother, learned it. Her daughter, my mother, saw traces of it but didn't rely on it, and her daughter, me, doesn't even know the value of it because it appears to be obsolete.

Women in general, I'm starting to believe, have a sense of being unfulfilled. The feminist movement has taken its toll. Even my compatriots who don't call themselves feminists pride themselves on the fact that the burden of the family is shared equally in the home. Two incomes come in, both mother and father rotate diaper changing, dish duty, and laundry. And yet, the woman is still unfulfilled. Rousseau persuaded women:

> *...freely to be different from men and to take on the burden*
> *of entering a positive contract with the family, as opposed to*
> *a negative, individual, self-protective contract with the state.*

Tocqueville picked up this theme, described the absolute differentiation of husbands' and wives' functions and ways of life in the American family, and attributed the success of American democracy to its women, "who freely choose their lot."

Allan Bloom goes on to say:

> *Modernity promised that all human beings would be treated equally. Women took that promise seriously and rebelled against the old order. But as they have succeeded, men have also been liberated from their old constraints.*[15]

He continues:

> *And women, now liberated and with equal careers, nevertheless find they still desire to have children, but have no basis for claiming that men should share their desire for children or assume a responsibility for them."*

Here's the truth:

> *The promise of modernity is not really fulfilled for women.*[16]

A career outside the home didn't solve it. But are the homemakers any happier than their careerist counterparts? Rarely.

Where is the answer? I think there are two of them: One is technology, the other, ideology. *[Oliver's handwriting appears in the margin right here: "Tiffany, you're creating, thinking, adding new information. Last year you just couldn't do that, but you are now. Keep up the great work! Push it even deeper. –od"]*

Technology has inadvertently caused a change in motherhood and home making. It used to be a necessity to set aside one day a week for washing, one day for mending, one day for baking, and one day for cleaning—besides the *daily* rigors of gardening, cleaning, cooking, and preserving food.

It was a necessity to the function of the home that mother and multiple children reside, work, and play therein. Because of technology we no longer have to spend as much time on food, clothing, and shelter. We have much more leisure time. Because of the sudden advent of technology, since the 1930's, something has been gained (time), but something has been lost (mom feeling and knowing that she is needed in the home). Furthermore, that "missing something" is tied to "systems". With the loss of systems in the home, the new homemaker, four generations later, feels lost.

We must create and find new systems that bring fulfillment.

There are many books on organization and home management for women—all because we have lost our organization, our management, and our vision of what motherhood is. Where are our gardens? Where are our seasons? Where are our preserves?

Is the only way to find fulfillment—our lost sense that things are right—to reinstate the old models using today's technology? All of the old models are tied to self-reliance: the reliance that says we are a community, we are in charge of our own, our education, our homes, our food, our animals, our land, etc.

Are we unhappy because something deep inside of us knows that the cycles of history do repeat themselves, that challenges will come again, and we realize we don't know how to make bread? Are we unhappy because in losing some of our models we have lost some of our liberties? One well-known form of government in America is our commercial focus. Jefferson recommended widespread private ownership with an agrarian bent and we adopted it in his time and up to the early 1900's. Then we shifted to Hamilton's industrial-commercial focus, with central ownership in a few hands along with a nation of employees. In the 1960's we heard of a new program, a focus on pleasure, which we have been adopting more and more. Is it the shift to the commercial focus, or the pleasurable (or both), that has caused the uneasiness of women, even in the "home-makers"?

We don't know how to grow food and store enough to see us through to the next growing season. We don't know how to care for animals, provide our own milk, butter, cheese, and eggs. We don't know how to knit, or sew, or mend. And most of my colleagues would laugh if they read this!

No wonder we have a sense of anxiety. Like Roosevelt said, "we do not believe that with the two sexes there is identity of function; but we do believe there should be equality of right."[17] Is it part of our function to know these things?

Over and over in the literature I read—Potok, Hugo, Stratton-Porter, Wilder, Virgil, Plutarch, Herodotus, Thucydides, Toynbee, Durant, and others—the women of all ages and times have known how to produce and store food, how to create clothing, how to exist in hard times.

The industrialization and urbanization of America has all but banished these abilities in women. I find myself looking more and more to those who came before me for knowledge of these systems. I want to purge out my slothfulness, my laziness, my ease of living and wake up to the reality that there is work to be done, and I better be doing it! I wonder if the problem of modern women, and men for that matter, is just that we don't sweat enough. Maybe really small things make all the difference, and we've lost sight and knowledge of a few really simple, small things.

The other difference that makes or breaks a happy woman in the home is ideology, the power of ideas. When Roosevelt went looking for the source of declining fertility, he found the ideas of Malthus, Mill and Nietzsche. Malthus taught the dangers of overpopulation, Mill the need for government to become utilitarian (do what is best for the most people, not for the individual), and Nietzsche started making the focus on pleasure credible (it had always been popular). Amazingly, Gibbon shows similar forces creating the fall of Rome, and Hamilton shows the same for Greece. History repeats itself, as Santayana warned, and may be poised to do so unless we get past ideology.

We haven't yet. Unhappy and unfulfilled womanhood can be traced to the power of "wrong ideas." Ideas, which are spread through words, are more powerful than the sword. This, of course, impacts men too.

The idea has reached the point that most young women actually believe that being a homemaker is more unfulfilling and personally damaging than an army at the door. I think it's great that my generation of women has so many choices. I just wish we hadn't lost so many skills and so much understanding.

My realization is that I am coming upon a new idea that I think will make home life more fulfilling to me. I want to embrace motherhood, with all its duties intact, even that of finding the simple models that all generations of women through time have known. I should learn the systems inherent in the georgic, or agrarian, tradition and in the entrepreneurial focus of widespread private ownership.

I've been asking myself a question as of late: "What makes a strong civilization decay and crumble?" This isn't a question that has an easy answer because there are various reasons. But my mind has hit on one idea that lends a little more understanding.

If educated people study the past they know that nations and civilizations crumble when the citizens become corrupt. When there is no trust between people, how can a nation prosper? A country can't grow when there is no trust in a person's word, bond, or contract.

This begs the question, "How can a people be so stupid as to believe that it's okay to be corrupt and still think that they won't receive the natural results: loss of freedom? Why do individuals think their civilization will survive their personal corruption?"

Demosthenes, in speaking to the Athenians before their downfall, tried to warn his countrymen of this very thing. He even said:

> *Our affairs have not declined from one or two causes only: but, if you rightly examine, you will find it chiefly owing to the orators, who study to please you rather than advise for the best.*[18]

Here's part of the clincher:

> *Some of whom, Athenians, seeking to maintain the basis of their own power and repute, have no forethought for the future, and therefore think you also ought to have none.*

It's a matter of timing. A skewed sense of timing happens before the fall. No forethought of the future takes place. Somehow a belief that serious decline won't take place in their lifetime is enough to console indulgent behavior. It's about justifying indulgence with a poor sense of timing.

Had the Athenians listened to Demosthenes, there was still time to change the pending doom.

> *If you will choose to perform your duty, it is possible to repair it all.*

It seems that all peoples are given choices, chances, to perform such duty and repair it all. Think about the American Colonies. They faced a similar choice as the people of Demosthenes. In Demosthenes' case the challenge was Philip of Macedon, in Patrick Henry's case it was the King of England. Either way, their cry for action was the same:

Mr. President, it is natural to man to indulge in the illusions of hope. We are apt to shut our eyes against a painful truth, and listen to the song of that siren till she transforms us into beasts. Is this the part of wise men, engaged in a great and arduous struggle for liberty? Are we disposed to be of the number of those who, having eyes, see not, and, having ears, hear not, the things which so nearly concern their temporal salvation? For my part, whatever anguish of spirit it may cost, I am willing to know the whole truth; to know the worst, and to provide for it.

Our petitions have been slighted; our remonstrances have produced additional violence and insult; our supplications have been disregarded; and we have been spurned, with contempt, from the foot of the throne! In vain, after these things, may we indulge the fond hope of peace and reconciliation. There is no longer any room for hope. If we wish to be free—if we mean to preserve inviolate those inestimable privileges for which we have been so long contending— if we mean not basely to abandon the noble struggle in which we have been so long engaged, and which we have pledged ourselves never to abandon until the glorious object of our contest shall be obtained—we must fight! I repeat it, sir, we must fight! An appeal to arms and to the God of hosts is all that is left us!

They tell us, sir, that we are weak; unable to cope with so formidable an adversary. But when shall we be stronger? Will it be the next week, or the next year? Will it be when we are totally disarmed, and when a British guard shall be stationed in every house? Shall we gather strength

*by irresolution and inaction? Shall we acquire the means
of effectual resistance by lying supinely on our backs and
hugging the delusive phantom of hope, until our enemies
shall have bound us hand and foot?[19]*

That is the clincher, "lying supinely on our backs and hugging the
delusive phantom of hope." Timing was everything. Patrick Henry
knew it, and Demosthenes knew it. Demosthenes said:

*If we really wait until he avows that he is at war with us,
we are the simplest of mortals: for he would not declare that,
though he marched even against Attica and Piraeus, at least
if we may judge from his conduct to others. For example, to
the Olynthians he declared, when he was forty furlongs from
their city, that there was no alternative, but either they must
quit Olynthus or he Macedonia; though before that time,
whenever he was accused of such an intent, he took it ill
and sent ambassadors to justify himself.*

*People who would never have harmed him, though they
might have adopted measures of defense, he chose to de-
ceive rather than warn them of his attack; and think ye he
would declare war against you before he began it, and that
while you are willing to be deceived? Impossible. He would
be the silliest of mankind, if, whilst you the injured parties
make no complaint against him, but are accusing your own
countrymen, he should terminate your intestine strife and
jealousies, warn you to turn against him, and remove the
pretexts of his hirelings for asserting, to amuse you, that he
makes no war upon Athens. O heavens! Would any rational
being judge by words rather than by actions who is at peace
with him and who are war? Surely none.*

*Defend yourselves instantly, and I say you will be wise:
delay it, and you may wish in vain to do so hereafter.[20]*

Why is it that in the time of choice and of opportunity, some choose
to act and some choose not to? More to the point, what is our
opportunity today, and do we see it?

*Excerpts from
my fourth Academic Journal:*

War intrigues me. More to the point, leadership intrigues me. Business focused many years on management, only to improve from management to leadership in the past thirty years. I just finished reading Sun Tsu's Art of War. I don't know if his book is definitive of the art of war, but it was enlightening. So many of the principles apply to many areas of life. As we're studying the applicational sciences—war, business, family and statesmanship—I am learning so much.

Our future depends on great leadership and statesmanship. Looking back over the last few years of pursuing a liberal arts education, I realize how beneficial the classes have been. One of the biggest "a-ha!s" I've had is the difference between arguing and debating. At first I couldn't tell the two apart, but then I encountered someone who forced me to see the difference.

When we all come together to discuss ideas or a specific book, it deepens our experience. For instance, when I read *Jane Eyre,* I hardly took notice of the relationship between Jane and Helen Burns at the boarding school. In a way it was a painful part, and I didn't allow myself to go very deep. On the other hand, I took great notice of Jane's relationship with St. John. When I read a book I have *my* experience with the characters in the book and with the author. And that is that.

When I discuss the book in a tutorial or a colloquium setting my experience expands. It takes in the other people's "a-ha!s" and ideas. Plus, I have to clarify my thoughts in order to articulate them to others or to persuade them of something. Colloquia take my learning to the next level. Then mentors push it even further. When we discussed *Jane Eyre,* I was able to express my disgust with the man I considered to be evil because he claimed to have God's authority and used it to try to persuade Jane to marry him. I don't know why this part made me so mad, I guess because I think it's awful to abuse authority, and I think it's even *more* awful if you claim to have authority from God and then misuse it. But my classmate was able to open my eyes to the beauty in the relationship between Jane and Helen at the boarding house and I went back and re-read that part, growing in my understanding of what love can be. That's the beauty of colloquia.

True argument gets nobody anywhere. One of my friends and I love to discuss books and ideas but half the time I leave the discussion with a bad feeling inside. Finally, I took a closer look and realized that one of us was debating and one of us was arguing. To me, debating is when both people want to arrive at the truth, and at the right. Both are willing to look at all arguments presented and then be open enough that if another view is proven to be correct and more truthful, so be it. At least they arrived at truth and right, which is the ultimate goal.

Arguing, on the other hand, is where one wants to prove that his or her point of view is right at all costs. It isn't about arriving at what is true and right, it is about *being* right. Webster says that arguing is to "persuade by reason" as well as "inventing and offering reasons; disputing; discussing; evincing; accusing." While both debaters and arguers show arguments to put forth their case, debaters have an attribute wholly to themselves, what Webster calls "discussion for elucidating truth." That is the key. I have found that I like to debate with someone whose highest goal is to elucidate truth, not just to *be the one* who is right.

Class was interesting. After pursuing a liberal arts education for several years now I can finally see how much I've grown and how worth it this has been. Some classes are pivotal moments for me. This class was one of those.

Oliver was at the front of the class lecturing about poetry. I'd come in late so I was on a hard seat at the back of the room.

"People in the West don't often view the difference between prose and poetry as I am going to define it, and of course there are other ways to define this, but there is merit in looking at it this way." *Hmm, what is he going to say the difference is? I'm way past just taking him at his word and he knows it. He'll ask questions and expect me to have original ideas—good ones, that are relevant and well articulated.*

He began making a list of the characteristics of poetry versus prose. "Prose uses clarity where poetry uses symbols. Prose explains what already exists where poetry creates. Prose is backward-looking and descriptive where poetry is forward-looking and predictive. Prose shapes ideas. Poetry shapes people. Prose appeals to the basis of truth by using reason, where poetry appeals to our emotions by using passion. Prose often sticks to the facts. Poetry uses universal truth that is applicable to individuals. Prose attempts to teach and inform the audience while poetry seeks to elevate and transform its audience. Prose tells, and poetry shows." *Okay, I could easily challenge these definitions—first on the basis of what the commonly accepted definitions are, and second because they're too narrow. But let's see where he's headed with this. It's interesting.*

He continued: "My whole point is that I want us all to understand Shakespeare better. He's deep, and shallow reading doesn't do him justice. Your education deserves better." *Years later, and still back to Shakespeare, Aristotle, Plato, Madison. And I learn more each time through. These really are classics.*

"Now let's really understand this. How does Prose view Poetry?" he asked. There were several answers from the students, like "Prose views Poetry as superfluous", "flowery", and "a bit too much." *This is an advanced class so I can expect tough questions. I had better be thinking because he'll expect great answers. He hates half-baked answers.*

Oliver paused for a moment. *I always like it when he does that, it means he's going to say something really important, or ask something important.* I took a deep breath and waited.

"How does Poetry view Prose?"

Someone commented quickly, "Boring."

Another blurted out, "Useless."

A third said, "Poetry views Prose as stale."

The Student Whisperer

I raised my hand. By now I couldn't help it, not only did I disagree with the comments, but I'd had an "a-ha" about myself, my writing, and about the great works I'd read. Besides, he would grill me anyway—so I might as well initiate it. When he called on me I think my answer surprised him.

"Tiffany, how does Poetry view Prose?"

"Poetry *uses* Prose. If Poetry is passionate about something, it uses reason to explain its passion. If it wants to be clear, it uses symbolism to carry its clarity. If it wants to predict it shows the past. It shapes people by sharing ideas, and it teaches universal truth by using the facts to show the whole. Poetry *uses* Prose."

"That wasn't what I was looking for," he said, "it's much better." I could tell that this idea was clicking for several in the class. For the others, well, maybe they'd have an opinion on it after they'd read more. I was excited. I could see clearly the difference between poetry and prose.

I sat there remembering several of the classics I'd read, and then Oliver asked, "When did we stop using poetry and start using mostly prose?" Oh, our ignorance! We sat silent. Oliver took out a book, I have no idea which one, and he began to list authors according to the oldest dates of any written works. There were several I'd heard of like Gilgamesh and Sinuhe, very few I'd read, and some I'd never known existed. It appeared that from the beginning of man's written word up until about Aristotle, the authors used lots of poetry (or prose in the poetic way). Aristotle used a lot of pure prose, and after him the practice grew.

My mind skipped ahead, or back, to many of the books I'd read. I began analyzing the books that had the greatest impact on me, asking myself, "Poetry or prose?"

Les Miserables? Poetry.

Jane Eyre? Poetry.

My great, great, great, great, great, great grandfather's journal? Poetry.

Laddie? Poetry.

The Bible? Poetry.

My list went on and on until I remembered . . . I got to *Billy Budd* and stopped.

I thought of how I struggled reading Melville. I thought about the storyline. I remembered when Billy Budd punched the first mate in the Captain's Quarters and he fell over, dead! I'd caught my breath and held it when the captain had to allow the punishment of death to fall on Billy Budd, on a clear day when the skies and seas were eternally blue and Billy hung from the gallows, though he meant no murder and the First Mate deserved a beating. The law had to be met.

It has been several years since I read *Billy Budd*, but I sat there yesterday in a Shakespeare class pondering about what Herman Melville had written a hundred and fifty years earlier. I realized that Melville understood at least in part how God must have felt when he allowed Christ to meet the ends of a broken law. Of course, my secularist friends would accurately point out that this is how Western Civilization feels about sacrificing Socrates to the cold, hard law.

What an amazing thing, I thought. *How powerful*, I mused. *How incredible*, I rejoiced, *that I could grow from something I read years ago. That is the power Oliver is talking about. Stories... they change people... they have myriads of levels... they stick.*

*Billy Budd...***Poetry!**

"Make your life into poetry," Oliver was saying. I tuned in when he paused. "Not in some artsy, dramatic sort of way, but in a world-changing realistic way. The world has problems. You were born to change them. You are educated to change them. But you still have to do all the hard work. *Good* poetry can happen in regular circumstances. But *great* poetry, great stories, great leaders, great lives—all are transacted in the currency of one word: sacrifice. Tell me what you're willing to sacrifice and I'll tell you how much you can change the world." I found myself holding my breath and had to force myself to breathe.

"Kim, what will your poem be?" he asked. We all knew him so well by now, and we knew he meant it. The energy in the room . . . well, it's hard to show in words. It was electric. Everyone was sitting up straight, but looking at their desks. He wanted an answer. Kim had tears running down her face and nobody said anything.

He asked several other students—still no answers.

"Tiffany, what will your poem be?" I had no answer. "What are you willing to sacrifice?" I kept my head down. It worked for everyone else. I had only tears as answers. But he kept looking at me. *Why doesn't he ask somebody else?*

"I require an answer, Tiffany," he said. "I'm done inspiring. Now I require." I looked up when he said that. "Tiffany, I require your answer. I will stand here as long as it takes. You're the leader now. What will your poem be? What will you sacrifice?"

I opened my mouth and words came out. I don't know where they came from. Maybe the hours and hours of study, of pondering, of discussing, of writing, of reading and wondering and asking. Maybe from even earlier, from childhood and youth and all my struggles to be who I was born to be. Maybe they came from the incredibly challenging studies and demanding mentors and projects. Maybe they were there all along. But suddenly I was tired of the classroom, tired of the safety net, tired of having people to go to when I had questions. Suddenly I wanted to give back even if it meant being on the high wire alone, to face the world and show them what I could do.

The scene of the classroom fades around me and I speak—not to a teacher, or a mentor, or a group of colleagues—I speak to the world, to those searching for answers, to those seeking real change. I keep talking for a lot of years. And when I finish speaking and sacrificing, sometime far in the future . . . the world is changed.

Life

by Tiffany Earl

I found myself bewildered. After feeling so inspired, after all my grandiose plans, life was . . . hard. It was my first time being out of school since I was five years old. My whole identity was tied to school. All my habits revolved around school. Now I was a mother, a wife, and *not* in school for the first time in my life. The home had children in it and my life was so full, but I felt so alone.

It was eleven o'clock at night. Rick wasn't due home for a couple more hours. The kids had just gone down for the night. I opened to the chapter I was on and resumed reading. Little Princess was in labor. She was having her baby.

Prince Andre had experienced a change of heart out on the battlefield and he'd come home to show his wife, and let her know that he loved her. The doctor wouldn't let Prince Andre into the delivery room. The Little Princess didn't even know he was there. *Why won't they let him in? Why won't they let him see her? She needs to know he's there.*

I read on. *Oh no, that can't be!* I went back and re-read the two previous pages. *It's true. How awful! Why didn't they tell her he was there? Why couldn't he have been holding her when she died?*

I shut the book.

I looked around me. I had a lamp turned on. I was curled up on the couch clutching my legs to my chest.

I opened the book again. *It's true. She died. He didn't get to tell her he loved her.*

I shut the book again.

I sat there trembling. Maybe it was that I had just recently had a baby. I don't know; but whatever it was, all of a sudden I loved Rick more.

He came home that night and found me in his arms.

Forty-two, forty-three, forty-four . . . fifty, fifty-one! Fifty-one things on the hall floor.

Legos, flashcards, Tonka trucks, ABC blocks, string, popsicle sticks, glue sticks, and garbage. And I was nine months pregnant!

"Jacob!" I hollered.

He came bounding around the corner kicking his soccer ball. I caught it with my hand before it hit my belly.

"Jacob? See this hall? This is your job. I want you to pick up all the toys and put them away before you play. In fact, if you get it done then you can play. And if you don't, you can't." He kicked the ball down the hall.

"Jacob, do you understand?"

"Yes."

"Good."

With that I went into the kitchen and began making breakfast. Twenty minutes later I went to go switch the laundry before we ate.

The hall! It was still a mess.

"Jacob! I said to get this hall cleaned. I mean it. You won't play until it's done."

I switched the laundry, and came out of the laundry room into the hall. The hall! It was still a mess.

"Jacob! I said to clean this hall and I mean it."

After breakfast I sat on the couch. I was beat.

The knock at the door was Sara's. I knew her knock. Jacob ran to the door excited. We let her in and I saw the hall in the corner of my eye.

Anger rose within me. Why was I such a failure? Why couldn't I get my child to pick up his toys? Why didn't he obey me?

I felt like I'd failed. This made me mad.

I picked up Jacob and took him to the hall.

"I told you to clean this or you couldn't play." I got on my knees and took my son's hands and forced him to pick up the toys. I knew I was shaming him in front of his friend Sara, but I felt more than justified.

After he trotted outside to play in the sand with Sara, I sunk onto the couch with a contraction, feeling guilty and angry. I took out a sheet of paper. I drew my chart:

Give assignment.

Child says "yes" and does it, and then receives a reward. OR doesn't do it and I make him.

Was something wrong with this picture? And could I fix it?

For two years I found myself repeating the cycle. I asked my son to do his job. Sometimes he chose not to. I felt angry and I pushed and pushed and pushed until he acquiesced and did it. He felt crummy, and so did I.

For two years I had been searching for the principles and solutions to the cycle I was following.

Furthermore, I struggled to understand why Rick disciplined the way he did. Two different people, coming from two different backgrounds, trying to unite into a single purpose, a single unit, a single family—no wonder it's a miracle when marriage works. Of course, I believed it could almost always work—but it was so, so hard.

The real difficulty didn't hit until Jacob was old enough to be given chores, and then our different backgrounds came out with a vengeance. We began to see that I was very permissive and Rick was more authoritative, neither of which were obvious traits of our

The Student Whisperer

personalities. Rick was quiet by nature, and I was much more open and opinionated.

"I think we should decide beforehand how we want to be with our children instead of just reacting," I said to Rick one day as we watched Jacob playing in the dirt. "We both agree that we should be united, that we should be one, the question is, which way is best for our family, mine or yours?"

"Tiffany, maybe neither of us is right. Maybe you are on one end of the spectrum, and maybe I'm on the other. Maybe we have to *find* the right course."

"But Rick, how? All the parenting we've ever seen modeled is from our own parents. And you are saying that maybe neither of our parents had it right?"

"That's not what I'm saying. Why don't we pick the best of each model?"

"Rick, they are opposites. Your parents gave the rules and there was no discussion. Bammo, you had to obey, or nothing. There was no leeway, there was no talking, there was just, 'The first rule of our house is obedience—you always obey your parents, no matter what!' And they enforced it! My parents were the opposite. They gave general guidelines, there was always open debate as to how we could follow those guidelines, and if we broke them, there weren't very many parental consequences. There was just a lot more discussion. How do we pick the best from each example?"

"I don't know, but somehow we've got to come to some consensus."

That's as far as we got but we kept looking. We had the same discussion or something like it at least a dozen times over the years. I knew I was doing something wrong—but what was it? I wanted my kids to obey. They usually didn't. I had failed. That was my mindset.

It was time to see my mentor.

I pulled out my diagram and showed him, explaining the cycle.

I pointed to the part where kids "don't obey" and said, "at this point I get angry and remind the child every two minutes to do his job."

"Wait right there. Why do you get angry?"

"What?"

"Why do you get angry when your son or daughter doesn't do the job?"

I stared at him in disbelief. I wanted to say, "*Why do I get angry? Why am I angry when their choices force me to live in a mess, manipulate them, or clean it all myself?*"

Instead I politely said, "For two reasons. One, because I feel like I've failed; and two, if they don't do it then I have to!" My voice got a little heated at the end of that sentence.

"You don't fail when your son chooses to disobey. Does God fail when his sons and daughters disobey?"

"Well, no."

"Okay. No. By feeling like a failure and choosing to be angry you cloud up your emotions and make a bad choice."

With that he turned over the paper with my diagram on it and started writing. Down one leg he wrote "Freedom to choose" and down the other he wrote "Forced to obey."

"There are only two choices, Tiffany. That's all there are. Don't you think your children should be allowed to fail?"

I caught my breath.

I turned my head to the side and looked deeper at my diagram. I could see where I went wrong. Instead of letting it take its course— my diagram of agency—I introduced force in the name of manipulation and shame.

"You mean that when I ask a child to do his job, he should be allowed the freedom to fail, to disobey, to choose not to?"

"That's exactly what I'm saying. But why are you asking me, instead of talking this out with your husband?"

"Well, we parent so differently. We both try to follow the best methods from our parents, but it never seems to work."

He smiled. "Maybe forget your parent's methods, and focus on the best principles of parenting taught by your parents, others, and whatever you believe. Methods are so often habits, not principles or ideals. I'd bet your parents and Rick's parents would tell you different principles to follow than you would think based on their behaviors." He started to laugh. "I know my kids would sure rather learn from the principles I believe about parenting than from the practice I too often fall into in real life!"

This makes so much sense, I thought as I laughed with him.

"Just remember the principles," he said. "You and Rick are the experts on your home—not me." He was still smiling.

I slowly let out my breath as I realized that what he was saying was no different than how he ran his classes. He would tell us our possibilities, what our life could be like, then explain the natural requirements for getting there—challenge us to do it—and then let us alone, let us act or not act. This was the model of teaching through freedom, not force, not manipulation, not shame. *I want this! I am going to learn to trust the process.*

I walked home in the dark. I ran it through my mind. I told myself my guidelines:

- Give assignments
- Explain the details
- Show the consequences and blessings for obedience
- Show the consequences for disobedience
- Let my child choose

I asked Rick what he thought the best principles of parenting were, and what ideals he thought his parents would suggest on parenting. We talked for a long time, and a lot of things seemed to click into place. We fell asleep in each other's arms.

The next morning, I tried a new way. "Jacob, your job today is to clean the hall. Any questions?"

He shook his head.

"Good. One more thing. If you get it done before breakfast you can play with Sara today. If you don't do your job then you can't play today. Do you understand?"

He nodded.

"Jacob, it is very important to me that you clean the hall, and that you learn to obey me and Dad, so I will follow through on my promise to reward or not let you play—depending on whether or not you clean the hall. Do you really understand?"

"Yes, Mom," he said.

"Good." I smiled and walked away. For the next fifteen minutes I bit my tongue in order not to nag and manipulate Jacob. It was hard, but it got easier with practice. After an hour I still frowned but then just moved on when I noticed the dirty hallway. He didn't clean the hall that day.

It was so hard not to get mad. It broke my heart when he sobbed as I sent Sara home. He even pleaded. I told him I loved him and reminded him how important it is to obey. He continued sobbing and acted like he didn't hear me. When Rick came home and wanted to lift the consequence and let Jacob go to Sara's, I told him the whole story. He immediately smiled and hugged me, then found Jacob and gently reiterated the whole lesson. Then he took Jacob to work with him in the yard. Jacob's big smile made me feel better, and I hoped the worst was over. At least Rick and I were happily on the same page.

It took a week before Jacob started doing his job, but our family life has been so much better ever since.

Rick came into the room one night to find me distressed.

"What's wrong, Tiffany? I can tell that something's been bothering you."

I looked up at Rick. I had just finished changing the baby's diaper.

"This is wrong." I said, pointing to the diaper.

"And this," I said, pointing to the laundry on the floor.

The Student Whisperer

"And that!" I emphasized as I pointed toward the dishes in the kitchen sink.

"And the fridge too," I said as I thought about all the meals I had to make day in and day out.

Rick sat next to me and made me stop folding the laundry I had started working on. He took my hands in his and made me look at him.

"What is it *really*, Tiffany?"

I struggled to swallow back the tears, but it was no use, "Rick, when will I get to use my brain? When will I get to use my talents? When will I get to do more of the things I know I was born to do?"

He just squeezed my hands tighter waiting for me to go on.

"When will I write? When will I work with the youth? When will I speak? When will I do anything besides folding laundry, cooking, cleaning, changing diapers, and reading to the kids?"

We'd had this conversation many times. Rick knew *me* too. He knew I loved our family. He knew that it was the most important thing to me. He knew that I wasn't trying to complain about being a mother and a wife. He knew that it came first and that I loved him and our children. He knew that that wasn't what the problem was. He knew we were both excited about the legacy of faith, trust, hope, and love we were instilling in our children through our example. He also knew that I felt a burning desire to work with the youth, to write, to speak, to understand more fully other pieces of The Call.

"Tiffany, it's seasons."

"What?"

"*This* is your season right now. Enjoy it. You are still preparing for others. I know you want to apply all the learning you have, all the many hours of study you do, and you will."

"How long will I prepare, Rick? How long?"

"Not long, Tiff. Not long."

He was right. It wasn't long.

*And when the day comes that you are called upon for what the **world** calls "great things," you will see clearly that they are no greater than the things you did at home. And by the way, that call **will** come . . ."* As my eyes scanned the words in Oliver's book, something touched my heart—a tickle from a feather almost.

I re-read the words. I knew they were true. I'd always believed they were true. That's why I could continue as I did. In the mundane face of laundry, dishes, pick-up, I made time to study and to ponder. In the important phase of rearing children—holding, teaching, nurturing, and listening, I applied the new understanding I gained. In my relationship with my husband and my friends, we did our best to support one another and uplift one another.

For years I'd heard the thoughts in the back of my mind, "Now is the time to prepare." And prepare I did—with hours of endless study and meditating, with constant checks on where to spend my time. There was consistent weekly analysis of "what should I leave out of my life—and has anything unnecessary crept back in?"

"No Mary, nothing. It's just so frustrating. He is only twelve. He can't continue to audit community college classes with his dad. Without his dad with him, it just doesn't feel right to have him take college courses—even though he does understand the material and does well with the work."

"I wouldn't recommend it anyway. What we've seen is that when they go too young they may have the skills and intellect to do the work, but they're not prepared in some really important ways to fully benefit from it. By the time they're sixteen or so, they get a 'been-there-done-that' attitude, and when they are eighteen and really ready in all those other ways for a great college experience, they are already burned out and leave."

I was listening to the familiar tune of a frustrated mother—only this time it was two of my best friends, and they were discussing a boy I knew personally. I sat back on the couch and concentrated with all my might to understand more fully what was taking place.

One thing was quite obvious: "the way" had been shown and yet mothers and fathers of youth were still stuck. Oliver's book, *A Thomas Jefferson Education,* had taught people the difference between conveyor-belt, professional, and leadership education. And yet, most moms had the choice of having playgroups where "Love of Learning" classes were offered, or public school, where they were in luck if they found an exceptional teacher who had a liberal arts education. Or they did it on their own—which from what I was hearing, didn't work with some of the older youth because the kids needed an academic and social environment where all five learning environments of lecture, tutorial, exams, coaching, and discussion were used. Sometimes parents sent a youth to a local college course, but then sadly watched him burn out early.

I noticed a familiar feeling inside, a gnawing thought that I had something to do with this, with the answer. There was something else though, a missing piece. I kept listening to my two friends talk.

"He wants to be with his friends. He used to be satisfied at home, with occasional friends. But now, he wants to be with them *more.*"

My mind wandered for a moment: *here was a pattern.* When the child turned twelve or thirteen, something took place, and that something was the desire to be with peers a lot. A thought persisted, *this is right. This is a good thing. The desire to be among peers isn't bad. Use it. Don't fight it. Use it. The synergy is right.*

Along with these thoughts an image came to my mind so powerfully I could see it right in front of me. I saw a mountainous heap of stone. I've been rock-hunting with my husband enough that different rocks with their different shapes, sizes, color, cleavage, texture, smells, and attributes keep my interest and are exciting to me. This heap was made of coal. On the top of a hill stood a gigantic ball of stone with its bottom edge sliced off parallel to the ground and hanging by a huge cable. With a loud crash it came tumbling down and as it landed on a large piece of coal, the coal was shattered into a million pieces.

Over and over the ball of stone came crashing down, breaking the coal into smaller pieces.

My mind zoomed into the heap, and under miles of topsoil and rock were hundreds, nay thousands, of small pieces of coal that through pressure and time had turned into diamonds. Their luster was shimmering, their beauty unparalleled.

Thoughts crept into my mind: *A youth craves to be a diamond. And deep inside he knows that the only way is through pressure. That is one reason he desires to be with peers: he wants to stretch his wings and fly. So use the peers for positive pressure. Instead of pressure to "fit into the crowd" or to do drugs, or to waste time, like the ball of stone crushing the precious piece of coal, shattering its wholeness, use pressure for goodness, for nobility, for excitement to learn. Create an environment where there is pressure to become someone good, knowledgeable, courageous, and wise. Where the pressure is love.*

I recognized the familiar feeling. *I must do something. This is what I was born for. This is why I am the way I am. This is why I crave and have always craved and lived this kind of education. It is time to act.*

This is what I yearned for as a youth, and it wasn't available. That was in the past. I will do something about it. I will help make a Leadership Education available to the youth.

It was cold outside, but I did have a coat on. It was one of those crisp nights where the stars shine clearly and the breeze cuts to the bones. Still, the conversation held my attention.

"How's your school coming along?" Oliver asked.

Should I tell him the truth or pretend that all is well? I decided to risk the truth.

"Actually . . . I . . . I just lost one of my best students."

"Oh." I could hear the disappointment in his voice. He wanted me to go on.

"I just don't get it. It was right when I felt I'd finally reached them too. You know, right when the ice breaks and the students are ready to take a dive."

He looked at me quizzically. The moon was bright this crispy, cold night. I went on.

"I had finally inspired my students to put the time in, to really pay the price that greatness requires, to seize the opportunity to really push themselves past mediocrity and find the joy in study! I know it hurts to study—especially at first if the brain isn't used to thinking on one thought long enough to see from many angles and in many lights. I felt like they were really grasping the concept. I could see their mouths begin to water. But then . . . I lost one."

"Why?"

"You won't believe why."

"Why?"

"It's a paradox, really. The parents come to me, and say, 'My child should be in Scholar Phase, but she isn't yet. Would coming to your school help?'

"I say, 'Of course! We employ all the principles of a Leadership Education, and a good portion of the students inevitably naturally discipline themselves and progress from the Love of Learning Phase into the more rigorous Scholar Phase.'

"They say, 'Good! That's exactly what we want!'

"Only it really isn't." My teeth were chattering a bit by now, but I forced them to hold still. I couldn't tell if it was the cold, or telling him I felt like I failed.

"They really *don't* want Scholar Phase. They're blown away if their child *really* studies eight to twelve hours a day. It's culture shock to them. Our society thinks high school is the time to play."

"You're right, Tiffany. We make them work, work, work at elementary school and then when they get to high school we say, 'Go to the football games! Go to the parties! I don't want my kids to miss out on the best time in their lives! They'll never have this time again, so have fun! Don't let learning get in the way.' Of course, youth should be fun. It should also be a time of great education! Too often, though, it's exactly opposite what it should be."

"That's right! We were doing role-plays and I taught the kids how to make a plan of action. They each listed how much time they thought they should realistically study each week. Then I had them list their three biggest stumbling blocks to studying.

"After that I had them come up with proactive plans for each stumbling block. I asked for a volunteer to share their plan and one student raised his hand and said, 'I know my biggest deterrent to studying, but I don't know how to solve it.' Then the most amazing thing happened," I related:

"Well, maybe the class can help you come up with a good plan," I said.

The student continued, "Every time I go to study, my mom calls me."

The class brainstormed some awesome ideas. The consensus seemed to be that he could have a chat with his parents and between the three of them decide how much he should study and when, and also to make sure all his chores were done and never use study as an excuse to get out of family chores. That way he wouldn't get interrupted. I thought we had really helped him.

"What happened?" Oliver asked.

"The next thing I knew, his mom called me to withdraw him from the school. She said, 'My son studies too much. He misses our family activities of watching movies together, sometimes he refuses to play with his friends, and I'm just afraid he isn't playing enough!'"

"Needless to say, I was shocked! I'd finally inspired my students to want to put in the necessary time and I lost one."

I was beginning to learn that one of my greatest stumbling blocks to reaching the youth and inspiring them to get a Leadership Education was figuring out how to get the parents to want it first, and to understand what it meant.

It was weird to think that very few people understand the truth that two hundred plus years ago boys like John Adams and Thomas Jefferson went to college in their youth, got a liberal arts education in their adolescence, studying upwards of eight to twelve hours a day, and only after graduating with proficiency in several core subjects (and by proficiency I mean that they had read the classics in their original language, debated many facets and views of the ideas that would lead to the emergence of the freest nation on earth, and many other things) did they go on to pick a profession—usually in law, or business ownership, or possibly the clergy.

We talked for a few more minutes and I was comforted to keep plugging away. I walked home under the moon with all the conviction in the world that though I was sad to lose one of my best students, I wouldn't give up.

When Susan asked me to mentor her I was leery at first. I'd learned quickly what type of student I was willing to mentor and they had to have a special quality, the quality that they were willing to *be* mentored. They had to want something bad enough that they were willing to *trust* me and to put the time and work into becoming what they desired.

I listened to her story: "Three months ago I read Oliver DeMille's book. I'm seventeen years old and have home-schooled my whole life, and never has a book had such an impact on me.

"I looked over the recommended reading list, and thought, 'Well, I better get started. I know I've read some classics here and there, but I want to be serious about my education now.' So I looked on my mother's bookshelf and pulled out Plutarch.

"It's been a slow process, but over the last two months I read Plutarch and annotated it."

She had my full attention now. She had actually done what Oliver recommended. She had started reading and annotating the classics. Still, would her work ethic be worth my time?

After interviewing her I discovered she hadn't grown her ability to study for extended lengths of time. In fact, one hour was pushing it.

I knew thirteen year olds who could study longer than she did.

On the other hand, she had something many people didn't. She had *desire*. My first test would be to double her study time, and then double it again. We would start with that.

"Can you block out two hours of uninterrupted study time?"

"Yes, I'm sure I can."

"Okay, you've told me you want me to mentor you in math. I have a broader vision of mentoring you so we'll have a trial period to begin with, to see if we like working with each other, okay?"

"Okay."

I pulled out a literature book that had math in it.

"There are three things I'd like you work on: Read in your core book for thirty minutes a day, annotating all math and science principles you find. You will discover that there are no greater math books than most people's core books—The Talmud, the Koran, the Bible, Analects, and the *Autobiography of a Yogi,* just to start." I gave her the math page out of the *Thomas Jefferson Planner* so she'd have a place to keep track of the math principles, assumptions, and skills growth. "I want you to get a math textbook such as Saxon math and work on your math skills. Just block out the amount of time you want to spend on this and grow your math skills every day. And last, do you like literature?"

There was a concept about math I knew she needed to know. "Susan, when people think of math, did you know that a lot of them have a skewed vision of it? Did you know that they only see about one-third of the picture?" She looked at me with her eyebrows bunched together. "Most people in America have been trained in what I've heard called 'Newtonian math.' They see the measurements and calculations and symbols of math, which is great. Measurements and calculations are an important part of math. But that's just it. They are only *part*. Did you know they are not even the *most important* part?

"Did you know that many math classics and great works by scientists talk about things like happiness . . . wisdom . . . philosophy . . . light

. . . and *truth*? Did you know that the bottom line for math is to find truth? Math can help us find truth in all fields! Math is not confined to mere numbers and calculations. That is the language of math, but not the goal of math. The *goal* of math is to know and elucidate truth. So if you are a truth-seeker, you will love math."

She smiled. She was excited.

"There's one more thing right now about this . . . logic. Logic is really important. It's important to be able to reason, to be able to see others' reasoning. To be able to take your mind from point A to point B, and then clear through point Z on to infinity. There's a famous mathematician right now who recently joked with his colleagues that though scientists have discovered twelve dimensions, he can only keep ten of them in his head at once. It's not easy to think this deeply. It's going to take a lot of work. Are you prepared for that?" I knew I was overwhelming her. It was okay. I needed to know what she was made of. She gulped a nod.

"Back to literature: Do you like literature?"

She nodded yes. "I'll give you a new literature book each week that will pique your interest in math. This one happens to be called *Fair Blows the Wind*, by Louis L'Amour. It got me excited about navigation."

She took the book, and her commitment, and within a month she'd read five more books on navigation.

I kept waiting for her to hit her first roadblock. She'd built her study hours to four already, and three months into our relationship she finally came to me frustrated.

"I just don't get it, Mrs. Earl. It doesn't *feel* like it used to."

"What doesn't feel like it used to?"

"Studying doesn't. I used to just . . ." She put her arms in the air like an eagle, took in a deep breath and said, "I used to feel like I was soaring when I studied. I was so happy. I loved it so much. And now, it feels different."

Yes! Yes! Yes! She is growing. This was what I'd been waiting for. It was the opportunity to impact her understanding of where she was and where she was headed. Roadblocks can be exciting!

"Susan, that's because you used to be in the Love of Learning phase and now you are in Scholar Phase. They feel different. In the Love of Learning phase you could stop and change direction when things got tough. It was okay to do that before, but Scholar Phase is different. In Scholar Phase you have the *duty* to see it through even when it's hard."

Her eyes lit up. "Really? It's okay to feel frustrated when I'm studying sometimes? And hate it? Well, you know, want to quit?"

"I should say so. The difference is, you *won't* quit. You'll plow through. When you get to a spot that feels that way you have three choices."

"I do?"

"Yes, you have to determine if," I held up my pointer finger, "you aren't *supposed* to be studying that particular thing at that particular time, or," I held up my next finger as well, "you need to develop a skill that is keeping you from understanding, so that when you are studying, you aren't wasting your time, or," and I held up my third finger, "it is time to see a mentor who can help you through the hard spot. When I hit those moments I usually get on my knees to determine which of the three it is."

I spent the next half hour teaching her about the different phases, what they looked like and how each felt. When she left the usual bounce was back in her step.

I skipped a step as I walked over to the DeMilles'. The baby was on my hip and the other three children were trailing along after me. Jacob had the plates, spoons, and cups, and Laura had Joseph's hand. The DeMilles had invited us over for Dutch-oven breakfast over their fire pit on this crispy fall morning.

I skipped a step, not because of Rachel's home cooking—even though I looked forward to her spiced eggs and cheese, homemade bread thickly buttered and toasted crispy golden over the fire, and the hash browns and hot chocolate. No—my heart skipped a beat because I had a premonition.

The exhilaration that encompasses me at such times is almost indescribable. It's almost as if a part of my brain is tapped that lies dormant unless triggered.

After we breakfasted and the children began playing, I ended up helping Oliver and son put together the goat pen for Nibley, their buck.

As Oliver pulled, twisted, pounded, shaped, and hammered the pen, he asked me a question—well, several questions to be more accurate.

As he began asking me questions I felt like Plato must have felt when he sat on the beach with Socrates. Only we weren't on the beach, we were at the goat pens. Oliver must have asked me over three hundred questions by the time I discovered the answer. I know how grueling it was for me and can only imagine how difficult it must have been for Oliver to re-word his question that many times and in that many ways in order to allow me to have the "a-ha" and discover the answer for myself.

He asked, "If you have a student who is in Core Phase and has been focusing on learning right from wrong, good from bad, duty, and relationships, and they're ready to move into the next phase, Love of Learning, what do you do?"

I thought for a moment. "I set the example."

"What do you mean?"

"I read. I write. I am excited to study, explore, and learn."

"What does that do?"

"It gets the student excited. When the student sees me excited, and sees my love of doing these things, then she wants to do them too."

"Is that all you do? Read, write, learn and be excited?"

"No, I invite them to join me. I share the experience with them and give them a taste of what it feels like to learn."

"Yes, you share with them *your* love of learning—by learning and inviting them to join you."

"Yes."

One side of the metal goat pen was tightened into place now. "If you have a student in Love of Learning phase and she's ready to move into Scholar Phase, what do you do?"

That is exactly what I spent my time doing with my students, inspiring them to go from the fun Love of Learning Phase into the more disciplined Scholar Phase. I began to analyze what it is that I do.

"I give really cool lectures that expand the student's vision of what is possible, hoping to help them want to become leaders."

"Yes, but what else?"

"I get them to read the classics and expose them to greatness.'

"That's part of it, but what else?"

"I hold them accountable for their commitments."

"That's good too, but it's still not what I'm looking for. What is it that teachers don't do often enough, and when they *do* it, the results are powerful?"

"They pay the price themselves."

"A lot of teachers do that. Keep trying."

"They teach through freedom. Instead of coercing the students they inspire them."

"Yes, but how do they inspire them?"

"By telling stories."

"What kind of stories?"

"Stories that inspire."

"Whose stories?"

"Stories of great men and women. A good teacher will expose the students to the great things that men and women have done throughout history."

"There's something else that teachers don't do often enough, and when they do it the results are powerful. Even if they do it they too often don't know how they did it. I've never heard this principle taught. What is it?"

Oh how I wracked my brain! I went through all my best teachers trying to figure out what it is they did that inspired someone to enter Scholar Phase and really discipline themselves. I thought of my Dad. He is one of the most effective teen teachers I've ever experienced. I started listing the things he does:

"Makes eye contact with the students."

"What else?"

"The teacher understands the content so well that he doesn't have to keep his nose in a book as he teaches."

"What else?"

"Reads his audience's energy and changes speed, dynamics, and direction as needed."

"What else?"

"Has an effective learning environment and spirit in the classroom.

"What else?"

"Loves his students."

"Right on. That's probably the best answer. But what else?"

"Help me out. Ask me another question."

"Okay, what is it that effective teachers do that helps a student want to become great and helps the student desire and commit to putting forth the effort required to really learn?"

Oliver's son had been listening to all this, and now he ventured an answer: "Have the students do their work over and over, in order to go really deep. And keep having them do it over a bunch of times on the same assignment."

"Good idea," Oliver said. "Not what I'm looking for though." He smiled as they both kept tightening the wires on the fence.

I thought of what Oliver does as he teaches.

"The teacher challenges the student."

"They do, but that's not what I'm looking for."

"The teacher listens to the students."

"That's another of the most important answers. But what else?"

"The teacher gets really quiet at the end and boils everything down and brings the whole lecture down to 'so what does this mean to me?'"

"That's good, but it's not what I'm looking for."

I was at my wit's end. He looked at me and said, "I am not going to tell you the answer, Tiffany. I asked the same question to a big workshop of teachers and they still haven't figured it out."

I knelt down by the goat pen and took a deep breath. I took a handful of dirt in my hand and gently let it fall between my fingers. I sighed, and as I did, I looked in Oliver's eyes before he could speak and said, "There *is one thing*. There's something I do—but I only do it with permission, and very sparingly. And when I do it, I feel a change in the room. I sense the determination of my students, and I realize they are on fire." I paused, gulped, and then said as I stared him in the eye, "I share with them *why* I do what I do."

He smiled widely and went back to pounding with the hammer. That was it! That was what he was looking for. The thing that inspires a student, as much or more than anything else! It is when a person buys into a personal mission so that she is willing to discipline herself and push harder. It is the taste of someone else's mission, especially the one doing the inspiring!

The goat pen was finished, and it was afternoon now. I'd been drilled, hounded, guided, led, probed, and pushed. Now I had another tool, which would make me a more effective teacher. It wasn't necessarily what Oliver thought he was giving me. I had that tool too, and I used it. I realized that the most powerful lecture can be ineffective without it. A well-prepared lecture can be life-changing when it includes a personal glimpse into the life of the teacher; but even more than that tool, I learned something else.

The type of tutorial I had just had with Oliver was incredible. I love it when my brain is questioned and questioned and questioned and the gears have to start turning, and the music starts playing and I become a creator—a creator of thought and ideas.

I want to learn to teach like that, to take the time to pull from my mentees what they have inside but don't know yet, to help them have life-changing "a-ha!s," to ask the right questions!

Months later I found myself sitting in the DeMilles' parlor. Usually I sat here with my kids and life was about being Mom, but today it was because my mission mentor had something to teach me.

"I want to make this kind of an education available to the youth in many places, *not* just one or two little schools. Don't get me wrong, Oliver. I'm glad I can reach the youth here and have an impact, but don't you see, I can't rest until all the youth have that choice!"

"Tiffany, your current plan won't work."

I looked at him, and he could see his words hurt. "Tiffany, there are at least four types of schools. There are traditional schools, mom's schools, private schools, and founder's schools. History shows that if you take a private school and try to duplicate it in other cities over time, once the staff is trained they will simply break away."

"But, but . . ."

"No 'buts,' Tiffany. It's happened many times, it's happened to . . ." He listed several concrete examples.

"That means that you are either a mom's school, which only lasts while your kids are involved, or you are a founder's school, which I don't even want to begin to describe to you. Or if you are a private school, you will try to duplicate yourself and fail."

"Well, I'm not a mom's school. I want to reach youth around the world. So you better tell me about a founder's school."

I could see his face was pained. He took a deep breath and for a minute he even looked down at the floor. When he looked back at me his eyes were different.

"Tiffany, a founder's school is something you give your life for. A founder's school is like the pioneers coming across the plains, stopping at new ground, and digging in their heels. They make camp. They cut trees. They build roads. They dig ditches. They plant seeds, and they sweat love, blood, and tears. And then, often, they move on and leave their improvements for others who come along and have it easier. Tiffany, you don't want a founder's school. It requires the sacrifice of all."

It was dusk as I walked home. *I know I'm not a mom's school. I've always known that. If duplicating private schools doesn't work, then do I have to be a founder's school? Am I to build a founder's school? Isn't there a way, somewhere in history where someone accomplished what I'm trying to accomplish? Something I could model? I know it isn't required that I give up raising my children, but I also feel the call to impact the current educational trends, among other things.*

So what if Oliver says these are the only choices. There are always limits on things until somebody innovates and does them differently. I'm not going to be limited by what Oliver said. I need to figure this out.

I felt peace. There was a *way*, and I would find it. I'd scrap the current plan and search for the one that would work. If that meant creating a new way that had never been done then I would do it, but if it meant searching until I found a way I could model then I would do *that*.

"Tiffany, I'm telling you, my parents don't want to pay *you* if I'm the one teaching."

I took a deep breath. This was the big test I was hoping I'd pass. I knew this is what would let me know if I'd found the solution.

"Why? I'm the one who created the stuff you are teaching. I'm training you. Without that, you couldn't even give it to them."

"I didn't say they didn't love your stuff. They do. It's changing their kids' lives, but they have a problem paying *you* if I'm the one teaching."

I only had a few pods, but I was treating them as if it were many. I knew that when my business partner, Aneladee, shared her critique, every positive remark and every criticism represented 100 teachers. Even though it was opposite to what I wanted to hear, I listened. I listened as if I got this call from 100 different teachers in 100 different locations.

Lucky for me Aneladee was a fighter. In fact, she'd finally found her match. She was usually too strong for most people and people couldn't handle her passion. It scared them. I understood there were times people just gave up rather than working things out. I liked to see things through, even when they got tough—and this was tough. Could Aneladee and I see it through? Would she stay on the phone with me while we looked at it from every angle?

Was it our presentation? Was it the business plan? Was it the structure? Was it the payment plan? Was it the foundation? What was it? Was it me? Was it her? Were the parents justified in feeling the way they felt? If so, what needed to change?

I knew my business had to be sound financially or I'd never reach the thousands I intended on reaching, so I couldn't just create a world-changing curriculum, and train for free. It had to be a sound professional model.

After thirty minutes of getting nowhere she said it again. "Look, Tiffany, my parents just won't pay you and have you pay a portion of it back to me. *I* know I need you. *I* know I can't do this without you. *I* know you have to be paid—but it won't work this way. The parents, the customers, just don't understand."

"Then, what?"

"I think you should do it like Suzuki did it."

My insides had been all knotted up throughout our whole conversation, but when she said this, I felt a little light come on inside.

"What do you know about Suzuki?" I asked.

"I know that he had an educational method he wanted to bring to the world, and he was successful—and people didn't pay him and *then* have him pay the teachers."

She had my attention. If what she was saying were true then I wouldn't have to be a founder's school. If what she was saying were true then I would have a successful model to follow. If what she was saying were true then I could accomplish what I'd set out to accomplish!

"Aneladee, you've got to tell me more. Tell me what you mean. Tell me what Suzuki did. Tell me how he did it. Tell me what it is you are really saying."

"What I'm saying, is this: I'm a trained Suzuki teacher. I teach the cello. My students pay me, not Suzuki. That's what I'm saying."

It was a start, a beginning. Over time I changed parts of the business structure. The students paid a certification fee, my teachers paid a fee for training and mentoring, and the teacher charged the students whatever they personally decided to charge, and they kept all that money. There was no reason to break away after training. They were already free.

Eventually we realized that our business structure at Leadership Education Mentoring Institute was only the foundation to training the real "frontier" type of school, the new form that was an educational form to match the needs of our time. Aneladee Milne eventually published her book about the New Commonwealth Schools[21]—and indeed *they* were Founder's schools. They were different than the one-room schoolhouse, public schools, and private schools. They were an extension of a mom's school that turned into an interdependent commonwealth school. The communities had to be interdependent to reach the scholar needs of their youth. We didn't know any of this at the time. We were focusing on the classroom and great teaching, not the school-form yet.

I looked at the numbers. There was no way I could spend an hour a week with each teacher.

The Student Whisperer

I'd seen this very thing slow down other businesses—even crush some; but I had an idea. I called one of my business mentors.

"Dad?" I said into the telephone.

"Yes, Tiffany is that you?"

"Yeah, it's me. Listen, I know you've done literally thousands of seminars, business presentations, and been on several radio talk shows, but have you ever done 'conference calls'?"

"Lots, why?"

"Whew. I think that's how I'm going to mentor my teachers."

We talked for a while and he told me some different ways to do the calls. It was nice to have one of my *expert* mentors be my dad.

"Thanks, Dad, you just made it so I can more effectively mentor my teachers."

I held my first conference call and felt like it was a fiasco. I called my mentor back.

"Dad, it was just awful. I had a list of things I wanted to teach my teachers and I taught it over the phone. Then I opened it up for questions and got bombarded. One question was negative and I answered it all wrong and had to e-mail her to tell the right answer. It was just horrible. What did I do wrong?"

"For starters, Tiffany, you've got to be really clear about what your goal of the conference call is."

"I have a couple of goals, Dad. The biggest is that I need to inspire my teachers to keep on paying the price themselves, to keep reading classics, to start writing every day if they aren't, to set boundaries so they don't lose sight of what's most important. You know, Dad—inspire my teachers to stay committed. I also have things I need to continue training them on. Not a whole lot because we cover most things in the seminar training, but things still come up. I also need their feedback."

"Do you use e-mail, Tiffany?"

"Of course. My teachers send a weekly report form through e-mail. It tells what they did to prepare, how class went, and what they would have changed for next time."

"Include on that weekly report form a place for them to ask any questions. That way all questions have to come through e-mail first. This gives you time to know if you want to respond through e-mail or decide that it's important enough to address on the conference call. That way nobody's time is wasted.

"You're the expert, honey. They call in to hear you, not have their time wasted by questions that don't pertain. If it is important enough to address for them all, then you can."

"So you're saying they can't ask questions on the call?"

"No, what I'm saying is that you lecture for the first 45 minutes. Then open it up to questions for the last 15 minutes, but only questions about the topic you just taught about. Any other questions should come over e-mail first."

"That's perfect, Dad. Perfect. Then anybody who needs private coaching can schedule to stay on the phone with me afterward. Dad, thank you so much!"

"No problem, Tiff. Let me know how it goes. Bye."

It worked wonderfully, and I found that I loved doing the conference calls. I couldn't believe that in the same time I spent training one school, I was now training schools in many states and two countries. I received e-mails from different teachers each week expressing how grateful they were to have this communication with me.

One teacher wrote: "It's the calls that keep me going, keep me focused, keep me inspired. I'd give up if I didn't have the calls to keep reminding me why it's worth it to work so hard. But the truth is, deep down inside, I know it's worth it. I'm seeing amazing things happen with the youth who are in my class. But what is even more surprising to me is how these calls are changing *me*, not just affecting my students. I work harder. I read more. I write better. I've organized my life and my time so that I can do the things I've always felt called to do."

Things were going well, but I realized the hard work never ends.

Aneladee sat at the table. She was half facing me. She preferred studying at the table. Her books were spread about her, notebooks (both paper and PC) and pens, her big black bag with all her things including her "Deluxe Teacher's Notebook" she was so proud of after working on it for so long.

Unlike Aneladee, I preferred studying on something soft. I lay on my belly with my legs bent at the knee. I was on the couch. My books were on the floor, on the back of the couch, and my notebook was in front of me.

We were getting tired. We'd been going at this, planning, organizing, brainstorming, writing, and re-writing the First Level Training for our teachers for six hours now—and we still had hours to go! The topic was getting pretty heated, though. Aneladee always made me work. Why couldn't we just talk and not have to get so impassioned?

"Why? Why, Tiffany? Why don't you want to teach the teachers the '5 paragraph essay form'? Why?" She pushed.

"Because, Aneladee, it's baloney; that's why. It's a bunch of non-sense!" *How could I make her understand?*

"I will not teach the '5 paragraph essay' to my teachers, or to my students. It's detrimental."

"How so?"

"It forces them to think in a box! Did you know that I was the perfect '5 paragraph essay' writer in high school? I could pump those babies out every time. But did I ever write the best papers? Was I a good writer? *NO.* Why? Because I believed my teachers and I stayed in the box. The box called '5 paragraph essays: Thesis, three supporting ideas, conclusion'! Stink!"

I continued: "That's not necessarily good writing! That's not thinking! That's parroting. Only the students who didn't follow that form wrote well. They could think outside the box. I couldn't!

"Good writing is grabbing your readers' attention, holding their attention while you carry them through your thoughts and then slam dunking your point! Or whispering, if necessary; but either way: *convincing* them! Or at least getting the reader to consider and to think—and even disagree! *That's* good writing. I want to tell the students about what C.S. Lewis uses to prove a point: historical evidence, personal experience, reasoning, and revelation.

"No boxes, Aneladee. No five-paragraph essay forms, unless you are going to give them at least ten other forms to choose from so that they are really confused and finally toss it up in the air and think for themselves. I've rarely read a great piece of writing that actually followed that form. Many classic persuasive essays don't even get to their thesis until the last paragraph; did you know that?

"I want these kids to write! I want to know if they can think. I want to feel their passion! See their reasoning! Question their premises! Not check to see if they followed a rote form."

Aneladee was smiling. She did it. She got me to convince her. I was standing now—pacing the room and had even thumped my hand on the table when I said, "rote form!"

A few minutes later I was sitting on the couch and Aneladee turned in her chair, "Tiffany, will you please stop humming? You're killing me."

"Sure; but why am I killing you?"

"Have you ever heard of 'relative pitch'?"

"Are you saying I'm off pitch? If I'm off pitch then sing with me. I may not know the next note if I'm singing by myself, but I can match your pitch if you sing with me." I knew I didn't have good relative pitch. My dad had told me so before—but it never stopped me from singing. How could it? I grew up in a family of singers!

She laughed and consented to sing with me. We were singing one of my favorite songs, and I didn't realize until later that it was giving me courage to keep going. Life can make it very hard to keep planning, keep brainstorming, keep fighting, keep teaching, keep working. I was in "The Hard Work Phase" and knew it.

Aneladee's voice was beautiful. The music filled all the space in the room—the corners, under the table, the cushions on the couch, the inside of the pictures. And I was singing with her!

It is about community. I know that Jefferson and Hamilton fiercely debated whether America should follow an ownership form or an employee form (agrarian versus mercantile), and that each would impact America's ability to stay free. The places in America where there is a true sense of community are becoming few and far between. Living among friends and neighbors who have a shared vision of the future, who have a shared story of their past, and who have shared values and goals, is becoming more and more rare. Knowing that your neighbor is watching your back as well as his own is almost unknown in many places.

The amazing thing is that those who are really learning Leadership Education and those who build Commonwealth Schools are getting something beyond a great education. They are forming communities. They are actually going through a "founding" era that requires tremendous personal sacrifice, a lot of personal growth, and they are learning how to *work together* toward a shared vision. They are gaining a shared story because of the *founding* work it requires to truly educate the next generation for leadership.

I read the biography of a woman who lived through the Cultural Revolution of China, *Red Scarf Girl*. Mao controlled the media and he controlled the education. Ji-Li Jiang said, "We were all brainwashed. To us, Chairman Mao was God. He controlled everything we read, everything we heard, and everything we learned in school. We believed everything he said. Naturally, we knew only good things about Chairman Mao and the Cultural Revolution. Anything bad had to be the fault of others. Mao was blameless."

It was the same with Hitler. He controlled everything the Germans read, everything they heard, and what they learned in school. And every place he conquered followed suit.

Perhaps less dramatic were the losses to freedom in many other nations of history. They occur among us whenever people get their information from just one autocratic source, or a few controlled sources. The near monopoly on education in our day has created an environment where less independent thinking takes place in the American citizenry than once occurred. Even as freedom is winning out over discrimination on the basis of race, gender, social class, maybe against disability, and possibly someday over educational status and religious conflict, people are thinking less—content to believe in and follow the norm in almost everything. Of course there are also exceptions to this rule, thank goodness.

Freedom can only survive and flourish where there is truly independent thought and action. That occurs less and less the more government is the provider of jobs, security, education, organizations and community programs that used to be voluntarily run by private citizens.

Aneladee and I set out to help educate the youth, to help them see their inner greatness and potential and ability to live great lives of service and benefit to the world. The longer we worked, the more clear it became how desperately the youth and their parents, and all of us, need to belong to strong, caring communities that instill the values of freedom, wisdom, service and enterprise in action and daily example as well as in books. But who would build such communities? And when?

Freedom

by Tiffany Earl

I had to be picky about which books to take on my trip to Hungary. I'd be lugging them around in my backpack along with all my clothes and other packed necessities for nine days.

I made a mental note of the rules for myself: I really wanted this experience to be what I called a "Louis L'Amour education." I wanted to learn not only from books, but also from the local people and surrounding lands. All three had a story to tell.

I remembered devouring Louis L'Amour's memoir called *Education of a Wandering Man*. The study of education as a by-product of studying great men and women throughout history had always been a focus of mine, and when I came across L'Amour's own biography on his education, I was blown away. I wanted to be able to reason like he did, command an audience like he could, understand human nature to the extent he owned it, and to think as broadly and yet minutely. Thus, I was exceedingly interested in his educational formula.

Most of it I recognized right away because of the recurring themes of other Greats and their education: Reading the classics of all times and discussing them was one part of the formula. He wrote, "My education in domestic and foreign affairs began at home . . ." He then mentions how his family was "constantly discussing and arguing about school work, reciting poetry, and talking of books [they] were reading.

"How many books we had in our home I do not remember, and doubt if anyone ever counted. We had collections of Longfellow, Whittier, Lowell, and Emerson, as well as the Stoddard lectures on travel. Reading was as natural to us as breathing." And also: "When I was in the fifth grade my father told me he would give me a three-volume *History of the World* if I would read it."

L'Amour's opinion of getting an education in the way he chose always made me chuckle, only because I agreed with him, and only because I hungered for knowledge as much as he did: "Often I am asked if I would recommend my way of learning to others. I certainly would not. A young man once asked me that question and I told him that the first time he read fifty nonfiction books for fun, in one year, he could think about it. I studied purely for the love of learning, wanting to know and understand."

I understood this part of his formula well: reading from the best places possible, the classics and histories, and then discussing and writing about the ideas, debating and thinking, pondering, learning, changing.

The part I wasn't so good at, but which was equally important in L'Amour's education, was another way in which he took in learning: through real life association with people, places, and countries. Because of my impatience with petty gossip about what the neighbor next door did last week, or the latest pop-culture movie, or some trite matter that doesn't even hint at ideas, I often tired at the table of human discussion (unless in an academic or "ideas" setting) and retired to a lone place with my book.

Somehow L'Amour found the table full of interesting "foods" and appetizing "drinks." He learned as much from the friends he made as he did from sitting down to dine with a stranger. He had an incredible aptitude for "living" as well as for "listening." I desired to learn this art.

After reading L'Amour's book I had a burning desire to get a traveler's education. I wanted experience, and I wanted to learn from people, from associating with them, from listening to their stories, and from touching the dirt of their homelands and feeling it fall between my fingers. I wanted more than just black on white. I wanted color! And Hungary was my first big chance. Thus, the rules for myself:

1) I would only bring three books on the trip

2) I wouldn't allow myself to read if there was someone nearby who was willing to talk

3) Don't complain. (This rule came because my husband gently told me I was a good complainer when it came to taking trips).

My burning secret desire and prayer was that I would meet someone who'd been in Budapest during the famous 1957 Freedom Revolution. I wondered: *What was it like to be part of such a brave movement? What did it feel like to win back freedom? What did you do when Russia sent tanks in 7 days later? Why were you defeated the second time? What did you do personally? How did you feel? Did you believe in God? Where did you turn for comfort? How did you find happiness? What was it like living under communism? What do you see for your country now and in the future?*

I had all these burning questions I needed answered. I secretly hoped I would find someone in Hungary willing to talk to me.

The first three days I stayed with an elderly single woman named Ildiko (the same name as Attila the Hun's Hungarian bride). I knew she was alive during the war and the years of communism but we had a language barrier. For some reason I hadn't counted on the language being a problem, but it was.

It was true, many knew some English; but it was the rising generation that knew English, not the generation I was hoping would enlighten me.

About the most Ildiko and I could communicate was when she had me believing she had just fed me dog.

I sat in her 4' x 9' kitchen, overlooking the piazza of Debrecen from the ninth floor of the housing condos left by Stalin. He'd built huge housing units for his workers to move to after being forced off their private farms and into the factories.

When we rode in the antiquated elevators to reach the top floor, the elevator paused and sputtered, only to resume after Ildiko stomped her foot. I held back a chuckle as I thought of Julie Andrews dancing with Mary Tyler Moore in *Thoroughly Modern Milly*, and I had to restrain myself from dancing a little tap next to Ildiko and bursting into song.

Sitting to breakfast I had quite a spread before me: a fruit basket with oranges, bananas, and apples, four different kinds of breads, from banana-shaped loaves to big bread bowls to home-made wheat bread made from her modern bread maker. There were plastic bags of milk, both chocolate and plain. There were several cheeses and an array of yogurts. There was also a long sausage.

For the first two mornings Ildiko left my son and me alone at breakfast, as is their custom. On the third morning she joined me. I delicately cut the sausage and placed pieces on my bread that I'd spread with peppered cream cheese.

The night before, my family had dined at Itsinaney's house and I remembered the hand motions she had made when my sister translated her story about how she made the sausage.

I made the same hand motions to Ildiko by taking my right hand and pretending to hold a handle. I rotated my arm around in circles, "Did you make this?" I asked as I made the "make" motion, pointing to the sausage. "Nem, nem." She said. And somehow I understood her to say that her parents used to make it—but in the story of the making she took the sausage and said, "Woof! Woof!" while she did the grinding motion.

When she said, "Woof! Woof!" I stopped chewing.

I'm sure my eyes went huge as I calmly told myself: *It's okay. It's okay. Dog. Dog. Dog. I'm eating and have been eating dog for three days!* I gulped my bite down as I calmed myself by thinking: *Lewis and Clark ate dog and they didn't die.*

Ildiko must have seen the look on my face, because she got a paper and pencil and drew something on it. She came over and, pointing at a fat pig, said, *"Woof! Woof!"*

The Student Whisperer

I took a huge sigh of relief and pointing back I said, "Oink! Oink!"

I then drew a dog and, pointing, I said, "Woof-Woof!" Her eyes got huge, recognition hit, and she laughed and laughed.

Thus, I knew I had little chance of obtaining my secret wish—to have a conversation with someone about what it was like to live in Communist Hungary. I didn't speak Magyar, and so far, the older generation I was coming in contact with didn't speak much English!

So when the chance came to talk to a Hungarian, I wasn't looking for it. And I almost missed it.

I lugged my fifty-pound backpack into the storage container of the bus, along with my son's twenty-five pound pack. I could only imagine how my son's shoulders were feeling, so I kept taking things out of his and putting them in mine. It was really nice on the sixth day of the trip when one of my brothers-in-law saw me nursing my shoulder—I had promised myself I wouldn't complain out loud on the trip about anything, and I kept my promise—and he showed me how to buckle and tighten the bottom part of the backpack so it took the weight off my shoulders. It wasn't so hard after that.

We climbed aboard the crowded bus in Budapest as we were headed toward Pecs. We'd been traveling on a train all morning since leaving my favorite Hungarian town of Eger and I was in a book-reading mood, so I wasn't sad when the bus was so crowded that I couldn't sit by my family. We had to spread out to wherever there was an empty seat.

Oh good, I thought. *I can read some more in Louis L'Amour!* I picked a seat near the front next to a woman who seemed somewhere around 60 or 65 years of age. The bus lurched forward and we were on our way to Duna and then Pecs. To my surprise the woman to my left spoke to me. "Is that your son?" she said while pointing to Jacob who was across the aisle from me.

"Yes, he's my son."

"He seems happy."

"Oh, he is. He's loving all these train and bus and *villamos* and metro and plane rides. Plus, he got to see a castle yesterday in Eger. He's really happy."

It was so obvious we were Americans that there was no use bringing that up. We simply didn't dress the same as the Europeans, from our tennis-shoes-instead-of-heels clear up to our backpacks.

I took a deep breath and went to dig through my lap bag for my book when she spoke again.

"I'm on my way to Duna to see the dentist."

"We are on our way to Pecs."

It was silent again and I went to reach for my book.

She spoke again, "Have you been to the baths?"

"The ones in Budapest? No. But yesterday we went to one in Eger. It was awesome. Do you go to the baths often?" Hungary is famous for the spas that have natural hot springs and healing waters.

"Yes, we live here for two months out of every year. My husband has arthritis and they can't do much for him in Canada or the States and so we come here."

"You mean that the medical care is better in Hungary than in the U.S.?" If this were true, I would really be surprised.

"Not on all accounts, but for arthritis we haven't found anything better."

"Wow."

I took a deep breath and reluctantly put my lap bag on the floor, realizing I wasn't going to get my chance to read. *Oh well, I'll visit then.*

I asked her how she could live in two places each year, Canada and Hungary, and she said that she and her husband were retired.

"My husband is an architect and I am an electrical engineer."

"You're kidding me! Where did you go to school?" When I asked that, we had already been driving for thirty minutes and had only one hour left of our bus drive.

"I went in Budapest and had just graduated when I was 21."

My brain did a little math and all of a sudden it hit me. "What year was that?" I asked, holding my breath.

"1957."

I turned to her wide-eyed and looked intently in her eyes, "You . . . were . . . *there?*"

It was quiet for a moment and then she said, "We didn't mean to start a revolution."

Omigosh. She was there. She was there. I can't believe I was going to read my book.

"What do you mean you didn't *mean* to?" I'd read the history books. I'd read several before coming, and as far as I could tell, the students had gotten fed up with their situation. They were war-torn from Hitler concentrating and exterminating the Jews. They went from one barbarian to another. Stalin came in on Hitler's heels only to tear families apart, steal lands, force labor, and murder all who opposed. The students at the university got together, listed several rights they felt were inalienable, and headed over to the radio station to have them read over the loud speakers. Before they knew it they were in a revolution, won, tasted freedom for seven days—and then got crushed into submission when no help came from surrounding countries or America.

"When the students started talking together about the fourteen rights we wanted, we thought that the only way to get the attention of the AVOs (the hired mercenaries who were trained in torture, abusive in their powers, and reigned with terror) would be to broadcast it on the radio, which was just across the street from their offices. So we were walking over to the radio station, when all of a sudden we were joined by hundreds and hundreds of the workers from the surrounding buildings.

"The AVO wouldn't even listen to us at the radio station. They refused to read our request over the radio. We said we wouldn't leave unless they did. Then the shot went off and things went crazy."

I knew what "the shot" was. A woman and her baby were in the crowd. One of the AVOs had fired his gun, and her baby lay dead in her arms.

"We grabbed whatever we could—sticks, bricks, books. Some made explosives. It happened so fast. We really didn't mean to start a revolution."

I was riveted to my seat, listening.

"When we realized we'd won we got together and the next day we started cleaning up the streets. They were a mess. Several bricks from our beloved buildings were scattered here and there. We organized ourselves and started cleaning."

"What was it like to feel free?"

"We couldn't believe it. We just kept thinking about rebuilding Budapest."

"What did you do when Russia sent the tanks in just a week later?"

Her eyes got glossy and I had to strain to listen. Elizabeth was her name. She had soft, soft blond hair. Her eyes were light green, and her voice was soft and airy. Now she was talking even quieter.

"They killed anyone and everyone who stood in their way. They simply massacred them, especially any students they could catch."

"How did you hide?" I asked incredulously.

"We didn't just hide. We fled. My husband had six co-workers. The eight of us decided to try and reach Austria. We could tell no one, not even my family. We had one loaf of bread and one circle of cheese. We hid in the day behind trees and walked at night. It took us eight days to reach the border. Two hundred thousand Hungarians got away before Russia closed the borders."

I sat there in disbelief. It had always only been words, black on white. It felt the same as the day before when I walked into my first European Cathedral.

The Student Whisperer

I had taken my son's hand in mine. I was telling him to make sure to only whisper when we stepped out of the broad daylight and into the Cathedral at Eger, when my breath was literally taken away. *Oh my. This is unbelievable. This is nothing like the pictures in the textbooks. The pictures don't hold a candle to this. This must be like what Plato was referring to. You have to be here to understand.* I looked at the mural on the walls, the sepulchers with Saints, the elaborate benches and antiques. All of it so real, so much depth, so different.

I felt the same as I listened to Elizabeth.

"What did you do when you reached Austria?" I whispered.

"I sent a note with all the money I had to my parents with someone who was going back in. I told them I was safe and not to worry about me."

It was silent for a moment. There was that familiar feeling deep inside of me: The hatred for things evil and the love for things good. I abhorred Stalin and the freedom he stole, the terror he reigned with, and the lives he ruined. I loved Washington, Jefferson, Adams, and Lincoln for the liberty they secured, the love with which they ruled, and the lives they blessed.

This is so much bigger than me, I thought. I felt so small compared to it all. *How could I ever think I could make a difference? This is huge. I'm only one person. How can someone like me affect the liberty and freedom of the world?*

I took a breath and just sat there. I'd always had such high hopes, and now none of it was making sense. The battle, the war, the many battles, and bigger war. I'd been so mad two months ago when I'd checked out twenty books about Hungary and read through its history . . .

"Angie, I hate Hungary. I don't even want to go there anymore. Their people are stupid! Did you know that they . . ." and then I started listing all the unwise things the peasants had done and how the kings and nobles had reigned unjustly, and on and on I went until my sister stopped me.

"Tiffany, what books are you reading? Are you reading textbooks?"

"Well, yes. That's what was available in my library."

"Well that's why you are getting a distorted view. I'm studying the same history and I love the Hungarian people. They are so beautiful, so alive, so whole and so real. They love the land; they love their children; they love their history. I just read about their poet Petofi. Oh, Tiffany you should hear his poems! I read about their beloved King Stephen. I'm reading an incredible book right now about the Hungarian revolution. It is just awful, but it teaches about their good-ness and sincerity. You've got to read it. Take back all the textbooks and get *The Bridge at Andau . . .*"

She listed several other good biographies and histories. We hung up the phone and I did what she suggested. Now my burning question was, "How could someone like Stalin take over an entire country? Why couldn't they stop him, and could it happen again, and what could we do about it? What could we learn from it? How could we secure our liberty against it?"

I sat there on the bus feeling small. I was one sand crystal on the beach of millions of crystals. Stalin's reach was like the waves crash-ing down. Why couldn't they stop Stalin? What did he do that made him invincible? *Why couldn't they stop him?*

"What Stalin did wasn't communism," Elizabeth said.

"What?" I said as she brought me back to reality.

"What we lived really wasn't communism. Communism is good and what we lived wasn't good." I couldn't believe I was hearing this. *How could she think communism was good after what she'd been through? Couldn't she see that it just didn't work? Couldn't she see that Engels and Marx were wrong?*

"Elizabeth," I said, "I guess I don't know what you mean by commu-nism. I don't believe that what Marx and Engels and later Lenin wrote was good. Yes, they wanted to help the poor against the crushing power of the aristocrats, and *that's* good; but the way they said to do it was all wrong. Their communism didn't work because it was *forced* on you. Community caring, loving and helping each other are good—but that's not the communism they taught. They promoted force, and Stalin just followed their plan. Force doesn't work. *Force is a lie.* For that reason alone, communism the way Marx proffers it will never work." She nodded, so I went on.

"Another reason it didn't work is because of human nature. It's human nature that when men get power they abuse it. That means that a truly communistic and 'equal things' state can't ever work because someone has to be in power and only a God, or men like angels, can stay good and be in total power without un-equalizing the 'things'.

"Communism won't ever be good because it is synonymous with force and terror. It won't ever work the way Marx wanted. Communism is based on lies. And lies don't work."

She was listening and still nodding, but I stopped.

"I'm doing the arrogant American thing, aren't I?" I asked.

She laughed and patted my hand. "Actually," she said, "I didn't know people your age even cared about these things. I'm surprised at your passion."

A little embarrassed, but encouraged, I said, "It's just that you said communism is good. I don't believe it can ever be good. I know that the alternative seems to be a free-for-all of capitalism where nobody cares about anybody or anything except the next dollar, but I don't believe in that either. I believe that we can build a world with *real* freedom, where people use their freedom voluntarily to help and serve each other because they *want* to. I know that sounds idealistic—maybe crazy—but I don't believe we should ever give up on the ideal. Utopia may not be possible, but kindness and friendship and real communities *are*. Governments have to protect freedoms, and people have to behave like friends and, well, like *humans*. We know how we are supposed to be. We even have words for it—like *humane*, or our *humanity* showing through."

We talked for the rest of the trip, clarifying when we disagreed but finding that we agreed on almost everything. We especially agreed on the truly important things, like hoping that what happened in the Soviet crushing of Budapest would never happen again anywhere. Ironically, we both knew it was happening in more than one place as we talked. Still, both of us agreed that no matter how dark the world seemed, better things were always possible and that each of us should do our best to build a better future.

I listened, I talked, we smiled. I made a friend. She taught me to always keep my head up—brighter days can and will come.

As we left the bus, Elizabeth said, "Tiffany, I think you are really going to gain something lasting from your visit to the Museum of Terror."

I left the bus with such strong feelings. Something about the long conversation with Elizabeth seemed to have changed me. I thought, *I'm only one, but I am engaged for the long haul. I don't care if I'm small. I won't shrink. I'll be like Paul and say, "I fought the good fight; I finished the race." I'll be like Jane Eyre when she ran into the storm and fell and got back up, but kept running. I'll be like Washington and stay atop my horse even as my men around me are falling and I'll cry within myself and pray, 'My God, I'm losing such good men'—but I'll keep fighting.*

That was before the Museum of Terror.

I was bundled tightly in my down coat. It was cold—cold enough to wear a hat and gloves, which I snuggled inside. There were thirteen of us: my mom talking to my sister Angie, my sister Katie talking to my sister Sarah, another sister Kami leaning on her husband Mark while she looked up at the tall buildings of Budapest, my brothers visiting together in a huddle, and my son Jacob running circles around his 6'7" uncle. My dad, as always, brought up the rear, making sure we stayed together and that all our needs were met. The thirteen of us stood in line outside the Museum of Terror.

That was its actual name: "The Museum of Terror." Already it reminded me of the haunted house I'd visited as a youth. As we made our way up the front steps I felt eerie as I listened to the organ music. *This is a haunted house,* I thought. There were statues that were half blown off, there were pictures of men hanging on a noose, there were molds of scenes of death and blood. *I want out of here*, I couldn't help thinking.

The Museum of Terror is the actual building where Stalin made his headquarters. I was about to walk through the rooms where Stalin's leaders made history.

I paid the fee for my son and myself and we got aboard the elevators. I put the red headphones over my ears, adjusted the sound, and snapped the box to my belt. All of a sudden the broadcast was in English instead of Magyar.

A man's voice trailed into my ears, "They herded us like pigs aboard the trains. We were shoved so tightly we couldn't sit down. We had no idea where they were taking us, and of course you know we ended up in Siberia."

What? I thought. *I didn't know Stalin shipped the men to Siberia!* I had a lot to learn. Up to this point I knew about Hitler and the concentration camps he ran, the death toll he piled up, and the mass extermination he employed. I hadn't grasped that Hitler didn't hold a candle to Stalin.

I choked back my horror as the voice continued, "We were deprived of all our rights. We were practically deprived of even our bodily needs."

Jacob and I stepped off the elevator and onto the third floor. I held his hand tightly in mine. The voice in my ears changed as we entered a new room. It now explained what the wallpaper on the walls represented. Each face—and there were hundreds and thousands of them, I think—was a person who was held in this building against his will. Many of them were exterminated, and many others were tortured. Some survived only to have a broken spirit and to wish for death.

The smell in the building was rank and old. It was unpleasant to breathe. In the middle of the building, to be looked upon from all levels, was a huge tank, immortalized. I soon came to hate its symbol. I'd never seen a WWII army tank up close. They were a lot bigger than I'd imagined.

The voice changed from the history of the wallpaper and tank to individual stories as I entered the next room. "We were forced off our farm and my husband was taken from us. I had to go to work in the factories. I lived in fear every morning, day, and night. You never knew if there would be another raid. I didn't want my son taken from me."

"We hid a pencil and paper in the floorboards of the room. We were afraid to be caught with them."

"There wasn't enough food. My children were so hungry that I often went two or three meals with only a corner of bread to suck on. I felt the life drain out of me."

"I didn't dare look the AVO in the eyes. That was reason enough for them to beat you, or take you away. In fact, I stopped looking people in the eyes almost altogether. Whom could you trust?" On and on the stories went. We moved on.

The next room was bright and cheerful, a circle of a room with wallpaper that reached the pinnacle at the ceiling. Once I realized the meaning of this room I was angry. On the walls were vividly bright pictures: a smiling mother holding a huge loaf of bread handing it to her child, a farmer loading huge piles of potatoes into carts, children playing on the playgrounds with warm coats and bright gloves and boots. On and on the walls lied to me. Newspaper clippings showing an abundance of food, magazines showing happy families, billboards showing communal living. I was sick inside. *Oh! The way the communist regime deceived them!* I couldn't believe the stark difference between this lying, stinking propaganda and the testimonies I had just heard in the room prior.

I forced myself to go on. I still didn't know how he did it. Why didn't anybody stop him? What strategy and technique did Stalin use to immobilize the people into such fear? I knew I'd seen two things already: force—the tank and other implements of force; and the lies, brainwashing and false advertising. But I knew there must be more.

I came into a room with benches lining both sides. We obediently took a seat and the voice in my ear began at the same time a movie screen came down in front of us and a video began. We were in a courtroom. Around us were hundreds and hundreds of files, real files, the *real files*, of the illegal trials we were watching.

The Student Whisperer

Omigosh, I thought. **That's** *how he did it. He gathered up all the leaders! The businessmen, the church leaders who couldn't be bought, the civic leaders, the community leaders, the education leaders—and he held illegal trials for them and shipped them off to Siberia, or tortured them, or massacred them!*

I sat there watching illegal trial after illegal trial. The men were lined up on the benches. They looked tired, dejected, worried. One by one they came up to the stand, the accusations were read, false testimonies given, and they were whisked away while the next man went up to the stand.

This is sick, I thought. *Just sick! I have to know and understand this better. I have to know how to fight against such injustice!*

We went through several other rooms and finally downstairs to the isolated prison rooms and torture chambers. *This can't be for real. People don't really hurt other people like this. That's only in the movies, like "The Princess Bride." Only barbaric nations tortured. I mean, didn't they stop torturing long ago? Could this really have happened less than fifty years ago? Could it be happening now?*

*I know it's in the news about the United States, but...*I swallowed hard. *We do it too. Maybe not the same, but we do it too.* I couldn't hold back the tears. It made me wonder how little I knew. I was acutely aware of this question since there were wars being fought this very moment about terrorism. And here terrorism was staring me in the face.

I looked at the two-foot-by-one-foot tiny room where men were forced to stand for days and days. The voice in my ears explained that iron "hot plates" were put on both sides of the wall so that if the victim fell asleep or leaned over he would be seared.

I saw the implements of torture: from whips to needles, to hot red pokers, to clubs and many other unidentifiable objects. They were hanging on the wall next to the antique mahogany desk of the AVO. The men were mostly beaten and then made to stand on their toes with nails under their feet if they came down and then beaten mercilessly if they fell to their knees.

What was the torture for? To make the men admit they didn't support communism? To make them tell where secret meetings were, or identify ringleaders of anti-communist movements? To force them to tell if they had weapons in the house with which they might have defended themselves? Or was it just to terrorize the country into submission?

On and on the inhumanity went. Finally we came to the last room. The video showed the ingenuity of one of the AVOs. He figured out how to kill more prisoners in less time. They had several nooses hung on vertical beams. The prisoners, dressed in light blue pajama-like clothes, would step up onto a removable stool, men standing behind the beams would put the noose and sack over the man's head and then hold tightly to the rope. When the gong sounded, other men at the front of the beam would kick the stool away. After the count of one minute the hanging was done, and a new group of victims would then be marched to the gallows.

I was sick of this place. It was depressing and all wrong. We came away and nobody spoke for a long time. Yet I knew something: I knew I would fight evil with every bit of life inside of me. I knew that one way or another I would do all I could to do good, to feed the hungry, to clothe the naked, to liberate the captive, and to administer relief to the sick and the afflicted. I knew I wasn't evil like Stalin; and I knew that wasn't enough. Not being evil wasn't enough. I knew I had to keep working, building, *living* for good.

Now I knew what my work boiled down to. It came to work—a whole lot of hard work. If there was one soul to save, one family to lift, one child to teach, one country to educate, one life to bring from ignorance to truth, there was work to be done. Like my dad kept repeating as we walked away from the terror, "Now I know that if the only weapon I had was my fingernails, I wouldn't quit fighting—not to end up like them." He was right. This was real, and no one wants to end up like them. *I have more tools to fight with than fingernails,* I thought, *and I'm not giving up either.* I wept. I sobbed. Then I stewed.

I stewed on the walk back to our boatel room on the Danube. I stewed my whole time in Europe. I stewed when we flew the seventeen hours home. I stewed on the seven-hour drive from the Phoenix

The Student Whisperer

airport back to our home. I stewed until I made up my mind to talk to Oliver. The next day, I got my wish.

"Oliver, what's your plan?"

"What are you asking, Tiffany?" We were used to each other by now.

"I'm asking what your strategy is, Oliver. I'm asking on a whole new level, *Why statesmen? Why social leaders? How do we get enough leaders? How can freedom last?* I know what you are fighting for. I know your heart and your love for freedom. And I understand on a new personal level *WHY!*"

I took a deep breath and intently looked inside Oliver's eyes while *my eyes* communicated what was in my heart. Then it all seemed to come out in a gush: "Oliver, I'm offering my help. I've got to help freedom. I've got to. And education is the answer. It makes all the difference. With widespread leadership education, the Stalins of the world just can't succeed. I can't do it alone. I'm just one person. I'm just one little person, in a big world full of those who hate and hurt and attack. But the families of the world, all those good people who just want to be happy . . . I have to do something. I have to—and it has to be effective. It has to actually and really help. It has to work!"

I was so intent on my expressing my feelings that I didn't notice Oliver. When I looked up he was just looking at me, and there were tears streaming all down his face and neck.

I was so surprised I just stopped talking. This was new.

After a long time he composed himself. He looked at me, and his lip trembled again. "Tiffany," he said, "I know what you are doing, and I think I understand a part of why you are doing it. Freedom must win, more people must take action, and it must *work*." He paused. He had turned my own questions back on me before, but this time was different.

"What are *you* going to do?" he asked. "That's the question now. It's not just about teachers, mentors, students. It goes far beyond education. It's about people, all people, people who make freedom work. You are one of those people. What are *you* going to do?" Then he stopped talking.

We sat in silence for a long time.

Eventually, quietly, he stood up, put the book on his lap into his valise, and walked to the door. He stopped, but didn't turn back. "It was an honor to mentor you," he said. "Thank you. You'll succeed." Then he left.

I cried for a long time. I felt like a whole part of my life was over and another was beginning. Somewhere during this time I glanced at the mirror next to the piano. The mirror was oval, the kind with a golden, ornate frame. But the thing that surprised me was my face. I expected to see the tear-stained mascara cheeks and the redder-than-usual nose, but the surprising thing was the big smile looking back at me.

The tears and my smile just didn't seem to go together.

"What are you smiling about?" I asked aloud.

I looked deeply into the eyes peering back at me, like I was trying to figure out Mona Lisa's secret. They were the same eyes as that little girl listening to my daddy's stories of Peter Rabbit and my pinky finger, the same eager eyes from high school and college study sessions, the same eyes that overcame business challenges and kept things growing, the same eyes that had been welcoming Rick and the kids home every day for years. But something had changed—slowly, surely, for good.

"You are ready," I heard my voice say.

I looked again into those reflected eyes.

"Yes, I am."

The Student Whisperer

BOOK TWO

"There are voices which we hear in solitude, but they grow faint and inaudible as we enter into the world."

—EMERSON

Student Whispering

by Oliver DeMille

Every person has inner genius, and quality education consists of helping each student discover, develop and polish her genius. This is the essence and very definition of great education. The highest level of teaching and mentoring is Student Whispering.

Student Whisperers are geniuses in this process. To some this genius comes naturally; it can also be learned. Student Whisperers are needed at all levels—from the education of children and youth, on up through college, professional and life learning.

How does one learn to be a Student Whisperer? The answer is both simple and profound. There are really only three kinds of education, and they are best understood from the student's perspective. Students get a good education for one of three reasons:

- They are forced to study long, hard and effectively (the "Stick")
- They are convinced, bribed or manipulated to study long, hard and effectively (the "Carrot")
- They love to study long, hard and effectively (the "Love Affair")

If the first two are *good*, the latter is truly *great*.

The Stick, the Carrot, or the Love Affair: These are the three types of education, and the Love Affair is by far the most effective.

The Heart of the Matter

All great learning is the result of the right kind of study. Even students with great talent fall short if they don't apply themselves. Those who know how to truly inspire such commitment and effort are Student Whisperers.

Unfortunately, most of what currently passes for education is based on either force or manipulation. This is a modern tragedy—one that deprives individuals of true fulfillment and societies of many of their brightest lights as people fail to develop and apply their true, innate genius. Imagine the opportunity cost when the creativity, innovation, passion and contribution of just one generation of the world's geniuses is snuffed out before they come of age—to say nothing of the assault on human happiness.

Imagine the impact on our world if Columbus had chosen to be "normal," if Joan of Arc had stayed on the farm, if Gautama had stayed in the palace like his teachers told him, or if Einstein had settled on being an accountant. It is, of course, *wonderful* to be a farmer or an accountant—if that is where your passion, purpose and genius lie. Indeed, many change the world from the "lowliest" of stations. In the case of Einstein, it would have been a tragedy—both for him personally, and for all of us.

Sticks, Carrots and Love Affairs

The Carrot and the Stick are, quite simply, *mediocre* forms of education. Only a true love affair with learning—and by this I do not mean a mere infatuation that is easily distracted, but a lifelong passion that endures the challenges and grows with time—empowers students to discover their great inner genius, to effectively develop it and to greatly refine it to become their best and to deeply benefit society. The old saying assures us that when the world needs something great, God sends a baby to grow up, learn and improve the world. I wonder how many such babies have been born, started to grow up, and then been forced or convinced to follow a different path than the greatness they were born to achieve.

How many have been persuaded that they needed to make it their life's purpose to find a job, follow a career, be normal, fit in, or seek security, prestige, power or possessions? What great blessings has the world missed out on because of these choices?

Actually, the answer is quite simple: How many have felt unfulfilled in their lives, their careers and their choices? How many have struggled to go to work each day, wishing for a different life? How many have rebelled at mid-life when the pain of not being their real selves and living their real lives finally became too much? Gallup reports that about 80% of people aren't happy with their work and life path, as discussed at some length by Marcus Buckingham.[22]

In other words, about 20% of us feel we are living life to its fullest, following what we love, content and passionate about our lives. It's worth considering that perhaps many of those who don't feel fulfilled or thrilled about their life path might be disengaged from their great purpose. Either they haven't discovered their true genius and purpose, haven't developed it, or aren't refining and applying it to a life mission.

Education has failed such people. Indeed, based on this statistic, around 80% of us are undereducated—or *mis*-educated. The years such people invested in studying and making the grade did not lead them to make the choices or acquire the knowledge, skills, habits and abilities that facilitated their happiness, fulfillment and meaningful contribution. Is such a process, therefore, perhaps mislabeled? Is this really what we want from "education"?

Choices and Consequences

Let's be clear about how this works. To some extent—and in the U.S., it is to a large extent—we all *choose* our education and path in life. Some choose because the punishments and pain of fighting for what they really want against the pressures of force are too much. Others choose because they are convinced that what they really want isn't the wise, accepted, or rewarding way to go, and because the promised rewards of choosing a different path seem preferable. Many people make both of these choices without ever really considering what they want or what they "should" do or be—never really understanding that *there is an alternative.*

To repeat: *True education* is discovering one's genius and purpose, developing it effectively, and refining and applying it to one's life and to benefitting the world. Why would anyone not follow this path? *Because they were forced or convinced to do otherwise.*

Enter the Student Whisperer. One of a Student Whisperer's most important roles is to know that each student has a great inner genius—even when the students themselves aren't aware of this fact.

By contrast, the mass conveyor belt attempts to bring all students to literacy by compelling parents to fit certain norms and children to meet certain standards. Everyone is herded in the same direction, impelled to conform by fear of not measuring up. The impetus is some form of negative consequence (you'll be looked down upon by your peers, you won't advance to the next level, you can't participate in extra-curriculars, you won't graduate, you won't be able to go to college, you won't be able to get a job, etc.).

The "professional" or "competitive" conveyor belt promises special rewards to the few who rise above the masses and follow a different assembly line (still conformist, but based on incentives rather than punishments, e.g.: scholarships, internships, job placement, etc.) to gain higher compensation, status and perks. Too often the result of both conveyor belts is widespread mediocrity and dysfunctional lives, marriages, families and societies. What else should we expect from a model that systematically teaches children, parents and teachers alike that to stray from "the norm" is pathology, and to test on level is the ideal?

Of course, on the bright side, the conveyor-belt models achieve a higher standard of living and more opportunity than the older class system where the masses were forced into child labor and education was withheld. Clearly ours is a great improvement on that historical system, and it is absurd in the present day to suppose that we can abandon public education. Thank goodness some of the best and brightest dedicate themselves to finding ways to improve on what we offer to 85%[23] of our society's children in the public school system.

But we can do better still. Bringing education out of sheer failure for the masses to general mediocrity is a significant accomplishment, and it is only a first step toward the ideal. We should be proud of a system that offers so much more opportunity to all than the educational models of history; and we must not be content with it or settle for it. We must build on what we have and make something much better.

I do not think it is an overstatement to assert that a professional educator of any merit, regardless of the system in which he or she works, believes that the ideal is an educational model that helps each and every youth in our world discover her inner genius, effectively develop it, and polish it to greatness. In our day, because of the gains of dedicated educators in history (and especially modern times), this ideal is within our grasp. Why would we choose anything less?

The great danger, of course, is that by promoting the conveyor belt too strongly we will re-establish the older class system. This would not be hard to accomplish. All it would take would be to systematically train the masses for jobs at the same time that the wealthy educate their children differently by offering them a much higher quality of education.

If the compulsory schools train the youth of the masses in rote thinking, conformity, fitting in, submissive obedience to superiors, memorized "correct" answers, clique socialization and the employee mentality, we are ensuring that most of those trained this way will remain in the under classes. Those who "fail" or just "get by" in this system will be in the lower class, while those who "succeed" will attain the middle class.

The upper class will, in contrast, continue to educate their children in the great lessons of history, the great classics from all fields of human endeavor, and the abilities and skills of creativity, independent and analytical thinking, persuasive communication, artistic and technological innovation, entrepreneurial initiative and ingenuity, and service and leadership, among others.

Through a fixation on conveyor-belt education, the class divide will be perpetuated and continue to grow.

Unless we build on past advances in education and continue to improve the system, a stagnated model will begin to devolve back to stronger class warfare between the "haves" and the "have-nots."

Another challenge is that in trying to improve on the existing system there is a tendency to prefer system-wide fixes. This is a major problem. Any attempt to remake the entire educational system from the top down will fail, because top-down mandates are, by nature, rooted in the class model—relying on dictates and regulations from non-teaching experts, and compliance by the technicians in the field. If *all* schools and teachers adopt truly great education in this fashion they will bring the entropy of bureaucracy, big-ness, systemization, and institutionalism into the fix. In other words, when passion and inspiration are structured, systematized and enforced, they lose their passion and inspirational qualities and become instead forced—or at best, manipulative.

For great education to occur, students must *choose* to study long, hard and effectively because they genuinely love it! It must be their passion and their delight. When students are deeply in love with studying, they learn in "the flow" and they absorb massive amounts of information, knowledge, understanding, connections and wisdom in a very short time.

Teaching Heart, Mind and Soul

Most of us have experienced times when learning just flowed, when it felt so right—and we seemed to be magnets of ideas and questions and knowledge. This is a normal state of learning when one is truly inspired. And it need not be a rare, spontaneous or haphazard occurrence. It can be the regular state of studying, virtually day in and day out.

This does happen regularly when students are actively discovering, developing and polishing their deep areas of genius. When this occurs, they feel passionate, dedicated and excited about studying.

Schools have long tried to duplicate this for every student, but even Anne of Green Gables or John Keating (Robin Williams' role in *Dead Poet's Society*) could only reach some of their students. And as soon as this type of great teaching is institutionally systematized, structured and enforced, it is fundamentally altered and essentially disappears. No

U.S. president can "fix" education, no law can systematize inspiration, and no amount of funding, policy or resources can structure passion.

Let me say again: No president can fix education, no law can systematize inspiration, and no amount of funding, policy or resources can structure passion. Great education defies structure because it is always (always!) individualized, personalized, interactive, nimble, responsive and inspired. The same great mentor will urge Student A to read and Student B to stop reading. The same great mentor will counsel Student A to read today and not to read tomorrow. Any institutionalization of inspiration *loses* its inspiration. Truly great learning is a miracle *every time*.

All the system can really do is set up the environment for predictable and consistent miracles, as Maria Montessori taught.[24] This includes establishing school buildings, providing budgets for schools, outlining general policies that ensure safety, and hiring principals and teachers (or presidents and professors at the college level) with proven passion and ability to inspire. These are the things the system *can* do. Presidents, laws, school boards and policies can do these. Parents can do the same in their homes. But beyond this list, great education can only happen if certain "sparks" fire, and they will only fire predictably and consistently if teachers understand and master their transformational role—and this only if they are left unfettered in order to carry it out. We recognize this phenomenon in coaching sports, theater and debate, for example; but we too seldom apply it to teaching math, science, literature and history, etc.

The irony here is rich. The educational system—from the professorial pools and expert theorists to superintendents and school boards, from principals to teachers to Congress, and from think tanks to educational lobbies—seeks a quantifiable, measurable system, while year after year parents, students, teachers and observers leave frustrated that schools so often fail to deliver that spark, that flow, that light that defies virtually all types of measurement.

We want something we can detect and observe, but can't objectively measure, and we use objective measures that consistently *extinguish the spark*.

Great education is not about institutions or bureaucratic policy. It is about individuals, one by one, becoming who they really are. Always.

As much as we would like a quick, by-the-numbers fix, a system-wide change in education won't solve the problem. Anything systematic changes can do to improve the *environment* is welcome, of course; but they will not fix *education*. This will happen only when Student Whisperers do their work.

Students can be forced in more innovative, progressive and techno-logically-leveraged ways; or they can be convinced/manipulated more deeply and in higher numbers. *This* is what the system can do. And the result will be more mediocrity.

For students to truly thrive, to consistently reach for excellence, something else is needed: *They need to fall passionately in love with studying.* To do this, they must be on the road to discovering, devel-oping and polishing their deep inner genius. This is always individual.

While it is true that The System cannot deliver this (*because it is a system*), there is one thing that can predictably, consistently and effectively deliver large percentages of students passionately studying hard, long and with enthusiasm that lasts.

This one thing is great mentoring. Great mentors understand what the students are seeking, what they deeply and completely want, and how they can get it. Great mentors understand this even when the students don't. Great mentors are Student Whisperers.

This is not haphazard or strictly metaphysical. It is duplicable and learnable—but once a mentor has learned it, once she is a Student Whisperer, the system must get out of her way and let her Whisper.

The system cannot accomplish this. The system can only keep being the system, trying its best to create a suitable and safe environment where students can discover books and rub shoulders with great mentors. The rest must happen naturally. It may arguably be much more likely to happen naturally with the system in place—as long as the system fully allows private and personal alternatives to schooling. The less (social) class-oriented the public schools, the better.

With such a system in place, we are ready to drastically revolutionize education. Not systematically, but personally and profoundly. This all starts with Student Whisperers.

Student Whisperers follow, knowingly or naturally, the Student Whisperer's Creed.

The Student Whisperer's Creed

1. Great mentors believe in freedom—in the world and in one's personal education.

2. Great mentors believe in individualizing the process and content of each student's learning.

3. Great mentors believe that each student has a unique and vital mission in life.

4. Great mentors believe that each student has untapped genius, with the seeds of what is needed for his/her personal mission(s).

5. Great mentors believe that most missions benefit from a superb, broad, deep, leadership education in the classics.

6. Great mentors believe that students learn more and better when they are inspired and intrinsically motivated than when they are compelled by requirements.

7. Great mentors believe that one of the most powerful means of inspiration is example.

8. Great mentors set an example of rigorous, passionate study of the classics.

9. Great mentors exemplify seeking truth and searching out principles in many worldviews, ideas, sources and perspectives, and comparing them with the principles taught in their core book.

10. Great mentors exemplify pushing themselves outside of their own comfort zone and consistently expanding their breadth and depth of knowledge and skills.

11. Great mentors set an example and encourage students to learn from all mentors—authors, teachers, innovators, artists, thinkers, scientists, classmates, spiritual insights, and any other enlightening source.

12. Great mentors foster a culture of friendship and cooperation in and out of the classroom. Mentors genuinely like their students, and they know their students will teach them and friends/classmates much of what is learned.

13. Great mentors use many tools to inspire and create an environment of learning, including group discussion, readings, writing, lecture, simulations, field experience, personal coaching, refinement of talents and skills, visiting speakers, assignments, small group tutorials, projects, etc. They feel successful when students leave their meetings (or classrooms) and passionately study with self-starting enthusiasm and rigorous tenacity.

14. Great mentors seek and revere quality, and therefore do not orient themselves by rote conformity or other arbitrary measures. They know that simple, inspired study is the surest path to excellence in learning.

15. Great mentors acknowledge the working of higher principles and inspiration, and operate in harmony with them in a process that literally changes the world—building leaders for all walks of life who will greatly impact the future of family, prosperity and freedom.

16. To all these, great mentors add their own personal style, gifts, interests, specialties and areas of passion and enthusiasm. They truly pass on a little bit of their best selves to every student they serve.

These are the things that can be codified and followed. Those who follow them become the greatest of mentors: Student Whisperers. The better each Student Whisperer, and the more Student Whisperers in society, the better the educational quality.

The better the quality, the more "sparks" will ignite every day of study. The better the quality, the more students will passionately and consistently study long, hard, and effectively. The better the quality, the more our youth will discover and embrace their life's mission. The better the quality, the more genius will be loosed on our world. The better the quality, the more we will see society fix its problems and overcome its challenges.

It all depends on Student Whispering.

Great education is achieved mostly *by the student.* Students must accomplish most of the deep studying, thinking, pondering, memorizing, debating, practicing and learning. But the *choice* to engage long, hard and effective studying is nearly always sparked by a Student Whisperer. And the choice to *continue,* day after day and year after year, is usually fueled by Student Whisperers.

Without them, few will do the hard and sustained work to develop their genius. This is true in music, the arts, sports, academics and all facets of life. It is true in every area of genius. Genius is developed and polished when Student Whisperers do their job. It seldom flourishes otherwise. When the world changes, it is because great leaders in many facets of life appear on the scene.

Before genius, there is long and passionate preparation. Before preparation there is a spark of inspiration. Before the spark comes a Student Whisperer. The future of education depends not on policy or the system, but on Student Whisperers.

The future of the world depends on genius. The genius is in us, in our children, in our students. It will be discovered, developed and applied in response to the sparks. Even those who live and die by objective measurement of systems understand this. They also know that it cannot be measured until years after the fact, and then only by the results.

The genius is in us. *The genius is in us,* endowed by the divine, waiting for an inspired Student Whisperer to loose it upon the world.

Great Education

Note that the various exercises or workshops in this book are designed to help you become a Student Whisperer. Just reading the text will only get you partially there. I strongly recommend that you get a new, blank composition book, notebook or journal and write "Whisperer Journal" on the cover. Or, you can visit Student-Whisperer.com and download the free Student Whisperer Journal binder insert.

Use it for all the exercises in this book. Each of the remaining chapters will teach concepts and then assign workshops and exercises that turn the ideas into skills and abilities—but only if you do the exercises. Once you have your notebook/journal ready, proceed...

Time to Record: MY WHISPERINGS

*T*hink of the best teacher you ever had. Was it Mrs. Cox in the third grade? Or Mr. Smolen in high school? Was it a coach? Your mom? A church leader? A counselor at camp? Was it a character in a book? Or a certain author? A friend? A great composer, singer or musical group?

~ What teacher most inspired you to greatness in your life? What teacher helped you decide to become your best?

Write down the names that come to mind. Highlight the most significant with asterisks or underlines.

~ Once you have your best teacher in mind, consider this: What made him/her/it the greatest teacher in your life? Was she caring? Was he demanding? Did she see great things in you that you didn't realize you had? Did it move you deeply and passionately and make you want to be great?

Write down the thoughts and experiences, characteristics and events that most inspired and impacted you.

Whatever your answers, they came to your mind because they Whispered to you. They spoke to your inner yearning, your greatest needs, your deepest hopes and desires. They spoke to you. They seemed to understand you. They moved you.

Not every teacher needs to be a Student Whisperer for each and every student; but *each* and *every* student needs at least one Student Whisperer!

Seven Mentors

by Oliver DeMille & Tiffany Earl

The first thing we need to know about The Path is that the key to success is finding and following the right mentors. There are many types of mentors, each with unique functions and purposes. One of our purposes in writing this book is to differentiate and explain these types. This enables a person to know which kind he needs (or is) and thus have more meaningful mentor relationships. Sometimes a person is trying to move forward on The Path and she knows she needs a mentor—but she gets the wrong one. This leads to frustration, stifled progress and disillusionment. That doesn't have to happen.

Before discussing the types of mentors, let us mention two overarching strategies they will use: Mentors are typically either Formal or Informal.

Some of our most important mentors in life never really consider themselves mentors—nor do we typically call them by that name. These include parents, grandparents, brothers, sisters, aunts, uncles, friends, teachers, coaches, colleagues, authors, artists, musicians—the list goes on.

Anyone who has touched our lives, influenced us for good, inspired us to do better, comforted us during times of struggle, or otherwise helped us rise to our potential can be called an informal mentor.

Informal mentors often plant seeds, some of which don't sprout for years or even decades. Informal mentors can shape, mold, refine, inspire, and influence us in profound and lasting ways.

While informal mentoring takes place naturally as we move along through life, formal mentoring is something altogether different. Formal mentors and mentees make an agreement whereby the mentee is held accountable for commitments. Formal mentoring develops the *character* as well as the *competence* of the mentee.

Often the most profound mentors are the ones who actually have an understanding with the mentees that formal mentoring is taking place, that the mentee is responsible to "go and do" and then "return and report."

The agreement (that the mentee will return and report about the assignment or commitment) is what makes formal mentoring *formal*. It is also the hidden impetus and power of the formal mentoring process. With a formal mentor, the mentee has a guide to create an effective plan and is held accountable for keeping to her plan. This leads to tremendous growth, and helps define a course and goals that can sometimes lead far into the future.

Seven Mentors

There are at least seven types of mentors. It is important to know the types because each has specific functions and purposes. Often people mistakenly engage a mentor, knowing that "successful people have mentors," only to find that their time, money or effort is wasted. It is not just *having* a mentor that can make all the difference between success and failure, but having the *right* mentor.

Knowing these seven types and how they can help you along The Path will help you identify and recognize the right mentors in your life. Potential mentors are always near. It is *your* job to recognize them. The seven basic types of mentors are:

1. **Parent Mentors**—Parent Mentors are basically informal mentors. Sometimes parents move into the role of Formal Mentor to an older youth or young adult. In such a case the relationship is

not that of parent/child, but of Mentor/mentee, along the guidelines of a formal mentoring relationship, and with all its characteristics and constraints.

2. **Soul Mentors**—Some people in your life just seem to have a lifelong supernatural link with you. Others intersect with your life for just a brief moment, but leave a lasting impact. When we connect with someone at this deep level, we've found a Soul Mentor. Soul Mentors are also informal; and yet, they are true mentors in every sense of the word because of the huge influence they have in our lives. When challenges come, as they do to everyone in life, we naturally turn to Soul Mentors to lean upon for strength. Soul Mentors have much to teach us. Most of us readily recognize that we have already been taught such valuable and needed lessons. Soul Mentors *listen* to us, *guide* us, and are there for us at our most vulnerable times. For example, Sam in *The Lord of the Rings*[25] was a Soul Mentor to Frodo, being there for him, carrying him, admonishing him, believing in him, and loving him.

3. **Expert Mentors**—Expert Mentors have expertise in a certain field and they help you on the mini-path of success within their arena of special proficiency. Interestingly, these mini-paths follow the same order and format as The Path, so they give us experience and practice for "the big one." For example, you may have had an Expert Mentor when you learned to play the piano or another musical instrument, trained your voice, went on a diet, trained in the martial arts, played on a team or in theater under a coach, learned specific skills for work, or engaged a business mentor to help you invest or learn about real estate.

Expert Mentors can help you in almost any area, from practicing your religion to putting your finances in order. Some Expert Mentors are more formal than others—such as professors, coaches, brokers, attorneys, and supervisors. Others are more fun, such as the uncle who taught you to ride a bike or the grandparent who patiently helped you learn to make a piecrust. In any case, Expert Mentors share with you their field of expertise, and they acclimatize you to the micro-version of The Path by helping you to progress according to (and in spite of) your strengths and weaknesses.

4. **Leadership Mentors**—Leadership Mentors guide you through the liberal arts, inspiring you to get a superb education that prepares you for leadership in your chosen life mission. They help you learn *how to think*. They guide and help you overcome Tests, Trials, and Traps along The Path.

   Another name for this mentor is the Liberal Arts Mentor, or the Forgotten Mentor (since nearly all but the upper classes in our day have forgotten the link between great education in the classics and becoming leaders). The Leadership Mentor inspires you to understand human nature, culture, and the connection between human action and results. She helps you to see your own potential—your true inner genius—and to develop it.

5. **Mission Mentors**—A Mission Mentor has a similar "calling" or life purpose as you, and is therefore uniquely qualified to help you on the specific Path you have chosen. When a Mission Mentor formally accepts you it usually means you are ready for the gifts and challenges he will give to you that help you accomplish your mission. With Mission Mentors you may have the opportunity to become more than a mentee—you may grow into a protégé.

6. **Gurus**—These are spiritual mentors. Often they are found in scripture or through your church or deepest beliefs. For the more secular-minded, gurus are figures of admiration who teach you at your deepest levels. They are usually informal mentors, but at times, and depending upon your Path or beliefs, they can become formal mentors.

7. **Epiphanies**—Certain things in our lives provide special, powerful mentoring that changes us, gives us direction or clear correction, and truly inspires us far beyond the norm. Epiphanies can be people, experiences, events or other life happenings that touch, teach, inspire and greatly help us to grow. These are important and life-changing *mentoring experiences* that we all need.

Time to Record: "MY MENTORS" EXERCISE

*T*o remember the seven types of mentors better, complete the following exercise. To help your memory, we'll list these in a random order. In your Whisperer Journal (and leaving space for additional commentary after each mentor type and mentor name), write the names of the first few people (or experiences, etc.) you think of with each kind of mentor:

~ Mission Mentors
~ Parent Mentors
~ Epiphanies
~ Leadership Mentors
~ Gurus
~ Expert Mentors
~ Soul Mentors

Take a few moments each and list the top epiphanies you can think of that you learned from or with each mentor. You may find that some mentors will be included on more than one list.

*[If you skipped this exercise, we encourage you to go back and do it before proceeding on. Learning **about** Student Whispering is not nearly as powerful as engaging the process of becoming a Student Whisperer.]*

Now, once you have completed this exercise, review the combined list and ask yourself if these truly are the most important people and events of your life. If you missed some, add them to the lists. You will find that as you ponder on their influence on your earlier life, they still have much to teach you now about being a mentor.

Trail Blazers

by Oliver DeMille & Tiffany Earl

Years ago, scholar Joseph Campbell outlined a fascinating pattern in his book titled *The Hero with a Thousand Faces*. This pattern shows up wherever you see a hero—someone who must face terrible odds to accomplish some great task. It is well illustrated in Bruce Wilkinson's *The Dream Giver*. It appears again in *The Alchemist* by Paulo Coelho. We call this pattern "The Path of All Success," or more often simply "The Path."

People who achieve great success do so by persistently and successfully meeting the challenges on The Path. Their stories are found in ancient mythology, classic and modern literature, virtually all genres of fiction, great movies, the sacred writings of the world religions, the biographies of great men and women, the lives of successful business people, entrepreneurs, teachers, parents, and the stories of "regular people" who have paid the price of greatness. In fact, a fair definition of "success" is the completion of The Path. There are many paths of fear (failure, mediocrity, anger, pain, ignorance, hatred, etc.), and against all these stands The Path of All Success.

At any point along The Path, those progressing are linked in a partnership of traveler and mentor—and the mentor is linked as a traveler to a mentor further along than he. Remove either the mentor or the traveler and forward momentum is delayed or reversed. The goal of this book is to help you truly transform into a better mentee, and also a better mentor. The two go together—and are indeed inseparable; it is The Path that binds them.

By learning about The Path, by understanding it and by completing the exercises in this book, you will master powerful tools that aid any endeavor—great or small. The purpose of this book is to teach The Path and the highest level of mentoring, "Student Whispering," in a way that you can pull the principles right off the page, add them to your DNA and psyche, and apply them powerfully in your everyday life.

Unfortunately, most people end up **stuck** on the sideline, off The Path altogether, or even stalled right on The Path! Choosing to submit to the right mentor makes passing Tests, Trials, and Traps possible (more on this later), and keeps you progressing. The mentor often shows up *after* you walk away from the road to mediocrity. Those who walk away from the common road in search of a better way come across the right mentor, who then helps them progress. To be on the common road and/or without the right mentor is to be blocked—unable to progress or succeed.

Some people stay at this point for weeks or months—even years. Others remain caught in this rut throughout their whole career or life, searching in vain for success and happiness. By knowing and applying the principles of The Path, its steps and pitfalls, the 7 Tests, and the Vital Choices (all of which we will cover later), you will have the power to succeed. You will effectively leave The Path of Mediocrity. You will identify and choose the right mentor, and she will help you leap over the numerous hurdles—and even show you where to find an alternate route with fewer hurdles.

If you are on The Path, you are headed for success. You have (or will soon encounter) the right kind of mentor, and you will be successful. It will be challenging, and you will achieve your goals and attain your vision as you complete The Path.

Which Path Are You On?

If you aren't on The Path, you may wonder why success continues to elude you—why other people seem to get all the breaks. Others may appear to get the good education, the great career, the successful business, the idyllic family. Or you may feel that you have a similar resume, background, life choices and characteristics, but few of the same great results. *Why do their tough breaks always seem to work out for the best?* "Maybe they had *this* or *that* advantage that made all the difference for them," you may be tempted to think—but that isn't it. If they are truly successful, it is because *they are on The Path.*

Just knowing about The Path is a powerful and valuable start. This is the epic story, the purpose of life. These Tests come to all of us so we may find happiness, live our dreams, and *become* our highest potential. The right mentors can help us see, prepare for, capitalize on and overcome what's ahead. Mentors help us along The Path, and being able to recognize the right mentors, and ultimately, *how* they can help us, often catapults us over many hurdles and saves us a lot of time— as well as keeping us on The Path.

The Blazed Trail

In past times, travelers on the frontier carefully chose their route to avoid delays or hazards and to have ready access to food, water and shelter. They relied heavily on the experience of those who had gone that way before—especially those explorers who knew the whole terrain, its dangers, pitfalls, bounties and sanctuaries, and who marked the trail for those who would come along later.

Such trailblazers helped and shared their experience with those who followed by climbing high in great trees and cutting off, or *blazing*, a section of bark—leaving a marker visible from far back on the trail. Keeping an eye out for these blazes made the journey much safer, easier and more direct for others. The key was to always walk toward the next blaze.

The Path has at least seven "blazed trees," steps, or predictable guideposts. We call these the 7 Tests. The Path also has 7 Vital Choices, one for each of the Tests along the way. And there are at least seven important types of mentors to guide us on The Path.

The 7 Vital Choices naturally present themselves to anyone on The Path. Knowing what the next Test is likely to be, and what the Choice will actually consist of (though it will probably *look* like something else at first), is powerful. It keeps you on The Path, following the marks of the trailblazers. Those who have this information are much more likely to surmount the challenges that inevitably come in any important endeavor. In the next chapter, we will outline The Path and go into detail on the 7 Tests and the 7 Vital Choices. For now, let us consider one feature on The Path that you are undoubtedly already familiar with.

The Law of the Wall

Roadblocks, pitfalls, hurdles and challenges can come anywhere along The Path and there is a proven formula for getting through them. It is called The Law of the Wall.

When you run into a roadblock, it helps to let the roadblock trip a trigger to:

1. Stop
2. Be still
3. Ponder solutions

First, rather than going into panic mode, acting impulsively or under duress, **Stop**. Find yourself a quiet place and time where you will be undisturbed. Still yourself and put your mind in a relaxed state. In this objective and detached mindset (free of judgment, panic, skepticism, etc.), make a list of questions. One by one, ask the right questions and listen for ideas. Make a note of the ideas you feel, consider, and think about. For many people, this is most effective in the form of prayer. Others prefer to carry on a mental conversation with a personal hero.

This deep inner reflection and spiritual seeking is vital to keeping you on The Path. Giving in to the urgency or the drama of the situation, listening to the ping-pong tournament of voices in your mind or heeding "the crowd" often puts you on The Path of Mediocrity. At the very least—and this is no small thing—it can waste your time. Sometimes you will recognize a mentor, or feel impressed to seek one out. This is different than "going to the crowd." The difference is that you become spiritually in-tune *before* acting. Going to your mentor after *knowing* it is the right thing empowers you to submit to her counsel—which ultimately gets you ahead on The Path.

If you are going through The Path on the *education* cycle, the roadblock may come on your first day of trying to do the actual work, when you discover that "this is going to be really hard," when you finally sit down to tackle the classics, when you first crack the big, thick book and can't seem to understand it, or when you first try to follow the new intensive study schedule.

If you have engaged an Expert Mentor for business, the roadblock may come when you find that you don't have time, or you have lost your job, or you discover that you haven't paid the price to be on the same wavelength with your spouse. Roadblocks are different for everyone, but they come to all of us.

A roadblock may come from outside sources—such as the competition, or the lack of capital. It may come from natural factors or substantive challenges to completing your plan. It could come from internal weaknesses such as your lack of certain critical knowledge, skills, habits or experience.

In short, roadblocks can come in many forms, but one thing is certain: They will come. They come throughout the entire Path. *There simply is no progression without them.* No success is ever attained unless you feel a Call (more on this in the next chapter), take action to achieve it, and then run into significant challenges. These challenges are not just standing in the way of your success; they are opportunities that catalyze submission, creativity and commitment and thus *ensure* your success.

In fact, the image of an obstacle on a flat plane that impedes your forward progress *is not accurate.* Roadblocks do not hinder you from proceeding to the next step, from forging ahead on your path. The truth is: The Path is *not* a horizontal plane, and the "roadblocks" are in fact the only way to ascend to the next level of progress, which is on a new, higher plane. There is no way to make the upward leap to the next level without these so-called "obstacles"—which are really stepping-stones.

Nevertheless, when the roadblocks come you will likely feel overwhelmed, frustrated, perhaps angry or upset with other people or with the situation, and in general, the excitement of The Call will fade away and be replaced with anxiety, fear, doubt, hesitancy, or concern.

This state of mind is the opposite of a relaxed, peaceful state and can keep you from obtaining answers and progressing. Remember, when you hit roadblocks:

- **Pray** or meditate: still your heart, your mind, and your body and put your brainwaves in a relaxed state
- **Pose** your questions
- **Feel** answers and consider solutions
- **Take** action
- **Seek** counsel from your mentor when appropriate
- **Do** what the mentor says

Keep in mind that whatever forms the roadblock may take, its purpose is to bring you more success. This is The Law of the Wall: If you respond to walls and challenges correctly, they will help you progress much better than you would without them!

As our friend (and one of our favorite authors) Dennis R. Deaton wrote in his excellent book *Ownership Spirit*:[26]

"... We may not control the winds in life; but we do regulate our own sails. When the gales blow against us, we can learn to tack into the headwind. When we ... reach our intended ports, the headwinds and crosswinds of adversity leave behind an unexpected windfall. The joy and satisfaction we feel upon arrival is much greater than from the tailwind-aided pleasure cruises. The joy of victory is always, and exactly, proportionate to the degree of opposition."

The Path to Nowhere

Many people never take full action on the Calls they feel, so they don't even get to the roadblock. Unfortunately, such people are likely on The Path of Failure.

Some of those who make it to the roadblock either don't learn how to get answers or fail to act on them and follow through. They are on The Path of Mediocrity—periodically starting new Paths but never completing them. Such people seem to be just as talented and earnest as the rest, and always working really hard, but never quite achieving the success they desire. They choose mediocrity not because they aspire to it—indeed they are usually seeking a better path, often trying very hard to achieve success. But the success they so desperately seek never to them comes until they learn and apply the lessons of The Law of the Wall.

It is important to differentiate between being on The Path of Failure and what most people term "failing." The Path of Failure is simply this: *not trying, not taking risks, not even attempting to follow the Calls of life.* This is very different than falling down and learning something from the experience.

Some people call this natural process of growth "failure." It is most decidedly not failure. It is experience. It is growth. Anyone who has ever considered the development of a child knows this. The child learns to walk by trying, falling, getting up, and doing it over and over until there is a shuffle, a steady walk and an eventual run.

Failure (or growth), in this sense, should never be feared, but rather encouraged! It is the avoidance of this natural growth process that keeps many from trying and binds them squarely to The Path of Failure. Unfortunately, one of the devastating consequences of the conveyor belt models in the past century has been to teach students to fear "failure," and thus, to avoid any risk. Leadership, personal growth, individual mission and life success *require* risks and mistakes! Of course, we do not hope to dwell on our mistakes, but we must allow the growth that only comes when we risk and try.

The Path is like an upward spiral, meaning that we go through it many times in our lives, each time at new levels if we passed each Test—and if not, then as a repeat of the last lesson, or beginning over.

As you read through the overview of The Path in the next chapter, ask yourself if you have ever experienced the features and process as described, recollecting the choices you made and the results that followed.

So far we have learned several key concepts:

• Mentors can greatly help us succeed on The Path

- The Path of Failure comes when we don't heed the Call, take risks or try to do the great things we feel we should
- The Path of Mediocrity occurs when we try but attempt to succeed alone without the right mentor(s)
- The Path of All Success has 7 Tests and 7 Vital Choices which help us succeed
- There are also seven types of mentors to help us—some informal and others formal
- When we hit roadblocks or problems, The Law of the Wall teaches us to see opportunities in challenges, and to use humility, creativity and commitment to learn from roadblocks and use them to progress

With these basics understood, we are now ready to learn the specific Tests and Choices on The Path.

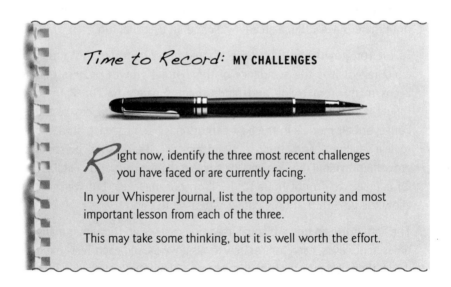

Time to Record: **MY CHALLENGES**

*R*ight now, identify the three most recent challenges you have faced or are currently facing.

In your Whisperer Journal, list the top opportunity and most important lesson from each of the three.

This may take some thinking, but it is well worth the effort.

The Path

by Oliver DeMille & Tiffany Earl

George Washington was successful as a leader, in business, and with his family—as well as becoming the Father of his Country. Yet Washington faced significant personal struggles, a major economic depression, business challenges and a society torn by a war that touched nearly every aspect of his life. He donated his full-time focus to statesmanship and public service for most of his adult life—to say nothing of prevailing in ground war over the greatest military power in the world. Like his hero Cincinnatus (and a future leader—Abraham Lincoln—who would follow him in the lineage of mentors), Washington was successful at least in part because he followed The Path of All Success.

Effective people follow The Path—and they attribute much of their success to great mentors. Name any number of men or women who stood for something, who changed society, who were raised up to accomplish a great mission, and a little study shows that they had a mentor who helped them along The Path:

Thomas Jefferson	→	George Wythe
Isaac Newton	→	Isaac Barrow
Abraham Lincoln	→	Sarah Bush Johnston
George Washington	→	Colonel Fairfax

We do not know if these great men and women of history knew

of The Path explicitly. Perhaps the societal traditions in their day of apprenticeships and wards naturally led to relationships that provided for personal training and professional advocacy—an example that we can learn from today. However, it is an historical verity that these individuals (and others like them) felt a Call, committed to a direction, faced roadblocks, and relied on the guidance of mentors to overcome. Whether by genius, luck, tradition or Providence: they followed The Path of All Success.

What is this Path? What does it look like? Perhaps most importantly: Where are *you* on The Path?

Let's take a look at The Path by defining the 7 Vital Tests it inevitably brings...

Test 1: The Call
You are given the Call; will you receive it?

The first Test on The Path is "the Call." Each time you start a new job, enter a new relationship, start a new project, engage the process of getting a great education or begin anything new, you are answering a Call. Something attracted you to the opportunity—to do better, to be better. *Something invited to you choose and begin.* This is the Call.

A Call comes packaged as desire. Never underestimate desire. It may look like a new idea, opportunity, direction or project. Some Calls are quickly rejected as a passing fancy. Others are considered in detail and then discarded for whatever reason. Still others catch hold, and you begin to want them, to seek them—and eventually you act on them.

How do you know if it is right to receive and act on a Call? Asking these questions can help:

• Does it lead you to that which is praiseworthy, beautiful, virtuous, good?
• Does it fit with you reaching your infinite potential?
• Does it match your core values of becoming your best and contributing to the happiness of yourself, your family, your community, your nation?
• And, is it your season?

The Student Whisperer

You may know a Call is received when you move toward a prospect, when you go beyond dreaming or thinking about it and take *action*.

The High

At the beginning of your undertaking, your energy and interest are high even though you really have very little clear or precise understanding of where you are headed or what it will require. But it feels great! You have felt a Call, made a choice—and now you are taking action!

This step on The Path is truly exhilarating, and it is a tragedy how few people make this a significant part of their life. It is true that difficulties will follow, but this is no reason not to enjoy the honeymoon!

If you have made a habit of passing on opportunity after opportunity in life, the excitement of acting on a Call will be wonderful. Have fun with it. You can receive many Calls throughout your life. Whatever your age, The Call is exciting and exhilarating—it feels good to know you want something and that you are going to take action to achieve it.

Blaze...

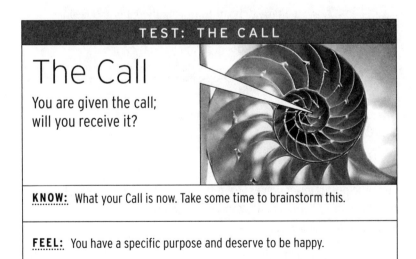

TEST: THE CALL

The Call
You are given the call; will you receive it?

KNOW: What your Call is now. Take some time to brainstorm this.

FEEL: You have a specific purpose and deserve to be happy.

VITAL CHOICE #1: Accept The Call if it is right. Prepare and move toward it. Take Action! What do you feel you should do to take action?

MENTOR FUNCTION: God or the Universe lights your desire. It feels right; it resonates.

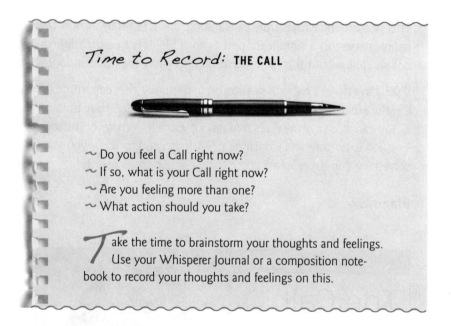

Time to Record: **THE CALL**

~ Do you feel a Call right now?
~ If so, what is your Call right now?
~ Are you feeling more than one?
~ What action should you take?

*T*ake the time to brainstorm your thoughts and feelings. Use your Whisperer Journal or a composition notebook to record your thoughts and feelings on this.

Test 2: Opposition

Will you abandon the Call?

At some point, inner voices, friends, loved ones, peers and others will question your involvement. You will be tempted to abandon The Call and do something else.

There is no mistaking this Test when it comes, because the excitement of The Call dies away and is replaced with frustration. *The honeymoon is over.*

"You can't do that," they say, or "That's crazy," "Be realistic," or "Please don't." Unfortunately, opposition may also come from a mentor. If the mentor is telling you something that is right, you need to listen. Sometimes, however, you need to use diplomacy, humility and creativity to resolve the concerns of those whose support will be vital to your success.

Whenever you decide, "the sky is the limit," it seems there will always be someone or something to burst your bubble. They will try to convince you that it won't work. They may even have a list of reasons. As you choose to get a superb education, to accomplish an important life mission, to pursue a business opportunity, or to improve your family significantly, this Test *will* come. Be prepared for it and stay on The Path.

This part of The Path tests your allegiance. Allegiance is the most important thing in your whole life because it is the driving force behind all your other choices. It defines who you are, what you want and how you go about achieving your goals. You can't continue to work toward your Call without passing this Test, making the 2nd Vital Choice, which is: Choose the Right Allegiance. If your allegiance isn't right, the best, worthiest and most relevant voices are drowned out, certain other voices have too much sway and power, and you stop progressing on The Path.

The four most basic "allegiances" to choose from are:

- Others
- Self
- Evil
- God/Good

Others

The allegiance to others manifests itself in either the desire to fit in or the need to stand out. Both of these define themselves in a context of conformity, or relation to the "others" in one's life. Whether as a pleaser or a maverick, a minion or a rebel, those with an Others allegiance are rudderless without the input of or comparison to people or trends outside of themselves. They crave input from peers or authority figures, whether positive or negative, to know that their lives are on track.

Self

The allegiance to self is characterized by a "me first" worldview—the idea that what happens to one's self is of paramount importance. Good and bad are defined in relation to impact on personal comfort, security, gain, power or status. Both the Others and the Self allegiance can appear to be generous, moral, courageous, sympathetic, etc., under certain circumstances, and the one who holds these allegiances therefore believes himself possessed of these virtues. At the same time, the tendency and capacity for self-deception in these individuals leaves them unable to meaningfully evolve and progress on The Path.

Evil

We'll spend the least time on this one, as we think it is self-evident that this is not the ideal and brings a host of problems. And while an allegiance to Evil is not common, it does exist. The nature of things is such that those who persist in the allegiance to Others or Self have a greater capacity for evil, and over a lifetime can even unknowingly serve Evil, just as if it were their chosen allegiance.

God/Good

The highest, most noble, and most rewarding allegiance is to God/Good.[27] This allegiance entails understanding and acting in accordance with sound principles and natural law. Such a course will almost certainly include work, sacrifice, courage and nobility. The rewards of such a life and allegiance are happiness and success—although not always in terms of physical comfort or personal gain. At the same time: no matter how successful somebody is, if his allegiance is to the wrong thing(s) his life's contribution is diminished and less meaningful. A society populated by individuals with an allegiance to Good is (or will ultimately become) more happy, free, prosperous and secure.

Blaze...

Opposition
Will you abandon the call?

KNOW: People you respect and love may try to dissuade you (with words such as, "We'll miss you," "It's stupid," "You can't," "You'll fail," "Let someone else," "Don't do it."). Or, possibly, another new path will look more enticing and you will be tempted to jump from one "honeymoon" to the next, to the next, and so on.

FEEL: Prepared to please the "Good" rather than "Others" or even "Self."

VITAL CHOICE #2: Choose your allegiance and pursue the Call. Answer these questions:
• Based on an analysis of your choices, what is your top allegiance?
• Is this the right allegiance, or are you compromising or rebelling in your choice?
• What should your allegiance truly be?

MENTOR FUNCTION: Encourage you to decide **whom** you are going to believe. Love the others, serve the others, and learn what you need to from them—but ultimately, pick the allegiance you are going to follow and orient your choices and responses to be consistent with that allegiance.

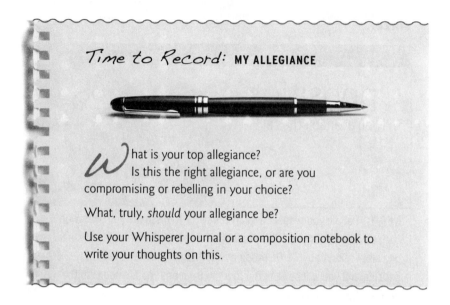

Time to Record: **MY ALLEGIANCE**

*W*hat is your top allegiance?
Is this the right allegiance, or are you compromising or rebelling in your choice?

What, truly, *should* your allegiance be?

Use your Whisperer Journal or a composition notebook to write your thoughts on this.

Test 3: The Great Chasm

How will you cross it?

When you are well on your way and moving toward the Call, you will reach a chasm separating you from where you know you want and need to be. As Bruce Wilkinson describes this in his book *The Dreamgiver*, a guard blocking the obvious pathway tells you *his is the only way across.*

You have a difficult choice to make. The guard is representative of what appears to bring happiness.

Not all roads lead to your dreams or your unique mission or Call. The decision to cross the chasm some other way *has* to be made, and until it is, the right way doesn't appear—and neither does your submission to the next mentor. That is why so few pass this Test.

What does this choice look like? It could look like not cheating even though "every" other medical student is cheating. It could be you choosing not to climb the corporate ladder because you're not happy there, or not unnecessarily getting food stamps even though you *could.* It could be humbling yourself to do either of these things (even when you don't want to), because you *should*. It could look like a dozen different things that have personal meaning to you. Passing this Test is not easy. The world believes one road is the only road, but it is not. The world in general doesn't even remember the need for the mentor who helps you get across the chasm.

Only after you pass this Test does another way across the chasm open up.

Blaze...

The Chasm

How will you cross it?

KNOW: Once you decide that—*no matter what*—you will *not* take the wrong path, another way will open up for you and a mentor will appear to help guide you. To make the right choice here requires what Robert Frost alludes to in "The Road Less Traveled." This Test requires trust—which makes "all the difference!"

FEEL: Determined that there *is* another way. YOU'LL FIND IT.

VITAL CHOICE #3: This is a two-part choice:

First, you must choose a *right* path across the chasm, which at first means *not* choosing the common road. It is *not* the only way. In fact, that road doesn't work at all. It is a dead end of wasted time and needless misery, because it doesn't end up where you need to go.

Secondly, you must recognize and submit to a mentor who helps you along The Path of All Success, including showing you how to cross the great chasm.

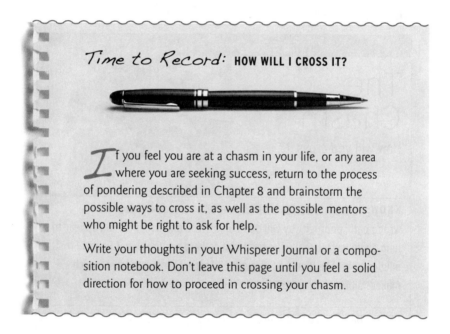

Time to Record: **HOW WILL I CROSS IT?**

*I*f you feel you are at a chasm in your life, or any area where you are seeking success, return to the process of pondering described in Chapter 8 and brainstorm the possible ways to cross it, as well as the possible mentors who might be right to ask for help.

Write your thoughts in your Whisperer Journal or a composition notebook. Don't leave this page until you feel a solid direction for how to proceed in crossing your chasm.

Test 4: Hard Work

Is this what you really want?

You have to work very hard to achieve any success, and most of us don't naturally want to do this. In fact, Tests 4 and 5 can be summed up as Hard Work, and it is usually through good mentors that we get help to make our work *effective*.

Blaze...

Hard Work

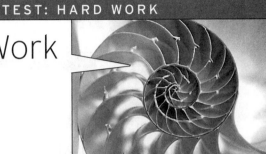

Is this what you
really want?

KNOW: This is about having new eyes and recognizing what you've asked for. This is the wilderness where you'll face Tests, Traps and Trials.

FEEL: Warning! It doesn't look like what you imagined. It is much harder. Don't get discouraged.

VITAL CHOICE #4: Work hard. Ask for what you need. Learn the Law of the Wall. Recognize the answers and receive them. Meditate. Ponder. Plan. And keep working.

MENTOR FUNCTION: Teach you to see with "spiritual eyes" or intuition, and how to ask the right questions. Teach you how to know and recognize answers, how to face your fears, how to ask for what is needed and how to recognize gifts from the Universe. This Call is from God/Good, and Good will help you achieve it.

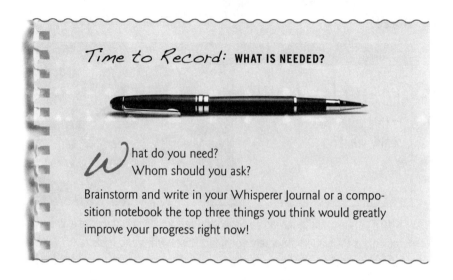

Time to Record: **WHAT IS NEEDED?**

What do you need?
Whom should you ask?

Brainstorm and write in your Whisperer Journal or a composition notebook the top three things you think would greatly improve your progress right now!

Test 5: Endurance

How much longer?

By this point, you've been at it long enough and feel you deserve to be done. Many people are asked to endure for decades. *Isn't there anyone to help? Why do I have to keep going? Nobody said it would take this long. I must be on the wrong path or something... Maybe I should turn back...? Wait—there's a nice looking Call. I could do that instead....*

Tests 4 and 5 on The Path can appear to happen simultaneously. They are summed up as the Hard Work phase and "TTT" (Tests, Trials and Traps). Hard work is part of any path to success, and in reality it lasts throughout The Path. After you are following the direction of your mentor, you'll be doing hard work *at a whole new level.* The hard work will take everything you have to give, but The Call will require even more.

As you continue to work hard, you will be faced with three very special kinds of challenges called *Tests*, *Trials* and *Traps*.

Tests

Tests are external challenges that must be overcome by making the right choices, working hard, taking risks, etc. This is easier said than done, of course, but the key is to squarely face them, work out your strategy to overcome them with your mentor, and don't give up—no matter how hard they are. When you feel pushed to the limit, consult your mentor and follow his guidance. Never give up. *All Tests can be overcome.*

Trials

Trials are also external problems, but instead of overcoming them you must *endure* them. They are an inalterable feature of the terrain for any success, and simply making the right choices does not negate their impact on your journey.

They hurt. All paths to success include Trials. Sometimes they are directly related to the field of your Path, and other times they are totally unrelated. You may have a child with a disability or you may have a lingering illness. A friend who has turned against you may make life painful. Like Tests, Trials come in many shapes and sizes. The best way to deal with them differs, but again you must face them, make a plan, and then take it one day at a time. Getting through each day of Trial is a victory.

Traps

Traps are *internal* challenges—personal weaknesses, flaws and blind spots—that must be conquered through self-honesty and discipline. This can take a lot of time and energy, and many people rationalize neglecting to remedy their Traps because it doesn't seem like it actually moves you toward your goal; but without due attention to our Traps, no true success will come. Conquering Traps, specifically your blind spots, requires a self-honest look at your life.

One of the most important things your mentor may do for you is also the hardest for you to take: revealing your blind spots. Remember to trust your mentor and work with her closely in the process of overcoming your Traps.

Blaze...

Endurance

How much longer?

KNOW: This is a desert, a wilderness. But it can be crossed! Keep on asking, receiving and working. There are Traps and Tests your mentor can help you avoid and get through. Don't give up. Think of the children of Israel in the wilderness, Washington at Valley Forge, Peter and later Gandhi in prison, or the book *The Alchemist,* by Paulo Coelho. Read *Free the Beagle* by Roy H. Williams.

FEEL: Gratitude

VITAL CHOICE #5: Endure, and Keep Working!

MENTOR FUNCTION: Inspire faithfulness and hope. Reprimand when necessary. Inspire you to have self-honesty, conquering Traps and not being derailed by endless "self-improvement," distractions or self-pity at the expense of doing the next right thing.

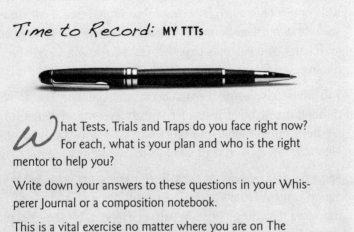

Time to Record: **MY TTTs**

*W*hat Tests, Trials and Traps do you face right now? For each, what is your plan and who is the right mentor to help you?

Write down your answers to these questions in your Whisperer Journal or a composition notebook.

This is a vital exercise no matter where you are on The Path, since TTTs are always present. Don't skip this! When you have completed all the assignments in this book, your Whisperer Journal/notebook will be a masterpiece of personalized Whispering wisdom.

Test 6: The Ultimate Test

What are you willing to sacrifice?

At some point on your Path to success, you will actually be asked to give everything back, even after all the work you've done. It may shock you, but at some point it will probably *seem* like you are asked to walk away from it all. You'll feel all alone. This comes in many different ways, but it is overwhelming and terribly hard.

When you face the Ultimate Test, you'll know. It will push you beyond your limits. It will require all you have to give—and more. You will go to your breaking point, and past. It will likely feel as if the Universe is against you, and every fiber of your being will want to cry out to be released from this Test. If you do abandon the call (for whatever reason), you will start over with a new Call. You will have the benefit of all the lessons you've learned in the first five steps, but you will not move to full fruition this time through The Path.

Whether you move forward this time or with some future Call, there will come a time when choosing to pass this Test is *vital*. To make it, you will stand alone, without the mentor—or at least without any *mortal* mentor. You will only pass this Test by refusing to give up, and by turning everything you are over to the governing power of the Universe.

You will receive some preparation for the Ultimate Test as you pass through the first five Tests of The Path. Everything you've learned in life from other people and other paths all help you prepare for the Ultimate Test. Still, it tests all of us to our utmost.

Some people break during such Tests, turning against Good or just giving up entirely. Others apply The Law of the Wall and use this Test to turn toward higher purpose. Whatever happens, these are defining moments. Sometimes the changes these Tests bring about are obvious and immediate, while other times they don't fully manifest for a long time.

Oliver: Mine came on a wintry day when my three-month-old son was injured in a car accident; I was the driver. I pled with God for him to live, and against all odds he did. It came day after day while I thought of him in the hospital, struggling, in excruciating pain, and with no prospects for normal function. It especially came at night when I begged for sleep but none came. Night after night. It came in the recurring dream that I still have, the same dream so many times— where I change the scenario somehow, and he isn't hurt. Each time I have the dream I wake up to find that no, the dream isn't true. He is still hurt. He is still in a wheelchair.

It came years later as I watched the neighborhood kids playing at the park, and then turned to my son because he was hitting himself repeatedly in the head. "What's wrong?" I asked. He pointed to the kids playing, then to himself in the wheelchair and chanted: "I stupid, I stupid, I stupid...."

A new recurring dream joined the older one after that day at the park.

I was on The Path. I was giving my all to the Call. Why did this have to happen? It's not fair. How am I supposed to do what I was called to do now?

Ultimate Tests are, well, *ultimate*. They tear at your very soul. If you've experienced such a Test, you know. And though it's not polite to say so, this book would not be complete if we didn't say:

If you haven't had one, you will.

Oliver: But know this: the Ultimate Test is not a punishment; and unlike the previous roadblocks—which are now completely trivial— it is not a deviation from The Path. During those sleepless nights I found myself. Really, deeply. In a way I never imagined. I also found something much bigger than myself. I experienced and felt things...; well, I won't share them here—but they changed me. I can honestly say now that I am so grateful for the challenges—and even for the pain that brought them. Those who have experienced an Ultimate Test may sometimes, like me, wish to change the details; but they never want to surrender the resulting blessings. The blessings of that pain are indescribable, profound and above all other things I've experienced in my life.

No earthly mentor can really hold your hand as you pass an Ultimate Test. For that, you'll have to rely on higher powers, whether internal or external. It is helpful to know when such Tests come that others have gone this way and passed such Tests, and that you *will* be able to choose to pass it, no matter how hard it is. Also that passing such Tests brings great, truly incredible rewards. Suffice it to say that you *will* be faced with your Ultimate Test and you will make *your* choice.

Blaze...

TEST 6: THE ULTIMATE TEST

Ultimate Test

What are you willing to sacrifice?

TEST 6: THE ULTIMATE TEST

KNOW: In order to give all you have back you must REMEMBER your allegiance and where you got The Call in the first place.

FEEL: You feel all alone. There seems to be no mentor besides God/the Universe. It feels like there is no one to help. TRUST. Seek higher power.

VITAL CHOICE #6: Remember your allegiance. Give everything you have. Give all you have back. By doing so you will ultimately and in time receive peace, become happy and full of love. The right choice will become clear. Choose it, no matter what it is.

MENTOR FUNCTION: The Universal Good, or God for believers, commissions you as an Emissary. You want to truly help others with all your heart. This becomes your focus in life.

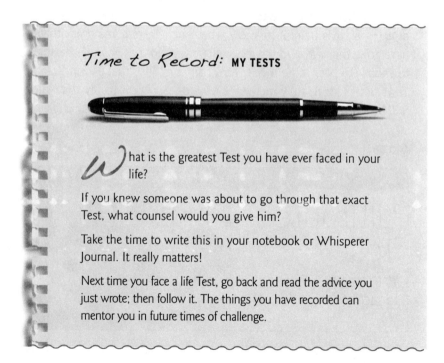

Time to Record: **MY TESTS**

*W*hat is the greatest Test you have ever faced in your life?

If you knew someone was about to go through that exact Test, what counsel would you give him?

Take the time to write this in your notebook or Whisperer Journal. It really matters!

Next time you face a life Test, go back and read the advice you just wrote; then follow it. The things you have recorded can mentor you in future times of challenge.

Test 7: The Pressure Lets Up

Do you?

At this point on The Path, after you have experienced your Ultimate Test, you can more clearly see which paths and choices lead people to unhappiness. It is time to take a stand and fight against them and for what leads to happiness, peace, and life. Now enters the Mission Mentor. Your Mission Mentor has the same field of Call you have. She has been successfully doing what you want to do; and now that you are ready, she is willing to give you what you need in order to join her in the work.

Of course, you have to recognize her, and then receive gifts from her. These gifts often come as difficult assignments! Armed with the gifts your Mission Mentor gives to you, you can hardly fail. Still, a few people are so relieved at this point to be out of the pressure cooker that they want to take an eternal break.

Tiffany: For example, I remember being in labor and experiencing desperate feelings during 'transition'—when all the prep-work was done and the baby was ready to be born. Just at this moment, there was a HUGE desire to just stop. Sound crazy? All I had to do then was push, and the baby would be born.

Just like the final stages of labor where the baby emerges and takes his first breath, Test 7 is challenging, but also often exciting and exhilarating. Most people sprint to the end. Others may walk, or crawl, but passing the Ultimate Test(s) changes a person forever. Such people finish The Path and achieve great success!

Blaze...

Pressure Lets Up

Do you?

KNOW: Learn to use the tools, trust the mentor, fight the fight.

FEEL: Prepared

VITAL CHOICE #7: Act. Keep going. Press forward. Be happy fighting your fight. Fully engage!

MENTOR FUNCTION: Your Mission Mentor gives you the necessary tools and weapons for the work ahead. Often this entails challenging assignments and more hard work. Sprint to the end, have joy in your work. Or, if you need to walk or even crawl, keep going! Smile. You have succeeded.

Time to Record: MY BATTLES

~ What were you born to fight for?

~ Are you doing it?

~ What battles should you engage right now?

~ How do the on-going vestiges of your Ultimate Test help remind you and strengthen you each day?

*T*ake the time to ponder, think about and write your answers to these questions in your Whisperer Journal/ notebook.

When a person completes The Path (or more accurately, one full turn of The Path), she sees at least three things. First, she sees that there is so much more to do. It can be overwhelming after such a challenging journey to realize that she has barely scratched the surface, but it is also exciting that she can keep going and make such a difference for good in the world.

Second, she feels gratitude to those making such a difference for good in the world and who helped her on The Path— especially to partners and mentors.

Finally, she wants everyone to experience The Path, the joy of success. She is saddened by those who refuse The Path, and excited to help mentees and protégés progress and succeed on The Path. Each time such a mentee or protégé completes a step of The Path, the mentor feels the exhilaration and joy once again.

In short, there is a Path of Success, and those who have taken it are taking it again. At the same time, they want to help those who are looking for The Path to find it.

This process, in all its levels and directions and individuals and potentials, is called Mentoring. Or, if you want to really get technical, you can call it Life.

Notice that nearly every great novel, movie, epic, play or profound story from history illustrates The Path, whether in its ideal, or in the various ways in which we struggle to achieve. Now that you know what to look for, you can see it everywhere there is triumphant success or an epic failure. It is The Path of leadership, and our nation and world are in the midst of such struggles right now. So is each family and individual that is on The Path of All Success.

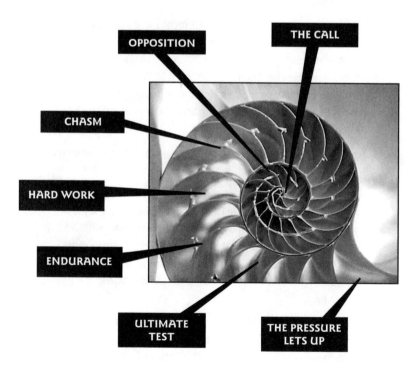

The Student Whisperer

A Whispering Language Lesson

by Oliver DeMille

As a mentor, it is essential to know the other voices that are Whispering to your children and students. For those who understand these voices, there is virtually no generation gap. For those who understand these voices, there is no smugness or arrogance. For those who understand these voices, predicting your own behavior and that of your mentees is simple. For those who don't understand these voices, others are a mystery. Indeed, if you don't understand these voices, you are a mystery to yourself.

Everyone hears voices—not in an otherworldly or schizophrenic sense, mind you, but in a very natural way. We all experience dialogues in our mind. Those who govern these dialogues, who choose and guide their thoughts, understand the secret to success in life's goals. Those who are eavesdropping victims of whatever these mental dialogues dictate struggle to accomplish their dreams in life.

There is an old saying that "those who can't do, teach." In leadership education, in mentoring and Student Whispering, the opposite is true. Those who *can* are the only ones able to really mentor. Student Whisperers understand the voices in their own mind, the prominent voices in the minds of their mentees, and how to persuasively communicate in the language of these internal dialogues. Because of this, they can Whisper effectively to themselves and those they mentor.

This is easier than it may seem at first. The problem is that few people pay conscious attention to the ongoing discussions of these voices. Student Whisperers not only pay attention to their own internal dialogues, they participate in the debate and actually lead the internal discourse in a constructive direction. They also pay attention to the same voices in the minds of their mentees, and they effectively join this dialogue.

Again, this is a lot easier than you might think. For example, stop and listen to what your own internal voices are telling you right now. Specifically, what is your Inner Critic telling you?

You know that voice pretty well, don't you? The truth is, most of us do. This is unfortunate. He is a bully, a pessimist, and he is always caught in the past. For some of us he is an incessant and annoying chatterbox. He is not someone you would likely keep as a friend in the real world. And if all this unpleasantness were not enough to turn a deaf ear to him: The Inner Critic hardly ever gets things right. But in the world of our minds, we seem to keep the Critic around all the time. Too many of us give him all the attention he craves, but has not earned. He twists facts, perceptions and truths to serve his agenda, and dismisses anything that would discredit his deceitful assertions.

We take him to work with us, to every social event, to our home, and even to the shower. We eat lunch and dinner with him every day—not to mention breakfast and snacks. We sleep with him every night. Worst of all, when a debate comes up in our mind, we often trust the Inner Critic above all other voices. We sometimes even trust him against all the evidence.

So yes, noticing our inner voices is really quite easy. We just have to pay attention. We need to give these voices the importance they deserve, be it great or small. In truth, they run our lives. We get to choose which voices we listen to, which we ignore, which we kick out of our lives, and which we follow. But once these choices are made, the inner voices we listen to determine our choices, our peace and our lives.

Some of the most impactful voices we tend to deal with are, of course, the Critic, and also the Judge, the Victim and the Rebel. While all of these voices are *technically* whispering (we hear them in our mind, though they make no sound), it often feels like they are shouting, demanding and even compelling. Sometimes they even laugh at us. These four negative voices are nearly universal, and have been discussed in depth in our culture since Jung (though called by various names).

A differentiation is in order here. It is true that at times the urge to "rebel" against something can be appropriate—even an expression of personal mission. There are situations where we *should* "rebel" against something, to change a long-held prejudice or question a destructive authority. When we are resisting in the right way, our feelings are positive, empowering, and even *peaceful*. You can clearly tell the difference by how you feel. This is not what we mean when we speak here of the Inner Rebel.

In the context of this discussion, the "Rebel" attacks things that are important to you—things that you really should not be fighting. Your feelings are negative, disempowering, and self-justifying, and tend to disregard the harm to others or ourselves by actions they urge on us. Agitation, anger and jealousy—these feelings typically come from the wrong voice: the Rebel.

Interestingly enough, the Critic, the Judge, and the Victim really have nothing worthwhile to contribute to the inner dialog. They consistently warn of dangers that will never materialize, they sensationalize faults, offenses and other tribulations beyond rational proportion, their motives and their arguments are base and unedifying, and they don't get anything accomplished. In short: they lie and they waste our time. To put it another way: If you are hearing one of these voices, you may know for a certainty these three things:

- You have no use for the information it urges on you
- The information it proffers is flawed, spun, incomplete, and wholly intended to mislead you
- There is another message (contrary to what the negative voice desperately shrieks at you) that you *do* need to hear and that will serve you well

Two other voices are part of this ongoing dialogue: the Real You, and the Inspirer. It is worth the effort to learn to tune out the negative voices and listen to these two positive voices.

How to Tell the Difference

There are two things helping us out in this battle, if we choose to accept their help. First, we are wired to only really listen to one voice at a time. In any given instant, we are playing only one channel in our mind, listening to only one voice. This allows us to tune out the negatives and tune in to the positives whenever we choose. We really do have this power. We just have to use it. Pollyanna[29] got it right, after all. We are responsible for how we feel and how we react, and by owning this we not only have power over our own happiness, but we are empowered to impact positive outcomes not only for ourselves, but for others.

Second, the negative voices always cause us to feel negative, or some incarnation of negative—selfish, justified, etc. *Always*. Once we tune in to the voice of Inspiration, we have a clear contrast to judge by. From this mature, enlightened perspective, "positive" and "negative" have intrinsic values, and do not refer subjectively to our moods. For example (in spite of the world's characterization to the contrary), feeling humbled and repentant is "positive," and feeling the exhilarating rush of revenge is "negative."

It is not just the sentiment but also its context, its intention and its consequence that determine its positive or negative value. In that spirit, if we are feeling negative, we are listening to a negative voice. If we feel positive, we are listening to a positive inner voice. Whatever happens to us externally, our feelings are determined by how our inner voices respond and which of these voices we hearken to.

This gives us great power. If we are feeling "negative" (as defined above), we know—without exception—that we are listening to a negative voice. This means we need to dismiss that voice, and we need to tune in to what our positive voices have to say. Some people do this almost automatically, while others have to consciously make this shift in their mind. Without this shift, the negative voices run our lives.

But, what about...?

Some people wonder if we should *always* listen to the positive voices. After all, what if we need to listen to so-called "negatives" in order to change, improve and fix things? The answer is that the positive voices—the Real You and the Inspirer—very often tell us to make changes, fix problems, stop doing something that is hurting us or others, or apologize and make something right. There is a huge difference between how we feel when we listen to positive chastening *versus* the destructive attacks of negative voices. Negative voices criticize and tear us down, leave us feeling despondent, futile, defensive, complacent, and inactive. Positive chastening leaves us in touch with the expectation that we can do better or be more, and is an invitation to be more authentically who we are. It is a validation of our highest aspirations.

The Real You and the Inspirer admonish and teach us in ways that lead to positive, effective and lasting results, even when we need to change. In contrast, the voices of the Critic, the Judge, the Victim and the Rebel lead us to negative, stagnating and destructive results even when we really do need to make the changes they seem to urge on us.

Negatives are negative, after all. It is through positives that we increase the positive results in our lives. In fact, it is often the positive voices that ask us to do the most difficult and challenging things that really make a difference. Even when the positive voices chasten and challenge us, they do so in a way that empowers us to do the hard things, and brings out the best in us. The negatives only, always, promote more negatives—no matter what their apparent message or intention.

Some readers may be skilled at detecting these voices, clearly recognizing which voice is speaking at any given moment, and always shunning the negatives and paying close attention to the positive, helpful voices. Most of us have to learn and practice such abilities. Even those who are skilled in this process can learn to do even better, or to be more consistent; and there are places along The Path that will challenge even the best of us on this point.

Time to Record: THE REAL ME

Sit down with your Whisperer Journal/notebook in a place where you can be relaxed and uninterrupted for an hour. Put the words "The Real Me" at the top of a page. Then picture the Real You in your mind, and ask him/her what important things he/she has been telling you recently. Write down in your notebook whatever comes. If negative feelings come, the wrong voice has taken over. Gently ask it to leave and firmly give it no attention. Listen to the voice of the Real You, and write down what it has to tell you.

~ Ask about difficult challenges you've faced, and what the Real You voice wants you to know about them. Write down the thoughts from this voice.

~ Consider how the Real You wants you to deal with projects or events that are ahead, and write down what this voice shares.

~ Ask the Real You if there are things you aren't giving enough attention, and write them down.

~ Ask for solutions and suggestions for the major challenges you face now, and also for the main projects you are involved in. Write the answers.

~ Find out if there are people you need to give more attention, and find out details. Write down what you learn.

~ Ask if there is anything else this voice has to share with you, and write it down.

It is okay if your answers fill much more than a page. I find that I usually fill 3 – 4 pages in this process.

Take the time to do this really well. This is a powerful and profound experience, and without the ability to really understand the voice of the Real You, your mentoring will always be weaker than it could be. This skill is essential to Student Whispering.

More importantly, the habit of doing this, at least weekly, for the rest of your life, is extremely valuable to effective Student Whispering. Those who learn to do this will see their mentoring skill drastically increase. The voice of the Real You intuits so much about great mentoring, and without it your mentoring will always be lessened.

Once you have completed this exercise, do the following:

Time to Record: THE INSPIRER

*N*ow put the word "Inspirer" at the top of a page. Then picture the Inspirer voice in your mind, and ask him/her what important things he/she has been telling you recently. I know of people who picture God, others who see themselves being counseled by a group of heroes (such as Moses, Buddha, George Washington, Joan of Arc, or whatever person or group of people you feel could be your great counselors), and still others who picture their best, most ideal and creative *future* self. Whatever your Inspirer voice, visualize it.

Write down in your notebook whatever comes. Once again, if negative feelings come, the wrong voice has taken over. Firmly dismiss it and give it no attention. Listen to the Inspirer voice, and write down what it has to tell you.

- ⁓ Ask about difficult challenges you've faced, and what the Inspirer voice wants you to know, feel or do about them.
- ⁓ Write down the thoughts from this voice.
- ⁓ Consider how the Inspirer wants you to deal with projects or events that are ahead, and write down what this voice shares.
- ⁓ Ask the Inspirer if there are things you aren't giving

enough attention, and write them down.

~ Ask for solutions and suggestions for the major challenges you face now, and also for the main projects you are involved in. Write the answers.

~ Find out if there are people you need to give more attention, and find out details. Write down what you learn.

~ Ask if there is one right thing that you are to do now. Write it down.

~ Ask if there is anything else this voice has to share with you, and write it down.

Together, these two exercises can drastically increase your ability to mentor and Whisper. They are profound and powerful. These two great positive voices, the Real You and the Inspirer, know so much about you and those you mentor. They seem to know a lot about almost everything. Most of us don't listen to them nearly enough, if at all. And to be a Student Whisperer, each of us simply *must* understand what these voices have to tell us—week after week after week.

But this is just the start of the process.

Amazingly: Negatives are, well, Negative

Note that I did not give you an exercise of hearing the negative voices and writing down what they have to say. I used to do this, to ensure that people clearly understood all six voices (the Critic, Judge, Victim, Rebel, Real You, and Inspirer). However, nothing that the Critic, Judge or Victim had to say was of any help; and it seemed that people didn't need any particular practice to hear these voices, anyway. These voices speak only to teach negatives, and so even when they point out something true they do it in a way that is destructive and/or misleading. Their counsel never improves anything. Indeed, I have learned to simply say, "Who cares!" to anything they say. They usually lie, and whatever truth they share is twisted. These are negative voices, and listening to them helps nothing.

My experience working with many, many people in this process has taught me that *everyone* already recognizes the negative voices. We may not consciously label them by their names, but whenever we listen to them we feel negative (again, using the definition above), so there is never any doubt that negative voices are speaking to us. Ask almost anybody what their Inner Critic has told them lately, and they have a long list of frequently repeated phrases. Same with the Judge and the Victim. People already know the negative inner voices.

However, if you ask what the "Real You" has been trying to tell them recently, most people grow silent while they search their memory. It takes them a while to figure out the answer. And even then, they wonder if they've got it all. They feel a little confused and concerned that they're missing something important. Ask them what the Inspirer voice in their mind has been trying to tell them, and they often blurt out one key thing. Beyond that, they aren't sure of anything except that they are certainly missing something. Being human is an interesting challenge: For some reason, we naturally tend to listen to our negative inner lying voices while tuning out the positive and inspiring. Most likely this is because the positive voices will not impose their counsel on us unbidden, while the negative ones have no such compunction.

We do not need any practice listening to our negative voices. Nearly everyone is an expert on this, highly skilled with a lot of experience. How unfortunate! We are mostly beginners when it comes to our positive voices. We need to learn to notice, pay attention, really listen, actually believe, and apply what our positive voices want to tell us. I am amazed at how often someone asks me in these exercises, "But how do I know if the Real Me and Inspirer voices are right? Maybe I'm just making this up." The amazing thing is that I've never had anyone ask me the same question about the negative voices! We tend to just believe our negative internal thoughts, but to question the positive voices! What's that about?

The positive voices tell us the truth, give us vital counsel about how to change and improve, and share essential information for our success. Their "version" of the truth can, by contrast with the negative voices, seem delusional, impractical, self-serving, naïve, or simply fantastical. But consider: the very essence of being a great leader, statesman, mentor, and Student Whisperer is to take the world from the imperfect reality to the dreamed-of ideal. *Which voices counsel in that realm?* The Real You; the Inspirer. They care about us, and want us to improve and succeed.

Time to Record: PLAN OF ACTION

～ Develop a plan to notice whenever you are feeling negative. Whenever this happens, stop, detect which voice you are listening to, and gently and firmly push any negative voice away by putting your attention on what your positive voices have to tell you—the Real You and the Inspirer.

～ Write this plan in your Whisperer Journal/notebook.

The key to mentoring is to be inspiring, and this occurs when you listen to the right—the *inspiring*—voices. Write out a plan to repeat this exercise—listen and write what the Real You and the Inspirer have to tell you—on a weekly basis. It helps to do this on a set day each week— such as Sunday evening, Saturday morning, or Thursday afternoon after working out.

Following through on this plan, making it a habit, is a must for great mentoring. For Student Whisperers, this is one of the basic weekly habits that make all success possible.

The Student Whisperer

Listening Matters

The most important skill of great mentors is excellent listening. Student Whisperers know that the first law of listening is to listen to the right voices, which includes not giving attention or energy to the wrong voices. The Critic, the Judge and the Victim have no place in success, leadership, mentoring or life. These voices are the things that hold us back.

In modern times, we often teach that we should consider all voices and listen to everyone equally. In contrast, ancient tribes would only listen to one voice—their own tribal perspective. Both extremes lead to negatives, either by giving too much weight to negative voices or by being closed and intolerant. The balanced ground is to reject the voices that are negative, and to give a lot more close attention to the positive voices of the Real You and the Inspirer. By truly listening to these voices, we are truly *listening*.

The second great law of listening is to really hear what our mentees say—not only with words, but in other ways also. Student Whisperers know how to hear what our mentees are Whispering, not just what they say. The next chapter is about how to do this.

The Whisperer's Dance

by Oliver DeMille

If your children, students, or colleagues were asked what kind of teacher or mentor you are, what would they say? Would they call you "easy-going, flexible, and relaxed," or "structured, demanding, and pushy?" Or would they ask, "What teaching?" For example, in high school I had a teacher who sat in the back of the room at his desk and never taught anything. At the beginning of each semester, he handed out a flyer that said we should bring something to read or study to his class each day, and that anybody disturbing the quiet would be sent to the office.

The last day of class he handed out another flyer with spaces for us to fill out our name and the grade we felt we deserved for the class. That was it. He was a very popular teacher with waiting lists to be in his class.

The one time I saw him actually teach was a surprise. The superintendent walked in, unannounced, and stood for about fifteen minutes at the back of the room. When he first came in, our teacher stood up and told us all to put away our readings. Then he taught us a twenty-minute lecture on diagramming sentences. When the superintendent left, the teacher kept lecturing for about five minutes and then told us to go back to our reading.

This was a challenging message for me to grapple with: Did he not value us as students? Did he feel the subject matter was not worth his/our time? Did he feel he had no business being a teacher? And why did he feel the need to "put on a show" for the authority figure? For some reason, he squandered his power for good; and yet, as a "teacher," he left an indelible impression on our young minds.

If your students wouldn't ask, "What teaching?" would they instead say that you are a Drill Sergeant, bossing every minute and controlling every second of studies? It is helpful to actually ask those you mentor this question. They will often answer it differently than you might think.

Yet, too often even the most earnest and committed mentor or parent struggles to meaningfully interact with her mentees. Understanding two axes and the quadrants they create is hugely empowering, and is sure to bring ready inspiration for those seeking to improve their mentoring.

This chapter will operate as a workshop. The information is essential for great Student Whisperers. I recommend that you do the full workshop. Those who do will learn more than those who skip the assignments.

The Manager/Artist Balance

Whether you're caught in the Drill Sergeant vortex or struggling to know how to lead out meaningfully, consider now a key balance that Student Whisperers understand: the Manager/Artist Balance. The following graphic illustrates these characteristics.

Manager	Artist
Concrete	Abstract
Steady Progress	Ups and Downs
Avoid Crisis	Crisis Feeds Creativity
Planning	Following Moods
Follow Through	Creativity
Routine	Eclectic

Time to Record: MY MANAGER/ARTIST BALANCE

*T*ake the time to consider each pair: are you more *concrete* or *abstract* in your mentoring? Do you promote *steady progress* or an organic cycle of *ups and downs*? Do you teach the student to *avoid crisis* or that *crisis feeds creativity*? And so on.

Of course, one of the skills of the Student Whisperer is to consciously manipulate this balance as you interact with and respond to each student's specific and changing needs. But as you are becoming agile in this process of personalizing the balance, you will find it helpful to know: What is your natural balance? What mix of these are you most comfortable following?

The question to ask yourself here is: **What is my default setting?** Write this question down and answer it in writing in your notebook. Also, copy this simple chart in your notebook and mark where on the line your balance tends to be:

Manager ———————————————————— Artist

Are you closer to Manager, closer to Artist, or do you tend toward one or the other? Or are you right in the center, balanced between Manager and Artist?

~ Now, ask yourself what your default mix of these *should* be? This is a very important question. Ponder and take the time to really consider if your balance is exactly what you think it should be or if you need to change it a little or even a lot. Write your thoughts in your Whisperer Journal.

　　　　　　　　　　　　　　　　　The Student Whisperer

Copy the same chart into your notebook and mark where you think you should be on it:

Manager ———————————————— Artist

~ Now compare the first chart, where you feel you are in this mix, with the second: where you want to be.

These are very important exercises, because to be a great Student Whisperer you need to be able to Whisper to yourself. If you don't know how to read and respond to your own mind, it is difficult to understand the thoughts and behaviors of those you mentor. While the research of developmental psychologist Howard Gardner shows that there is a significant difference between the introspective and interpersonal skills,[30] a deeper understanding of one does improve the other—if the mentor is trying to develop both.

~ Now select one person you mentor and write his or her name on the same page in your Whisperer Journal/notebook. What is your usual Manager/Artist balance as you work with this student? Mark it on a new chart:

Manager ———————————————— Artist

~ Once that is done, here is a new question: What balance does your student/mentee need from you right now? Mark it on another chart:

Manager ———————————————— Artist

Of course, this balance should be what your mentee needs right now. Over time her needs will likely change. Indeed, as the student goes through various levels of development (and in response to the various Vital Choices, Tests, Trials and Traps she encounters on The Path), the balance she needs from her mentor will likely change dramatically. For now, the two charts give you insight into what you are giving the mentee and what the mentee actually needs.

~ Consider the difference between these two. If your marks are in the same place on both charts, my bet is that you don't fully understand what your mentee needs. If your marks are in the same place on both charts, do the following additional exercise: teach this simple model to your mentee, and without suggesting what you think about your mentoring, have her answer these same questions about you and mark two blank charts. Then take a good, hard look at her charts. If her charts agree with yours (and they seldom do), then you are likely delivering what is needed.

If not, if you think your mentoring balance is what your mentee needs right now, but her charts disagree, try going with her charts for a while. Alter your Manager/Artist balance to try to meet what she wants. The results will likely surprise you (and perhaps, her), and you will be on the path to Student Whispering.

It is not always advisable for a mentor to gear his approach to "what the student wants," but in the process of connecting with your emerging Student Whisperer, the information you get from this exercise will be invaluable in the process of your becoming.

If both your charts *and* hers indicate that your mentoring is where it should be, skip down to the next section. Once you have two charts, one showing where you are as a mentor to this one student and the other recommending where you should be, sit down with your Journal/notebook and brainstorm how you can shift your balance. Note that the middle is not always the best goal. In fact, it seldom is. Each mentee at a given time needs a blend of Manager and Artist, and the mix is seldom a precise balance.

~ After brainstorming, make a specific plan of ways you can alter your mentoring to be at the ideal blend the student needs. Be sure to cross out any brainstormed ideas that are actually action items for the mentee. Focus on how you can change *your* attitude, expectations, plans and mentoring to be at the ideal blend of Manager and Artist that your mentee needs. Write these down.

By doing these exercises with a specific mentee in mind, you are practicing Student Whispering. You are identifying your mentoring balance between Manager skills and Artist skills, you are questioning and thinking about the specific blend of these that your mentee needs right now, and you are brainstorming and planning ways to alter your mentoring to give your mentee the ideal Manager/Artist mix they need at this point in their progress. This is a powerful start to Student Whispering.

Complete all these exercises before moving on.

Time to Record: WHISPERING EXERCISE

*R*epeat the series of exercises you just did for *each* person you mentor. This is the work of Student Whispering.

~ Consider each mentee. Chart how you mentor each, and what mix of Manager/Artist each student needs from you right now. If you think you are mentoring any student perfectly right now, have this mentee do the same exercise.

~ Brainstorm and plan how to be the ideal mentor for each

mentee by altering your Manager/Artist balance to what
the mentee needs.
~ Take good notes on your thoughts about each mentee, and
create a written plan, as described above, for each mentee.

I highly recommend that you do not skip this exercise. My purpose in assigning it is about more than plans for your mentees. Going through this exercise for each person you mentor will have a huge impact on how your mind works when you mentor. By doing this exercise repeatedly, and planning differently for each mentee, you will learn the process of Student Whispering using the Manager/Artist mix.

Think of it as Whispering Training Wheels: with this exercise as a prop, and using the repetition of doing it over and over, once for each mentee, you are actually training your thoughts and intuition in a skill that will become more and more natural to you. You will make thinking this way into a mental habit in a very short time. Once you have done this at least seven times in a few hours, your mind will naturally begin asking these questions and others like them whenever you mentor. You may need to use some hypothetical mentees—like friends of your children, nieces, nephews, etc.—to meet your "quota" and really anchor these techniques in your thinking processes. By doing so you will be adding a new go-to tool to your belt that will be readily available, as the circumstances require.

Completing this exercise will significantly improve your subconscious and conscious Whispering habits and skills. It will make you think more like a Student Whisperer. Most who do not complete this exercise will have to consciously sit down and go through the charting and planning each time they mentor a student, and over time they will be less and less likely to follow this process. This is because without a sufficient amount of time and repetition in one sitting the mind never fully embraces the whole process, and it will continue to be laborious, even after repeated short bursts of effort in the process.

Those who have done the full exercise, in contrast, will be more and more likely to use these tools, ask these questions and go through this planning process. They will also be naturally inclined to ask these questions automatically in their minds in every mentoring setting. If you are professional teacher with twenty-five or more students, you will do this at least twenty-five times. In fact, because you will typically have less time to dedicate to each individual student, you need more practice in this exercise so that thinking this way will become more automatic for you. Even if you only have one or two mentees, practice this at least seven times by using test cases of people you know and perhaps could mentor someday.

I do encourage you, if you want to be a Student Whisperer, or a better Student Whisperer, to do the exercises. When you have completed them, go on to the next section.

The Healer/Warrior Balance

Another vital balance in mentoring is the blend between your Healer and Warrior characteristics:

Healer	Warrior
Soothes	Provokes
Embraces	Pushes
Comforts	Challenges
Loves	Trains
Relaxes	Leads
Laughs	Analyzes

As children and youth grow and go through the various stages of development, the ideal balance naturally changes. For example, children under 8 (what I call "Core Phase" in my books in the *Thomas Jefferson Education* series) need a lot more Healer than Warrior from their parents and mentors. From ages 9-13, Love of Learning Phase, most students need a little more Warrior than before—but still more

Healer than Warrior. During Scholar Phase, ages 14-18, most mentees need more Healer than Warrior—but a lot more Warrior than during their younger ages, and with the Warrior rapidly growing in influence.

Some youth need more Warrior than Healer during certain periods of their teenage years.[31] Of course, a blend is always needed for each mentee, and it is the role of mentors to discover the needed mix and deliver it. Those who master this process are Student Whisperers.

Let's go through a few exercises concerning these important Whispering characteristics. It is very important to do these exercises. Like those above, they are designed to train your mind to use the tools of Student Whispering.

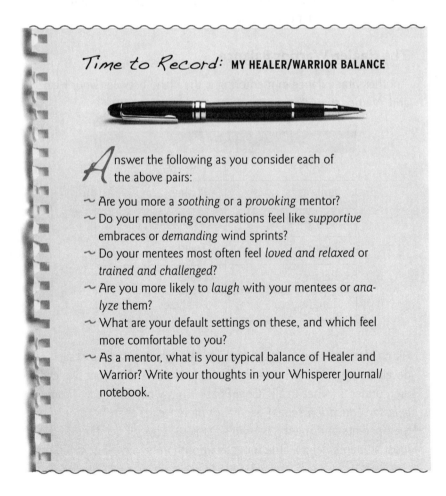

Time to Record: **MY HEALER/WARRIOR BALANCE**

*A*nswer the following as you consider each of the above pairs:

~ Are you more a *soothing* or a *provoking* mentor?
~ Do your mentoring conversations feel like *supportive* embraces or *demanding* wind sprints?
~ Do your mentees most often feel *loved and relaxed* or *trained and challenged*?
~ Are you more likely to *laugh* with your mentees or *analyze* them?
~ What are your default settings on these, and which feel more comfortable to you?
~ As a mentor, what is your typical balance of Healer and Warrior? Write your thoughts in your Whisperer Journal/notebook.

The Student Whisperer

Copy this chart and mark where your balance on it usually is:

Healer

Warrior

~ Are you closer to Healer, closer to Warrior (or do you tend toward one or the other)? Or are you right in the center?

~ What should your default blend of these be? This is a very important question. Ponder and take the time to really consider if your balance is exactly what you think it should be or if you need to change it a little or even a lot. Write your thoughts in your notebook.

Copy the same chart into your notebook and mark where you think you should be on it:

Healer

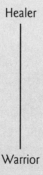

Warrior

Compare the first chart (where you feel you are in this mix) with the second (where you want to be). These are very important exercises, because to be a great Student Whisperer you need to be able to Whisper to yourself.

Consider the specific student/mentee whose name you first analyzed in the Manager/Artist exercise above. What is your Healer/Warrior balance as you work with this student? Mark it on a new chart:

Healer

Warrior

What balance does your student/mentor need from you right now? Mark it on another chart:

Healer

Warrior

Consider the difference between these last two charts. If your marks are in the same place on both charts, teach this model to your mentee and without suggesting what you think about your mentoring, have her answer these same questions about you and mark two blank charts. Then compare charts. If hers agree with yours, you are probably delivering what is needed.

If not, if you think your mentoring balance is what your mentee needs right now (but her charts disagree), do the same thing suggested above and try going with her charts for a while.

The Student Whisperer

Once you have two charts (one showing where you are as a mentor to this one student and the other recommending where you should be), sit down with a blank page in your Whisperer Journal and brainstorm how you can shift your balance. Remember that the middle is not always (or even usually) the best goal.

After brainstorming, make a specific plan of ways you can alter your mentoring to deliver the ideal blend the student needs. Be sure once again to cross out any brainstormed ideas that are about how the mentee needs to change. Focus on how you can change *your* attitude, expectations, plans and mentoring to be at the ideal mix of Healer and Warrior that your mentee needs.

Leave room for additional notes from upcoming exercises.

Remember that by doing these exercises with a specific mentee in mind, you are practicing Student Whispering.

Complete all these exercises before moving on.

Time to Record: WHISPERING EXERCISE

*R*epeat the series of exercises you just did, this time with each person you mentor. This is the work of Student Whispering. Consider each mentee. Chart how you mentor each, and what mix of Healer/Warrior each student needs from you right now. If you think you are mentoring any student perfectly right now, have this mentee do the same exercise. Brainstorm and plan how to be the ideal mentor for each mentee by altering your Healer/Warrior balance to what the mentee needs.

Take good notes on your thoughts about each mentee, and create a written plan for each mentee. Write all this in your Whisperer Journal. Leave room with each entry for additions from completing upcoming exercises.

Those who do this exercise will make thinking this way into a mental habit in a very short time. Once you have done this at least seven times (for your current and/or hypothetical mentees), your mind will naturally begin asking these questions, and others like them, whenever you mentor. Completing this exercise will significantly improve your subconscious and conscious Whispering habits and skills. It will make you think more like a Student Whisperer.

The Whispering Quadrants

Great mentors draw on their gifts as Managers, Artists, Healers and Warriors. Like a sound engineer on an audio console, they are able to tone down or dial up any of these as needed by a specific student at any given time. Student Whisperers also know how to detect what blend a student needs. Most importantly, Student Whisperers automatically ask themselves what each mentee needs in every mentorial interaction and between mentor connections. Student Whisperers also know how to deliver what is needed in language the mentee understands.

Student Whisperers understand the overall balance of mentoring styles and the general needs mentees have in each Quadrant.

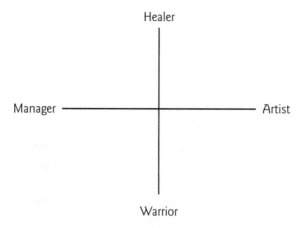

Each of the four Quadrants is different and important, and Student Whisperers may simultaneously have mentees in each.

Manager-Healer Quadrant

When a mentee is in the **Manager-Healer** Quadrant (as defined by what he *needs*) he benefits from:

- A more relaxed schedule
- Slowing down and focusing on quality
- Finding more balance and happiness in life

He is likely quite efficient and even driven, but needs to do *fewer* things *better*. He needs to learn to be more effective and do projects that really matter in a way that are deeply important.

Students in the Manager-Healer Quadrant are commonly found to be:

- Transitioning from one phase to the next
- Students in early Scholar Phase
- Students who are renegotiating lessons missed from a previous phase, but who are not in a Hate of Learning or gravely out-of-sync

Manager-Warrior Quadrant

Mentees who need the **Manager-Warrior** Quadrant benefit from:

- Order
- Structure
- Close guidance
- Lots of personal attention

These mentees need less personalization and more fitting in to a group or a challenging mentor-devised individual routine. The younger the mentee, the more frequently the personal interaction is needed with the mentor. For example, a ten-year-old might need hourly interaction, a fifteen-year-old might need mentor meetings twice a day, and a twenty-five-year-old might need mentor meetings twice a week. Mentees in this Quadrant need to see their mentor in action, doing things, setting the example, and being effective in achieving the things the mentee is striving toward.

Manager-Warrior Quadrant is commonly called for when a student is:

- At a Wall
- An adult student in Scholar Phase
- Just finished successful renegotiation of a lost phase[32]

Artist-Warrior Quadrant

Mentees who need the **Artist-Warrior** Quadrant of mentoring are typically creative, talented and accomplished, and they benefit from:

- Real discipline to go to a higher level of quality
- The focus to be on excellence through the basics, and doing the small things, the "wax on, wax off"[33] things that greatly impact quality

Student Whisperers need to really work within this student's talent fields and help get the basics right on. A helpful tool in this process is to have the mentee give feedback on the mentor's projects, as well as vice versa.

Students in this Quadrant are usually:

- Fully in Scholar, Depth or Mission Phase
- Ready to benefit from a high-quality, mentored formal classroom experience and/or a private coaching environment with high accountability
- Not in a transition between phases

Artist-Healer Quadrant

When a mentee needs the **Artist-Healer** Quadrant of mentoring, he benefits from:

- Being given a great deal of freedom
- Knowing that his mentor cares for him on a deeply personal level (not tied to achievement, talent or potential)
- Knowing that his mentor will be there for him if he needs any help
- Knowing that his mentor is busily working on things that are important to the mentor
- Feeling that his mentor will encourage and support his whole-some choices
- Feeling that his mentor is completely happy to let him go at his own pace
- Structure on only the most basic level of personal needs (meal-times, necessary chores, reasonable cooperation on family schedule)

This is the "summer break quadrant," where the mentee can pursue projects that are fun and interesting without the constant oversight of "authority" or high-touch accountability. He needs to relax, have fun and learn to *enjoy* things.

For older mentees who are moving out of a successful Manager-Warrior period, a week or more of sun, sand and quiet reading or surfing television channels is in order. A little romance is helpful for anyone old enough for it during this time. For younger mentees, this means having a wide variety of resources and unfettered creative play, while intersecting with expectations on such things as moral choices, personal grooming, sibling/peer interactions, family work, etc.

Most people need Artist-Healer mentoring at certain times in their lives. It is common to find in the Quadrant:

- Young children aged 0 to 8 or 9
- Students "detoxing" from a Hate of Learning
- Students recovering from trauma, ill health, or adapting to major change (adoption, foster care, death, divorce, blended family, move to new home, loss of friends or social status, etc.)
- Special needs students
- Students with highly exceptional, prodigy-level aptitude in a given area or areas

Regarding the last on this list—prodigy-level students: Such individuals often possess a high degree of introspective wisdom. They often feel isolated, misunderstood, and that they have no true peers. An objective consideration of their abilities, gifts and social needs reveals that these personal assessments are actually quite accurate.

They tend to identify more with older, accomplished people, and yet find that such people do not acknowledge them as peers. Yet, even when they are accepted as a peer in the area of their exceptional achievement, the lack of social skills or emotional maturity can tend to leave them ineffective at creating emotional or social bonds with those who respect them on an artistic or achievement level. In fact, one of the more challenging aspects of mentoring this type of student is that the mentor is often *not* as talented, intelligent, creative, etc., as the student—and there are no likely available mentor candidates that are.

To really help this student fully develop both as an artist/creator and as an individual, the best thing for a mentor to do is to create a strong emotional/social bond, and to be a true peer/friend on the social level. Note that in most cases this is the worst possible thing, as it interferes with the student's ability to accept meaningful counsel or to grow from praise/reprimands when they are called for; but in this case (where the mentor is not actually at a higher level in the area of the student's expertise, and *is* on a higher level in terms of relationship skills), it is of more enduring value for the student's development if they learn to function in a healthy friendship.

For this latter kind of student, the best mentoring includes giving her a lot of freedom, setting an example of the mentor self-guiding lots of learning, and meeting with her once a week (but usually not more often). Meetings should not be used to give assignments (which such students won't do anyway) or to make them feel guilty. The mentor can and should share his own personal triumphs and challenges, and revel in the achievements of the student—however small.

Such students respond positively only to honest affirmation, so praise is really the mentor's only effective feedback tool. Such students nearly always tend to be wary of praise at first, then warm up to it over time, and finally to seek it (if secretly). Continue giving honest praise, even when it looks like it does no good. Keep in mind that you are building rapport and trust with these affirmations, so any inflated or insincere praise could be disastrously counter-productive.

It is important to note that such students often purposely test the authority of mentors and parents, as well as their commitment to the relationship—usually by doing things that certainly deserve punishment, and even by denying that they've done anything of value. Their comfort zone is isolation and disappointment, and they are uncertain what may happen if they don't repel or disappoint the adult who is making overtures—so, even though they do long to be understood, appreciated, loved, etc., they are conflicted about whether they want the relationship to work. They feel safer not hoping for or counting on it.

The only effective response to misbehavior that requires a reaction (and be restrained and wise in determining if it actually does) is for mentors to be relaxed, even-tempered, and give firm, caring consequences without anger.[34] Parents and mentors must treat consequences as just natural, and separate them from the way the mentor feels about the mentee. Anger or passion on the part of the mentor sabotages growing trust and the will to try. The goal is firm, obvious and reasonable consequences applied by relaxed mentors who follow up immediately with quick smiles and genuine care.

Some people might argue that this kind of hands-off mentoring is just neglecting the student. While this may appear to be so at first glance, in reality a high percentage of this type of student constantly struggles in structured public and private schools. They generally fail to accomplish much in their youth (though they may have played the game in earlier years only to later become disillusioned, rebellious and/or inactive) no matter how much attention they are given, even in boarding and military schools.

One reason so many prodigies are at risk in our educational system is that their precociousness too often leads to a neglect of Core Phase. Their high aptitude impels the adults in their life to urge them to scholar-level accountability that completely eclipses the development toward Love of Learning.

Then, when they discover their personal power at the age when they should have been transitioning to Scholar Phase, they gain the perspective that they have been objectified by their most trusted adult caretakers and mentors, and that their "gift" is the bane to their happiness. They have missed out on early learning of critical social skills, they have not developed peer relationships, and their relationship with the adults that did not teach them to meet their spiritual and emotional needs grows contemptuous or distant. All of this leads to a most dangerous type of genius: the wounded idealist.

I once attended a seminar on educational psychology where an expert, one of the presenters, mentioned that in counseling incarcerated juvenile delinquents he noticed that nearly all of them were creative, artistic, or casual types. He wasn't sure what exactly to call this group, but as he researched it he learned that the place where schools most often failed their students were those who struggled with authoritative types of learning.

My point is not that this type of mentee is more likely to fail or to be delinquent, but simply that, of all types of students, those needing the Artist/Healer Quadrant fail to thrive in an environment of regimentation and pressure. What does this mean for a Student Whisperer? Through patient, personalized and inspirational mentoring these sensitive non-conformists not only *aren't* casualties of the system, but they can actually achieve brilliance.

What's more: once their emotional needs are met and they mature into a more complete individual (not defined solely or primarily by their virtuosity), they can ultimately choose to grow to a place where they can benefit from other types of learning environments and mentoring approaches. With appropriate nurturing they do not remain forever in their first (or second) developmental home, so to speak.

When wiser mentors give the Artist-Healer/freedom approach a try, the results can be astonishing. It often turns out that such students are among the very best and brightest of their generation! I have personally worked with dozens of this type of student, and I have only seen the freedom fail once—and the failure occurred because of long-established habits that led to legal problems for the student and removed him from the mentoring environment before the process had come to fruition.

Quadrant Mentoring Exercise

To start establishing the habit of identifying each mentee's Quadrant and planning for her needs, please complete the following exercise. As with past exercises in this chapter, I urge you to complete this exercise before moving on. It is designed to impact the Whispering mind and help prepare you to be an effective and even great Student Whisperer.

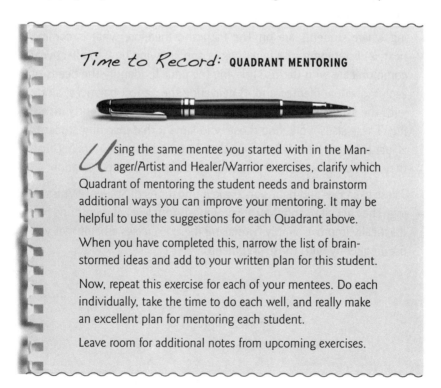

Time to Record: **QUADRANT MENTORING**

Using the same mentee you started with in the Manager/Artist and Healer/Warrior exercises, clarify which Quadrant of mentoring the student needs and brainstorm additional ways you can improve your mentoring. It may be helpful to use the suggestions for each Quadrant above.

When you have completed this, narrow the list of brainstormed ideas and add to your written plan for this student.

Now, repeat this exercise for each of your mentees. Do each individually, take the time to do each well, and really make an excellent plan for mentoring each student.

Leave room for additional notes from upcoming exercises.

If you have more than fifteen mentees, this may take a lot of time. Let me again assure you that it is worth the effort. The investment of your time and meditative thought will yield exponential returns in your effectiveness and your mentee's progress—and will ultimately save you and your mentee lost time and wasted effort.

This work is the basic weekly work of great mentoring and is central to Student Whispering. Without it, you just haven't done *your* homework as a mentor. The understanding, planning and individual insight that comes from asking these questions about each mentee is vital to Student Whispering. Those who don't want to do these things or don't make time for this work cannot as effectively Whisper, and are probably not ready to accept mentees.

Remember the three types of learning: the Stick, the Carrot and the Love Affair. Our purpose is to help the students fall passionately in love with studying and learning, and this is no simple feat. It requires consistent inspiration for transformational mentoring.

Mentors who understand and consistently apply the skills of 1) knowing where students are on The Path and therefore what is coming next, 2) listening to the inner voices and knowing how to effectively communicate with them, 3) paying the price to identify the needs of each individual mentee and 4) delivering the perfect balances, along with the skills we will cover in later chapters, are consistently *inspiring*. These skills work, and those who lament that inspiring students is just too hard have failed to do their homework as mentors because they did not fully comprehend the value of their own preparation.

These exercises and habits are basic foundations of Student Whispering. They are vital, and they are profound. Your level of mentoring will drastically improve simply by making these exercises a habit that you use frequently with those you mentor.

Seven Questions

by Oliver DeMille

Professors profess, usually in lecture and other times in written materials from articles to monographs to books. Teachers, in contrast, teach, and researchers research and publish. So, how are Mentors different from Professors or Teachers? *What do mentors do?* The answer is enlightening, and too few people really understand it. In fact, when most people in modern times hear about mentoring *versus* professing, they assume that mentors must be a lot like bosses at work—they give assignments and follow up on them. Add to this the idea of individualized mentoring, or personalized studies, and people picture mentors as tutors—working through the assignments with needy learners.

In fact, both of these visions have elements of truth, but neither is complete. Mentors do give assignments and follow up. They also tutor, coach and give personalized help and guidance. These are merely some of the *external* behaviors of mentoring. Mentors don't start with these things. They start by asking questions.

It would be impossible to list all the questions mentors ask. They ask their mentees a number of questions each time they interact with them; but most of all *they ask themselves questions about their mentees*. Indeed, if mentoring starts with the Socratic method of questioning students, Student Whispering begins even before that—by asking the basic questions about the mentee that the student herself isn't even aware of.

Indeed, most mentees aren't clear on either the questions *or* the answers to these deepest Whispering questions. Such questions require Student Whispering, and are seldom achieved by simply asking questions out loud and waiting for the mentee to answer.

We are already familiar with such questions from the earlier chapters. For example, the first set of Whispering questions a Student Whisperer needs to ask, answer and understand about each mentee include the following:

- What kind of mentor am I for this mentee right now?
- Where is my mentee on The Path?
- What Walls or Roadblocks is my mentee facing?
- What is the next step for my mentee on The Path?
- What is the Inner Critic telling my mentee?
- What is the Inner Judge telling my mentee?
- What is the Inner Victim telling my mentee?
- What is the Inner Rebel telling my mentee?
- Does my mentee seem to be listening to some other negative voice, and if so what is that voice telling her?
- What is the Real Her telling my mentee?
- What is the Inspirer telling my mentee?
- Where is my mentee on the Manager/Artist balance?
- Where do I tend to be as a mentor on the Manager/Artist balance?
- What kind of mentor does my mentee need me to be right now on the Manager/Artist balance?
- What changes do I need to make to effectively be the mentor she needs right now on the Manager/Artist balance?
- Where is my mentee on the Healer/Warrior balance?
- Where do I tend to be as a mentor on the Healer/Warrior balance?
- What kind of mentor does she need me to be right now on the Healer/Warrior balance?
- What changes do I need to make to effectively be the mentor she needs right now on the Healer/Warrior balance?
- What Whispering Quadrant does my mentee need right now, and what does this tell me?

- What Whispering Quadrant am I in right now, and how do I need to progress in order to be the best mentor I can?

These are all Whispering questions. Few professors, teachers, researchers, mentors or parents in the world deeply consider, ponder, answer, write down and plan from these questions for each person they mentor—each month, or more often if needed. Those who do are doing the work of Student Whispering. Those who learn to do it reflexively, consistently and persistently are Student Whisperers.

Of course, not every answer you feel and every plan you make based on Whispering questions will perfectly hit the spot. But those who are applying these techniques are Student Whispering, and over time your persistence in asking and applying the answers to such questions will make you a great Student Whisperer.

If you find that this is difficult at first, and even after you've been using it for a long time, you know you are on The Path. Of course it is challenging; but as you persist, as you refuse to give up, and as you see how often you get it right and truly help a mentee to make drastic leaps forward, you will relax, enjoy and come to trust the process— and she will come to trust you.

Another way to see this is to consider how you would be as a mentor right now without these questions. However much you struggle to mentor, you will do much better if you are consistently asking these questions and truly trying to understand your mentees and help them with all your heart.

By taking the time to ask the Whispering questions about each mentee and then planning accordingly, you will without a doubt take your mentoring to a higher level. You will care more, invest more, give more, help more—and eventually you will truly and deeply understand more about each person you mentor.

Key Questions Exercise

There are other key questions Student Whisperers ask, in addition to those listed above. One of the best ways to master these questions is to ask them about yourself and experience what it feels like to ask, answer and plan accordingly. It is extremely valuable to simultaneously answer the same questions about someone you mentor.

Time to Record: MY KEY QUESTIONS

Key Question #1: Your Biggest Dreams
Please do this exercise in your Whisperer Journal.

First, draw three columns on a blank page. Label the columns:

Questions   *Me*   *Mentee's name**

(*Write the name of one person you mentor, whichever name comes to mind, in the third column. You might choose your most successful mentee, or the one who seems to be struggling most, or just the first face or name that comes to mind. Later you will repeat this exercise for each person you mentor, so don't worry about skipping someone.)

In column one write the following:

"What are your three biggest dreams?"

Once you have written this in the first column, take a few minutes and ponder on the following prompts for yourself:

~ What are your three biggest dreams?
~ Your most important dreams?
~ What do you really dream of being, or doing?
~ What do you really want the most?

Whatever your three biggest dreams are, write them down in the second column. It's okay to write more than three if you prefer.

When you are done with these, spend some time pondering your list of big dreams.

The Student Whisperer

~ Why are they important to you?
~ Who would you be without them?
~ How important are they?
~ Are they central to your life?
~ Are they a lot of fun?

Don't listen to the Inner Critic or Judge on this. These are *your* dreams, and it doesn't matter what the negative voices say. Also, don't worry about whether or not you can achieve them—the Victim voice has no say in this either. Sometimes having the dreams is enough, regardless of whether you achieve them or not. This isn't a goal-setting exercise. You don't have to plan your dreams. You are just trying to get to know yourself better. Whatever your dreams are, smile and enjoy that you have big dreams.

If you have a hard time with this exercise, keep trying until you can write three things you dream of—they can be as simple as having extra money each month after the bills are paid or winning a free trip to Paris. Or they can be more elaborate.

When you are done with this portion of the exercise, answer the same question about your mentee (the one whose name is at the top of column three): What are his biggest dreams? Write down at least three of his dreams in column 3.

I am always amazed at how hard this is for most people. When I teach this in teacher trainings in an institutional setting, I usually get lots of blank stares from teachers when I first assign this. It is even harder for parents, it seems; but for those who try, it works in a big way! I learned this on my own, and I have seen it repeated by many others.

This exercise was hard for me when I first did it. I knew my mentees as students, including their attitudes in class, their level of writing and thinking skills, their punctuality or lack of it, what kind of clothes they usually wore, and a number of other little things gleaned from interviews in person and comments in classes. *But their dreams?* I was clueless.

Still, I tried to figure them out; and frankly, the harder I tried, the more surprised I was at how much I *did* know.

- *The young man who dreamed of building a successful business.*

How did I know that? Was it even true? I kept trying.

- *The girl whose main goal was to become a wife and mother.*

- *The girl who wanted to be a doctor and was at the wrong school in the wrong major.*

I had no idea until I tried. When I talked to her, asking lots of questions without telling her what I thought, she independently came back to me with the same conclusion.

- *The professional who felt that his life was missing something, and yearned to enter politics.*

Again, he hadn't mentioned this to me, but it just felt accurate.

I did the exercise, wrote down the dreams I could come up with, and wondered if I was making them all up. Then I applied the same exercise to my wife and each of my children. (I should clarify here, just so I don't run into trouble, that I do not consider myself a mentor to my wife.)

These were easier in some ways, because I know my family members so well. In other ways it was even harder, because some of my mental habits and misperceptions had so much history and momentum behind them. Still, I made myself do the exercise, pondering and writing down what I thought were the dreams of close family members and those I mentored academically.

Then I scheduled meetings with each of them and asked them point blank, "What are your three biggest dreams?" Some of them hemmed and hawed a little, but I was patient—and they eventually began sharing. I didn't tell them what I had written until they were done, and I shared many amazed moments with students and my kids when we compared their lists to mine.

The Student Whisperer

I was actually right on a lot of things. There were, of course, many that I had missed, and a number that I'd written down but the student had never even considered. Yet, *all* of these were fuel for some fabulous discussions as we came to wonder why I had not considered something, or why I had. Some planted seeds for future dreams, and others were rejected outright and I had to re-evaluate my understanding of my mentee. All of them led to greater understanding, meaningful dialogue and deeper learning about the wonderful people I was mentoring.

I have repeated this exercise many times since, and have found it to be one of the most important tools of quality mentoring. After all, if you don't know the dreams of those you mentor, what exactly *do* you know about them? On what do you base your counsel and assignments? Student Whisperers need to know the dreams of their mentees, and the best way to understand this is to:

- First, try to brainstorm what you think their biggest dreams are, and write them down
- Second, without telling them what you've written, ask them directly what their biggest dreams are, and to write them down
- Third, meet and compare lists, starting with their lists and then sharing yours
- Fourth, discuss each dream on both lists, ask questions, and really get to know your mentee on a deeper level

This is an extremely powerful exercise! I recommend doing it with each mentee at least annually, and referring back to it and updating it monthly. You are simply a different kind of mentor when you know (or even just try to know) the biggest dreams of all those you mentor.

Time to Record: MORE KEY QUESTIONS

Key Questions #2 – 7: Your Biggest Fears, Angers, Goals, etc.

*W*rite the following question in column one (allow ample space for revisions and additions):

What are your biggest fears?"

Repeat the exercise outline above for Question #1 by answering this new question, first for yourself (column 2) and then for your mentee (column 3).

This is a sensitive question and should never be asked to a mentee in a rote way, as part of checking off this question on a checklist. Indeed, in some settings you won't ever want to ask this question directly to your mentee. For example, parents of public and private elementary through high-school children get upset (and I think reasonably) when teachers ask such questions. Be smart about the time and way you use this, if at all. This is primarily for college and adult (Depth Phase) mentees.

With all of this said, this is a powerful and important question if used in the right way. At the very least, go through this exercise for yourself. If you are mentoring adults in a college or professional setting, this can be a valuable question if used wisely. For parents, it is a great question to ask about your children every six months or so.

As we did above, start by asking yourself what things your child or mentee most fears, and then, if it feels right, ask them and discuss both lists. Of course, many adults won't answer with their deepest fears, but the ones you do discuss will be valuable and helpful. You are probably not a counselor, so this isn't about *fixing* them. It's just a get-to-know-you process that helps you to do a better job as a mentor. The easiest way to do this may be to ask your mentee what his Inner Critic voice says about him a lot.

Write the following in column 1:

> *"What is your biggest anger?"*

Follow the pattern above, first for yourself and then for your mentee. Again, use discretion in how, when, and even if, you use this. With adults, especially twenty-somethings, it can be extremely valuable. I am amazed at how often anger at a certain situation or experience pushes a young person in the direction of his career field. A conversation about this with a mentor can make all the difference in helping a young person understand herself and her deepest motivations.

As a mentor, facing your own fears and angers is vital. Even if you never have such a conversation with anyone you mentor, doing these exercises for yourself can significantly improve your ability to mentor, lead, empathize, care, understand and Whisper.

Parents, above all, can benefit from knowing the answers to these questions about fears and angers.

In column one (you will probably be on your 2nd to 5th page by now), write the following question:

> *"What four things do you most need from your mentor in the next few months?"*

Take the time to really answer the question for yourself, and write your answers in column 2.

When this is complete, answer the same question for your mentee: "What four things does 'John' most need from his mentor in the next few months?" Write the answers in column 3.

Repeat this exercise, using the following question:

> *"What five things do you need your mentor to be?"*

Of course, *being* is very different than *doing*, and all of us need our mentors to be certain things. List what you feel you need from your own mentor in column 2, and what your mentee ("John") needs *you* to be in column 3.

In column 1 write this question:

> *"If scientists discovered that the rotation*
> *and revolutions of the earth were changing*
> *slightly and that we all would have one*
> *more hour in each day, what would you*
> *do with that hour?"*
> (That's 7 hours more a week, 30 more hours
> a month, and 365 hours more a year. What
> would you do with the extra time?)

Really think about this, and write your answer in column 2. Take the time to do this well.

Now, what would you recommend that your mentee do with this extra hour? Write it in column 3.

Finally, go back and consider all your answers for yourself in column 2, all the answers from questions 1-6. Using this information:

Write down one major thing you want to change.

Write the one thing you think will make the most difference in your life if you change it now, or the one thing you feel you really *should* change.

Then write a plan to do it and follow the plan.

Once you have done this, do the same for your mentee. You can't compel him to make the change, of course, but you can set up a special meeting and tell him you've really been thinking about him and you have a suggestion for him—one thing you want him to consider. I probably would not *assign* it to him, but simply share your feeling and ask him to think about it.

If he follows your suggestion, that's great. If not, trust his decision. Mentors are guides, after all, not sergeants. Your purpose in all this was to become a better mentor, to understand your mentee at a much deeper level, not to take over his life decisions. Just to be a more effective and inspiring guide—that is the role of the Student Whisperer.

These Whispering questions are so powerful! Imagine a mentor who doesn't know the dreams of his mentee; he is severely limited in his ability to really guide. Or imagine a parent who has no idea what her child's biggest fears and angers are; she has perhaps lost a vital connection and the ability to help, love and even protect her son or daughter in some situations. Imagine a teacher, professor or principal who has lost touch with what her students actually need her to do and be, or who doesn't even bother to wonder about these needs.

Imagine the classrooms full of glazed-over eyes and the nation full of bored, frustrated, or at best, brown-nosing students who lose their love of learning and fall short of their potential. Mentors can do better, simply by asking the great mentoring questions—consistently and frequently. Student Whisperers learn to ask them deliberately *and* instinctively, helping students see more in themselves than they could have or would have on their own.

Such mentees become so much more than they would have without Student Whisperers. All because their parents, teachers and professors didn't settle for mediocrity—but instead sought out greatness by simply doing one key thing with dedication and commitment: *Asking questions*. Week after week, month after month, year after year—great mentors ask the key Whispering questions about each student. This is the internal and external work—and the genius—of Student Whispering. Through this process both the mentor and her students come face-to-face with greatness.

Now, repeat all seven exercises in this chapter for each person you mentor. Keep all your notes in your Whisperer Journal.

Inspiring Archetypes

by Oliver DeMille

In the introduction I noted that many years ago a gentleman at a convention had felt impressed by the message I presented on Leadership Education, and—professional consultant that he was—urged me to focus my efforts to help parents and teachers grow into inspiring mentors.

I started that night developing a seminar called "The Student Whisperer," and Tiffany and I went to work bringing together other exercises and ideas for this book. We pulled from our favorite books on great teaching, previous research and articles on what is inspiring in education, and all our experiences as mentors in the Leadership Education model.

As we have taught different parts of this material in various settings and to thousands of people over time, one element has often stood out as a favorite among many seminar participants. The idea that is often the most exciting to people is the concept of *archetypes*.[35]

I am certainly no expert on archetypes, but I have read everything I can get my hands on about them. They are truly a fascinating idea, one that was popularized mostly by the thinker Carl Jung. Jung taught that human beings all have a conscious as well as an unconscious mind, and that the major parts of the unconscious mind include our genetic inheritances, experiences, beliefs, and values—among other things. Along with these, he taught, each of our unconscious minds has a collective consciousness, a set of ideas and ideals that we have in common with most other humans.

One of the key ways to organize the ideas and ideals of the collective consciousness is *archetypes*. For example, many children play games where they are orphans—even if they've never met an orphan. The idea of being a child estranged from a parent is somehow part of our societal heritage. Other universal archetypes include such iconic roles as Thieves, Warriors, Maidens in Distress, Pirates, Rescuers, Mothers, Healers and Young Lovers. There are many others.

Since Student Whispering is about understanding the quiet, often hidden, voices that influence our students—and using these voices to help inspire students—the use of archetypes is extremely helpful.

Whereas "archetypes" is a new word for many people, it may at first feel a little abstract; but most people get the hang of it pretty quickly. To make sure we're on the same page, let's get straight to an exercise using archetypes.

"My Archetypes" Exercise

Read through the following Archetype List[36] to familiarize yourself with it. Then make three copies of the list. I suggest not writing in the book because most people who use this list once end up wanting to use it over and over again. With the three copies you can use one or two up and still have a master to tuck inside the back cover of this book for future duplication. (You can download a pdf of this list at http://student-whisperer.com/free-gifts/.)

ARCHETYPE LIST

Abuser	Destroyer	Liberator
Actor	Disciple	Loser
Addict	Dreamer	Lover
Adonis	Drifter	Magician
Advocate	Elder	Martyr
Alchemist	Enchantress	Master
Amateur	Explorer	Matriarch
Amazon	Father	Mediator
Ambassador	Flit	Mentor
Analyst	Friend	Mercenary
Angel	Gambler	Merchant
Architect	Glutton	Messiah
Artisan	Goddess	Midas
Assassin	Guide	Minister
Avenger	Guru	Miser
Beggar	Healer	Monk
Black Widow	Hedonist	Monster
Boss	Herald	Mother
Bully	Hermit	Mystic
Caretaker	Hero	Nomad
Casanova	Heroine	Nun
Charlatan	Icon	Nurse
Chef	Innocent	Nymph
Child	Inventor	Olympian
Clown	Judge	Oracle
Companion	King	Orphan
Comrade	Knight	Patriarch
Coward	Leader	Pilgrim
Critic	Legislator	Pioneer

The Student Whisperer

ARCHETYPE LIST

Pirate	Servant	Traitor
Poet	Shaman	Trickster
Preacher	Shape shifter	Tutor
Prodigal	Siren	Vampire
Prince	Slave	Victim
Princess	Sleuth	Visionary
Prophet	Soldier	Wanderer
Puppet	Spy	Warrior
Queen	Stepchild	Weaver
Rabbi	Steward	Widow
Rock star	Storyteller	Wizard
Ruler in Exile	Student	Workaholic
Savior	Teacher	Wounded Child
Scholar	Tease	Wounded Healer
Seeker	Temptress	
Seer	Thief	

Time to Record: **MY ARCHETYPES**

*T*ake a copy you made of the foregoing List of Archetypes and write your name on it to use for this exercise. When you have completed your work with it, include it in your Whisperer Journal/notebook.

Now read through the list again and underline each archetype that seems or feels like "You"—which you identify with—whether you like the archetype at first or not.

Once that is done, slow down and go through the list again. This time narrow the list down to the top 12 that seem the most like you. Circle these to set them apart from the others.

Now, narrow this down to one—the one archetype that seems the most like you right now in your life. Take the time to ponder and determine this. Put a box around this archetype, or write it in your own handwriting in the margin.

Finally, pick the one archetype you would most *like* to be. *Of all those on the list, which do you most wish to be?* Put asterisks on either side of it, or write it down in bold letters in your own handwriting.

At this point, we are halfway done with this exercise. Now repeat all these items, this time about your mentee, the "John Doe" mentee you used in the last chapter. With this mentee in mind, do the following:

~ Use an unmarked copy of the list of archetypes, and write your mentee's name on it.
~ Circle the twelve archetypes you think are most like your mentee.
~ Narrow the list down to 1, and put a box around it.
~ Consider which you think your mentee would most like to be, and put asterisks beside it.

Please don't skip these exercises, or you will miss a great opportunity to improve your mentoring and become a Student Whisperer.

With this exercise completed, both for you and your mentee, you are ready to answer the following great Whisperer questions. As in earlier chapters, please write the answers in your notebook with the mentee's name at the top of the page.

Time to Record: MY ARCHETYPES

*W*hat type of mentor do you need to be to help your mentee with her archetype? List at least 5 to 6 things about this.

What are some specific changes you should make to achieve the archetype you want?

What does your top archetype tell you about yourself? Ponder, brainstorm, and take the time to really think about this. You will likely be surprised at how much this one-word archetype can tell you about yourself. If you aren't getting much, start listing characteristics of the archetype (like powerful, noble, wise, regal, protector, imperious, and strong for the King archetype). Ask yourself how these apply to you.

What does the top archetype you chose for your mentee tell you about him? Again, take the time to really consider this and think deeply about it. Write your notes and ideas as thoughts come to your mind. Of course, your mentee would probably select a different archetype for himself than you choose for him, but that's okay. In this exercise you are exploring your view of him.

Once you have completed all of these exercises, give a third copy of the archetype list to your mentee and have him fill it out: 12 things, then the one that he thinks is most like him, and finally the one he most wants to become. Do not show him your list for him until he has completed his. Have a long discussion with your mentee about why he chose the 12, 1 and 1. You will almost certainly learn a great deal about him that you never knew before. Share your list about him and discuss the differences between the two lists.

These discussions are often profound and even fun. As you use this method over time you will come to see what an effective mentoring tool it can be. Sometimes just telling people that this is a kind of personality test—which almost everyone has experienced nowadays—will help take the strangeness out of it. It might also be helpful to show them your own list and explain why you think your 12 and 1 are the most like you.

Again, the purpose of this is to help you understand your mentee better, Whisper more effectively, and inspire more consistently. Few things are more inspiring, especially for youth, than learning more about themselves, and pondering who they might want to become—and why. Archetypes are a profound way of helping with this process, since they naturally connect with universal themes, ideas and ideals. If you are dealing with adults as opposed to youth, the exercise is just as valuable—if you can get them to engage it and invest in the process.

The critical catalyst of great education is inspiration, and the central role of mentoring is finding ways to effectively inspire. Student Whisperers are those who know how to excel in this challenging role. A combination of the following can greatly help: The Path, the Real You and Inspirer voices, the Artist/Manager and Healer/Warrior balances, the Whispering Quadrants, the key Whispering questions, and inspiring archetypes. Each is a major source of potential inspiration on its own, and together they ensure that no mentor who is truly trying should fail to inspire strongly and frequently.

Now, repeat the archetype exercise for each person you mentor. Again, this is the work of Student Whispering, and it is effective and often profound.

Getting the Most from Your Mentors

by Oliver DeMille & Tiffany Earl

Mentoring is an art. So is getting the most from your mentors. Our purpose here is to learn more about improving both of these essential and profound skills. People who succeed are successful on The Path, and nothing is more helpful on The Path than great mentoring.

Studying mentoring from the viewpoint of the *mentee* is very important to Student Whispering, and is the focus of this chapter. As mentors, we learn many things about mentoring by seeing the whole process from the mentee's perspective. In the next chapter, we will reverse viewpoints and study mentoring from the mentor's view. Both are elemental to understanding the whole process.

Let's take a moment and do some self-reflection. There are at least eleven lessons that are very helpful to anyone trying to work with a formal mentor—especially if this is your first time (or if you feel that you failed at it the last time). This functions like a workshop, and each assignment is designed to help you get more out of your mentored experience. For best results, do not move on until you have completed each exercise, as each lesson builds on the last. We recommend that you use your Whisperer Journal or notebook for this project.

Note that these lessons are "classic," meaning they are worth studying over and over—because you learn more each time. If you ever feel frustrated with your mentor or your progress on The Path, you will almost always be able to find the solution by repeating these eleven exercises.

The first time through, do them at whatever pace feels comfortable and right to you. You can do them all in one day, one a week for eleven weeks, or anything in between. Just do them in order, and take the time to do each lesson well.

Once you have completed all of them, we highly recommend that you discuss them with your mentor(s).

Here are eleven of the great lessons of being a good **mentee**! Get out your Whisperer Journal and go to work.

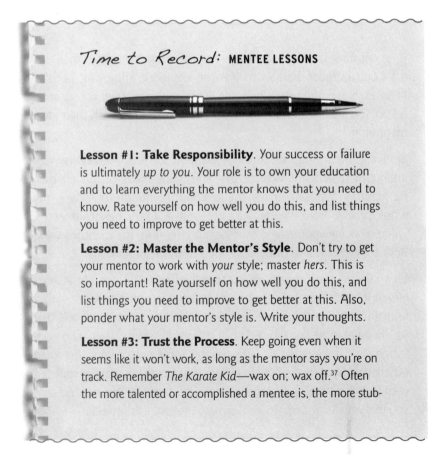

Time to Record: **MENTEE LESSONS**

Lesson #1: Take Responsibility. Your success or failure is ultimately *up to you*. Your role is to own your education and to learn everything the mentor knows that you need to know. Rate yourself on how well you do this, and list things you need to improve to get better at this.

Lesson #2: Master the Mentor's Style. Don't try to get your mentor to work with *your* style; master *hers*. This is so important! Rate yourself on how well you do this, and list things you need to improve to get better at this. Also, ponder what your mentor's style is. Write your thoughts.

Lesson #3: Trust the Process. Keep going even when it seems like it won't work, as long as the mentor says you're on track. Remember *The Karate Kid*—wax on; wax off.[37] Often the more talented or accomplished a mentee is, the more stubborn he is about trusting the mentor. Rate yourself on how well you do this, and list things you need to do to be more humble and teachable. Then, if possible, ask your mentor to rate you on this and give you suggestions for improvement.

Lesson #4: Keep the Mentor in the Loop. Don't waste his time, but *do* keep him informed step-by-step. Details make all the difference. Oliver: For example, I remember counseling with an individual who was struggling as a mentor, and giving a specific suggestion that seemed like the perfect solution. When the mentor returned frustrated, it was only then that I found out that I was giving advice for college age when the mentee was actually 12 or 13 years old!

Seriously, details make a lot of difference. Most mentors learn to ask right away: "boy or girl, how old, etc.?" Make sure you tell your mentor the details! Rate yourself on how well you do this, and list things you need to improve. Then, if possible, ask your mentor to rate you and make suggestions.

Lesson #5: Ask the Right Questions; Follow Through. When you need help, ask your mentor. Don't ask questions when the mentor has already given you the answers. Don't return over and over again for help when you haven't done what you were counseled to do. Rate yourself on how well you do this, and list things you need to improve to on this.

Lesson #6: Act. When you feel an internal tug to do something, *act*. Great mentors want to work with people who have a bias toward action. Don't act against your gut or mentorial direction, but don't sit around waiting for it. Rate yourself on how well you do this, and list things you need to improve to get better at this.

Lesson #7: Welcome Correction. When you make a mistake, or even just when your mentor says you've made a mistake, welcome the mentor's feedback. Act on it and change. Rate yourself on how well you do this, and list things you need to improve to get better at this. If possible, get your mentor's rating and ideas on this also.

Lesson #8: Under Stress, Listen! When you are frustrated, follow the mentor's counsel. This is true always, but under pressure it is easy to ignore this lesson. Don't! Stressful times are when you need your mentor's advice the most. Most mentees (us included) have made the mistake of ignoring this lesson, and the results are needlessly painful. Remember that word: *painful.* Listen to your mentor. Rate yourself on how well you do this, and list things you need to improve to get better at this.

Lesson #9: Under Stress, Really Listen! When *your mentor* is frustrated, REALLY follow the mentor's counsel. This is when you will learn the most important lessons. Ironically, when parents are most concerned about substantive issues is when their children tend to tune out their counsel. Don't make this same mistake. Rate yourself on how well you do this, and list things you need to improve to get better at this.

Lesson #10: Get Past the Myths about Mentoring!
First, closely read and study this chart:

Common Myths	Reality
Mentoring implies one-on-one.	Mentoring means getting you to progress on The Path. Sometimes this requires one-on-one coaching, but mentoring is much, much more than this. Really great mentors incorporate multiple mentoring environments beyond the common one-on-one.
"I'm a unique mentee—I should challenge all my mentor's systems."	You'll only waste his time—and yours. Smart mentees master the mentor's systems and style, not the other way around.

Common Myths	Reality
All mentors are the same.	Each mentor is unique—effectiveness on The Path means learning and adapting to your next mentor's style.
It's my mentor's fault.	It's your life; it's your Path. The burden of action and results rests on the mentee, not the mentor. Great mentors do make mistakes, and they will usually admit them and apologize. Don't waste your time getting caught up on them.
The mentee picks the mentor.	The mentor picks the mentee, or there *is* no relationship.
Mentoring only deals with competence.	Great mentoring grows both character *and* competence, especially when formal mentoring is combined with informal mentoring.
My mentor's core views don't matter.	Your mentor's core views don't have to be identical to yours, but they do matter greatly. Communicate about them, and consider and perhaps discuss openly how the differences inform your approach to the relationship and the process.

The biggest key to being a great mentee and getting the most from your mentor is to get the right mentor and then do what the mentor says. Be humble. If your mentor is ahead of you on The Path, there is a reason. Trust her.

Consider how well you do in not following each of these myths, and write your thoughts on how to improve.

Lesson #11: Learn From Both Sides. Mentees are better if they've also been good mentors themselves. That's not surprising, of course, but so few people think of it when it will help them the most: When they are mentees!

Write things you've learned about mentoring from being mentored, and things you learned about being a mentee by mentoring.

If you did your best on all these exercises, you gained some valuable self-knowledge to apply to your Path.

The Art of Mentoring

by Oliver DeMille & Tiffany Earl

While on The Path, we often find ourselves helping others along The Path. This is very fulfilling and challenging work.

In this section we'll cover a number of essential lessons about the art of mentoring, and guide you through exercises designed specifically to help you become an even better mentor than you already are. We'll keep it focused and brief, because mentoring is an art and *you* are the expert on your own skills and development as a mentor.

For best results, we recommend that you don't approach this intellectually as much as emotionally. Despite the fact that the culture we all live in has often taught the contrary for at least the last forty years, our emotions and intuition matter to our learning. Honestly, even though you've probably read or thought about many of these ideas in the past, we offer them as opportunities for you to become a much better mentor by helping these concepts get deeply into your heart. Feel them!

We suggest that you go slowly, and follow each exercise as outlined. We've seen these help some truly excellent mentors become even better! As mentors we can always improve, and we've witnessed these special exercises work over and over.

We also recommend that you limit yourself to only one exercise a day, one each for the next nine days. The time between exercises will allow your subconscious to think about, ponder, consider and more deeply incorporate each lesson. Again, just browsing these intellectually or even memorizing them won't do you much good. The goal of these exercises is for you to deeply experience, feel and incorporate them into your life.

Like we said at the beginning of this book, we want the things you learn here to leap off the page and transform from ink and letters into your DNA and psyche! So please do yourself the favor of going slowly—not more than one exercise per day, and even more slowly if you feel the need.

As with the earlier exercises, use your Whisperer Journal or notebook to record.

One more thing: *Enjoy!*

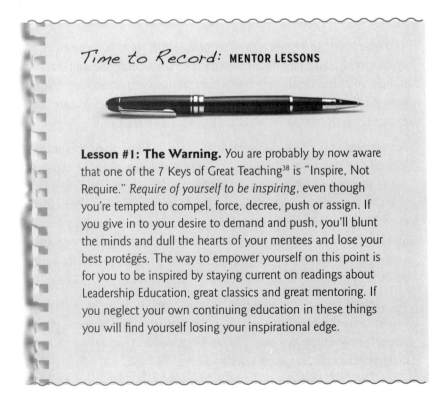

Time to Record: **MENTOR LESSONS**

Lesson #1: The Warning. You are probably by now aware that one of the 7 Keys of Great Teaching[38] is "Inspire, Not Require." *Require of yourself to be inspiring,* even though you're tempted to compel, force, decree, push or assign. If you give in to your desire to demand and push, you'll blunt the minds and dull the hearts of your mentees and lose your best protégés. The way to empower yourself on this point is for you to be inspired by staying current on readings about Leadership Education, great classics and great mentoring. If you neglect your own continuing education in these things you will find yourself losing your inspirational edge.

The Student Whisperer

Think of it as you do daily rest and nutrition, or feeding a fire. A complete intellectual understanding of these processes does not fill the need for daily nourishment or fuel. If you are to be consistently inspirational, you need daily inspiration by returning to the source and experiencing the classics of mentoring on an ongoing basis.

By daily immersing yourself in the paradigm of being a transformational mentor you will trust the process, and the tendency to manipulate or compel progress from your students will be foreign to you. That doesn't mean you aren't sharp or demanding at times—just that such times are more powerful because they are the exception and not the rule. You want to work with leaders and protégés, not mere "underlings". Brainstorm and list ways you can improve on this.

Lesson #2: The Contrast. The difference between you and the protégé is that you see the whole picture while the protégé only sees part. Help him see the whole as often as you can. Brainstorm how you can improve on this, by listing each person you mentor and brainstorming ways to help each see the "bigger picture" that most applies to him.

Lesson #3: The Role. Know your role! Your job is to *inspire* the mentee or protégé to greatness. Remember that as a mentor you are a teacher, not the boss. Mentoring is an *educational* process, even if it is carried out in a business or a home.

There is a myth in modern education that underpins most failures in schools, business and leadership. You must understand and avoid this deadly myth in order to help your mentees or protégés achieve success. The myth is: *It is the teacher's job to educate the student.* It isn't. The truth is that *only the student can educate the student.* The teacher's job is to *inspire* the student to do the hard work of self-education.

The solution is for you to be very clear that *your job is to inspire.* If, as the mentor, you are trying to manage details or control outcomes, you will give less energy and focus to inspiration, and the results will be inferior. Mentors must inspire—indeed, great mentors put their whole effort into inspiring. The mentee does the rest.

Brainstorm how you can improve on this (list each person you mentor and brainstorm for him individually).

Lesson #4: Go with your Gut. Trust your own style. You succeeded by going for it—now is not the time to second-guess yourself or to change your style. If you need to improve, do it. This book is full of suggestions to turn your mentoring into effective and inspiring Whispering. Use *your* strengths to mentor.

Brainstorm how you can improve on this.

Lesson #5: Use the Classics. Go to the greats yourself, the masters in your field—and other fields. As they inspire you, you will be more inspiring.

Brainstorm great works in your field, and beyond, which you have yet to master but should, and list them. Then read and study them.

Lesson #6: Be Educable. Your mentees and protégés will likely teach you as much as (or more than) you teach them. Remember—they have genius and greatness within them, and are destined to be leaders. Their nascent insights can be some of your most valuable teachers. Be willing and open to change when it is called for.

Brainstorm how you can improve on this, and list each person you mentor and the most important thing you have learned from her (or should learn from her).

Lesson #7: Use many Mentoring Environments.
Identify what the mentee needs, and help her experience it. Consider the 5 Environments of Mentoring[39] (including field experiences and simulations), and adding to those: outdoor treks, service projects, etc.

List each person you mentor, and brainstorm new experiences, opportunities or events that might greatly help her.

The Student Whisperer

Lesson #8: The Challenge. The hardest and most important part of your role is leading the mentee or protégé to *"aha!"* An "aha!" is a paradigm shift that literally transforms his perceptions, direction, abilities and vision. These "aha!s" come perhaps most frequently as the mentor and student(s) "debrief" (consider and discuss in depth) the student's impressions and experiences with: classics, the 5 Environments, conversations, student teaching opportunities, projects, relationships, assignments, guest presenters, formal events, casual social occasions, etc. Student Whisperers use the ever-important Debriefing process to help the mentee truly capture the lessons from these environments and experiences. Debriefing helps to anchor these lessons through associations and applications that bring them to life in the student's psyche and soul. This is, "aha!"

Brainstorm how you can improve on this (again, list each mentee individually).

Lesson #9: Know your mentee. You know your mentee is learning if he is laughing, crying, sighing, grunting, or dancing. These are good signs. Sometimes we get discouraged when we see tears. Sometimes we hold back and don't laugh. Laughter can be great mentoring. Growls and grunts can be wonderful. Know and recognize the many ways a mentee can demonstrate that he is learning and that you are having influence.

Brainstorm how you can improve on this with each mentee.

After you have completed all nine exercises, take some time to collect and copy the information about each individual mentee in a section especially for them. This is more than a data entry job. This seemingly "extra" step is actually the most important one in the whole process. It will most likely open your mind to new insights beyond those you got from mere pondering, and anchor the thoughts you had even more deeply. Do not miss this opportunity to review and record. It is a form of Debriefing that will yield the most valuable insights of the whole exercise.

The rest of the material in this chapter will greatly help you as you seek to master the art of mentoring.

Thirteen Mentoring Improvements

Following are thirteen key things that can help you immediately and significantly improve your effectiveness as a quality mentor. With each, please take time to consider how you can improve your mentoring with each person you mentor (list them by name, and then brainstorm and write how you might be a better mentor to each). Successfully completing this workshop will make you a Student Whisperer.

1. **Pass on a Legacy.** As a Formal Mentor, you are passing on a legacy, not just skills or information. There are various types of legacies, including: assets, position, confidence, vision, and many others. Vision is by far the most important of these.

    If a mentee doesn't share your vision (e.g. of a great liberal arts education, or of your mission in the world, or of the role of martial arts or visual arts in a society, etc.), she is probably not the right mentee for you. Your mentees either need to catch the vision, or you need to release them to find other mentors. Vision is incredibly powerful, and contra-vision mentoring isn't really mentoring—it's indoctrination.

    Write your thoughts and ideas for improvement with each mentee.

2. **Be a Mentor.** As we stated in the introduction: You can't pass on vision without mentoring. You can tell stories, and a few people might listen. But to really pass on vision you must mentor protégés over a period of time. Not all of them will catch your vision, and a few people you don't personally mentor *will* catch your vision; but if you're not actively mentoring over a long period of time, your vision probably won't get passed on. If your vision is important, you need to be a mentor.

    Write your thoughts and ideas for improvement with each mentee.

3. **Develop a Cadre.** There are no perfect protégés—just like there

are no perfect mentors. That's why you want to develop a cadre of protégés. Not only will you be a better mentor if you're mentoring more than one person, but the mentees will learn from and help each other. They may even argue with each other, and some of their greatest contributions will come from these debates (e.g. Thomas Jefferson and John Marshall were both protégés of George Wythe, and their spirited debates about the role of the Supreme Court helped establish the entire American constitutional model). Look at great mentors in history and you'll often find a cadre of protégés, not just one or two.

Write your thoughts and ideas for improvement with each mentee.

4. **Teach The Path.** Mentors must invite mentees to The Path. In other words, you should teach them what The Path is from your unique perspective, find out where they're at on it, and get them working on the next step(s). This is the role of mentoring.

    Write your thoughts and ideas for improvement with each mentee.

5. **Be an Advocate.** You should be your protégés' advocate. This means different things to different protégés: you will need to make introductions, open doors, facilitate rapport and in general help them make the connections that will take them to the next level of impact. Invite them to a fellowship of craftsmanship and friendship, and teach them to shun the false "inner rings," like cliques, that C.S. Lewis despised.[40]

    Write your thoughts and ideas for improvement with each mentee.

6. **Be Selective.** Since you're going to give a lot of your life, time and energy to helping protégés, you need to know you really want to support and promote *them*. That's why you give them an impossible test when they ask you to mentor them. Tell them "no, I won't mentor you right now, but I want you to . . ." This story line is so prevalent as to be archetypical, even in modern cinema and popular entertainment—consider movies like *The Karate Kid* or *Finding Forrester,* and contemporary television programs like *The Apprentice, Top Chef,* the modeling and design shows, etc.

Do you have the right mentees? Why or why not? What should you do about it? Record your thoughts in your Journal.

7. **"No," and an Assignment.** Choose a test that really needs doing and is very difficult. If they don't do it, don't mentor them (we're talking to Mission Mentors here; other types of mentors should do tests, but not quite so *impossible*).

   This "no" with an assignment is the planned weeding out. Understand that you are not only testing them for your benefit. The mentee will also gain critical self-knowledge about her level of commitment, her response to challenges, her passion for her Call, etc. Without this type of self-knowledge the mentee cannot know what she can commit to, or if she really wants what you have to offer. Those who complete the assignment will have confidence in their ability to work effectively with you, and a trust and respect for you and themselves that will make all the difference in the success of your mentoring relationship.

   Write your thoughts and ideas for improvement with each mentee, and also make plans in a way that you will remember to do this in the future.

8. **From Impossible to Mundane.** A natural weeding out will also occur when you say "yes." When a mentee or potential protégé has completed the impossible test and you decide to mentor him, now put him to work doing the mundane basics. This will weed out the ones without the stamina, trust or conviction to follow through.

   Write your thoughts and ideas for improvement with each mentee.

9. **Fish in Your Pond.** Gather your target market and fish in your own pond. That is, your protégés are going to come out of your target market—whatever that is for your life mission. They may come from far away, but many will come from next door, speaking figuratively. The one thing you can be sure of is that your protégés will surprise you. You'll waste a lot of time if you try to find the perfect protégés and groom them. Let them come to you, and be prepared to accept them once they meet your tests.

Write your thoughts and ideas for improvement with each mentee and plans to do this in the future.

10. **Planning through Tests.** When your mentees are going through tests, help them strategize and plan. They need your expertise during tests.

Write your thoughts and ideas for improvement with each mentee.

11. **Rigor through Traps.** When your mentees are going through Traps, teach them high standards, and hold them to them. They need your leadership to escape Traps.

Write your thoughts and ideas for improvement with each mentee.

12. **Empathy through Trials.** When they are going through Trials, be there for them. They need you to be more of a soul mentor at this point, to really care and show humanity that transcends the mentoring relationship without compromising it.

Write your thoughts and ideas for improvement with each mentee.

13. **Stay the Course.** Remain on The Path yourself. You are on a further iteration of The Path, a later turn, and your leadership and example will be a great encouragement and inspiration to them.

The Work of Student Whispering

Mentoring on The Path is not easy, and even the best and most experienced mentors have to personalize their mentoring to each and every mentee.

Student Whispering is hard work, specifically the hard work contained in the exercises of this book. If you skipped them, you will likely struggle to Whisper and wonder if Student Whispering is even real. You may even doubt that greatly inspiring all students is possible and turn back to the force and bribe methods of Stick and Carrot. But those who do all the exercises, or learn the same lessons some other way, will have a very different experience. They will be Student Whisperers, knowing how to consistently inspire, and their mentoring will reflect this.

Finally, remember that there is a powerful relationship between mentoring and The Path. One does not truly exist without the other. There is no mentor without a mentee, and no mentee without The Path. People may use different names or details when describing The Path, but the principles are the same.

Learn as much about The Path as possible, looking for it in its many derivations in life, the experiences of others, readings, entertainment and indeed everywhere. Great mentoring is an art, and its canvas or stage is The Path.

Spirals

by Oliver DeMille & Tiffany Earl

If the ideas in this book are new and challenging to you, it may be advisable to spend some time mastering the principles in the previous chapters before taking on this final one. For some "holistic" type thinkers, however, this final concept may be the element that brings it all into synchronicity. This final section is something of a master class for those who are in Mission Phase[41] and need to see the whole picture at once.

Even though this is a book about Student Whispering and The Path that leads to success, we want to clarify that "success" is only the goal of The Path—not of life.

For example: draw a diagram on a piece of paper using a circle to represent The Path with the 7 Tests spread around it. You now have a working model for success in whatever goals you seek. Do a separate page for each of your major goals. When you have made a Path chart for each goal (past, present and future), you will have a stack of papers.

If you consider the overlaying relationship of these from a side or three-dimensional view, these cycles create a spiral. It is this Spiral of Paths that charts your happiness in life.

A person who succeeds in every individual circle on every goal can still be unhappy. Mentoring helps us succeed on The Path; but the real key is to find happiness in the Spiral that is our life.

Some may picture a computer-generated spiral with each level increasing in size as it rises upward or spools down, but that isn't what we think of at all. Instead, picture a tornado. Or visualize a whirlpool drawing things into its depth, strong and willful. Now that's a spiral! And it is closer to life and reality than a mathematically constructed spiral image.

In reality, spirals contain few straight lines or equally spaced progressions like those printed out on engineering paper. They are organic, moving, changing, percolating, shifting. Like fire, they defy prediction. They feel *alive*.

Whatever they are, the spirals of our lives *feel*. Or at least we feel *them*—usually deeply and profoundly. This feeling is what makes us know we are alive, regardless of what science or theology or anything else may tell us. "I feel, therefore I am" is good philosophy, and we believe it is true. Or: "Feeling is knowing," as Oliver's first martial arts instructor was fond of saying.

Usually, The Path of a particular Call will eventually end. We may abandon it—right or wrong. We may become stuck on it, circling like a rat on a track—missing out on the upward progress in the Spiral due to our failure to meet the Tests, Trials or Traps. Or, with the help of a great mentor and commitment to the principles of progress, we succeed and move upward on the spiraling Path. Hopefully our journey takes us to another right Path, and then another; but each Path, vital to all success, is also finite in some respects. Most meaningful goals do, in fact, have a completion, a fruition—a resolution.

In contrast, the Spiral is us—the great journey of our souls. We are always on it, at some level, and we always will be. Even the "enlightened ones" of the great world traditions spend their days on many Spirals, helping others on their journey.

Where is your Spiral taking you? Is it lifting you up? Is it pulling you into its depth? There are many ways to visualize this, and we favor whichever one works for you.

Consider the great Spiral of your whole existence. It may include experiences from before this life, your genetic or experiential connection to ancestors and posterity, or futures you're only beginning to conceptualize. Whatever your whole existence is to you, picture it as a spiral.

Now, in your mental picture, place yourself on it right now. Where are you? Where are you going? What are you supposed to be doing here, right now? We all need to ask if we are at the right place, doing the right things, going in the right direction.

Are you? Picture the Spiral again, in your mind, and ask these questions. Then make life choices accordingly.

This pattern of inviting us to conceptualize, ask and choose is the crux of Student Whispering.

Iterations

Each full Path is only one "iteration," cycle, or turn on our life's Spiral. Each iteration of The Path teaches unique lessons; it also reinforces common themes. For example, most people live several of the following iterations: physical growth, mental development, social maturation, educational attainment, romantic relationships, work training, career experience, family building, and others.

A successful pregnancy is an iconic microcosm of The Path, while a great marriage is perhaps the great macro-version of The Path. One takes months, the other a lifetime; and both, hopefully, follow The Path of All Success.

Other common iterations of The Path include grandparenting, the business cycle, economic cycles, crossing an ocean or desert, building an organization, raising a child, developing a friendship, creating a true community, progressing through the seasons of a year, fully experiencing a day (with its entire 24-hours), doing a project, taking a trip, going through college, reading a book, raising a garden, assembling a car, taking a class, getting in shape, leaving a legacy—and the list could go on and on.

Knowing The Path helps us succeed in any goal we pursue.

We wish we could say at this point that there are certain essential iterations of The Path—like physical growth, education, marriage or career; but who are we to judge the life of a baby whose life is tragically short, or the woman enslaved in the fifteenth century? Do such tragic circumstances dictate that such a life cannot have meaning on The Path? We say not. Each person has a right path (and perhaps several options for what the right path may be). Success comes from embracing the path and staying true to it—but the types of path people take are incredibly diverse.

We are so amazed and inspired by the variety of Paths people have followed! We are humbled and moved to be able to learn from their examples.

We also wish we could provide a general order that would guide readers on which iterations of The Path to take first, second and so on—but humans are often mistaken on what the best order may be for anyone else. Challenge enough it is to find our own Path!

Oliver: For example, my son Hyrum, who is brain injured from the terrible car accident I mentioned earlier, certainly follows a different order of iterations than the norm. But his successes on The Path through multiple iterations are constantly amazing and so inspiring! He laughs daily at the pain and eagerly greets each morning with excitement and anticipation. He even sings at the top of his lungs before the rest of the household is up and about.

My own order of planned iterations changed the day of his accident. As I have worked with mentees over the years, I have witnessed many orders of iterations. People choose an iteration when a Call comes, and the order is what it is.

Spiral Lessons

Some people choose a few iterations, while others elect to engage many. We don't know if any "Spiral rules" exist, but our view is that no single way is inherently best—people must choose their own best way. We each choose what is right for us, and let others do the same. Then we help each other along the way.

Few plots are older or have worse endings than *Romeo & Juliet*-type parents trying to control or micromanage the iterations of their children for selfish reasons. The same applies to spouses.

People may pursue multiple iterations at once, or sometimes have the rare luxury of focusing on just one at a time. When a Call comes, each of us must consider and choose wisely. This is clearly a key principle of the Spiral, along with other basic guidelines such as:

- Stay on The Path in order to succeed
- Get the right mentors at the right times
- Make the correct Vital Choices

Of course, key advice on The Path is simply to trust God (the Universe)—especially in the midst of an Ultimate Test.

Perhaps the best axiom of the Spiral may be to consider the full Spiral as we make significant choices, especially at three key places in life: during an Ultimate Test, at the beginning of a new Path, and *Now*— in the present moment.

When you find yourself in a Path or Spiral repeat loop, where you seem to be dealing with the same test or problem over and over, recognize this explicitly and set out to resolve the situation or learn the lessons you have failed to grasp in the past. Specifically: try naming the problem, draw up a Seven-Test Path diagram about it, seek inspiration, and perhaps get a Call and mentors to address it. Then follow through. If it truly is a Test (and not a Trial), you should be able to move on from such a loop. We were meant to learn and progress, not to continually repeat negative loops over and over.

If you find yourself doing so many iterations of The Path at once that you are spiraling backwards instead of progressing, you know what to do. Put each Path iteration on its own diagram, then prioritize. Listen to the same voice that issued the Calls—your allegiance. Plan, organize, choose wisely, get the right mentor, and then take action that moves you forward on the Spiral instead of backwards. You may find that some of the objectives you have chosen are put on hold, or turn out to be Tests, rather than true Calls.

If too many voices are telling you what to do, thank them all politely and get clear on your allegiance—then act accordingly. Keep an eye on the trees blazed by your true and right allegiance, not by Others. Follow The Path, not the trail with the loudest camp counselor. Whatever you do, don't listen to the voices of fear.

Too many human Spirals are commanded by fear and anger. These weaken and darken a Spiral.

Human beings feel vulnerable. Having experienced loss and pain, we seek to avoid future pain or loss. People develop many strategies for this—thinking that if they have enough money perhaps they'll be immune to loss, or that if they cynically expect nothing they won't be disappointed. Other such strategies include thinking that if they just have enough faith, a higher power will always keep them from experiencing pain; or if they are in a high enough position of power they can control everything and never be hurt.

The list goes on—and none of it works. Ultimately, everyone faces pain and loss as part of the human experience. Rich, poor, tall, short, smart, etc.—we all experience life struggles.

Adults often fear loss more than children do. Because the memory of past injuries is very real to us, adults feel more vulnerable. Children tend to seek for joy now, not worrying about tomorrow. They believe they will live forever, while many adults subconsciously know that their lives and those of everybody they know are temporary. This sense of vulnerability, fear of loss, anger over loss (often before it comes!) and attempts to avoid loss and pain whatever the cost, create many of the miserable and dysfunctional careers, lives, relationships, economies and nations of this world.

What a tragedy! So many people heed these things and spend more time on them than anything else in their lives. The world this builds is not ideal.

The gurus among us, those who have overcome the fears and do not dwell on or act from them, say something very different: "Become as a little child; fear not; as a man thinketh, so is he; give no thought for tomorrow; ask and ye shall receive; let not your heart be troubled," and so on. Such ideals were taught and lived by Abraham, Krishna, Moses, Buddha, Jesus, Gandhi, Yogananda, the Dalai Lama and many others including "secular" sages like Cicero, Aurelius and Einstein.

These ideals were, and are, believed and lived by those who got past the fear. As Einstein put it: "Hail to the man who went through life always helping others, knowing no fear . . ." and "Everyone has been given an endowment that he must strive to develop in the service of mankind."[42]

These concepts are powerful.

Is your Spiral of life increasing your happiness? Solidly? Constantly? Effectively? What do the Real You and Inspirer voices say?

We have spent this much time on the topics of Spirals and Fear because these are two of the voices many people listen to. They Whisper to us day and night, whoever we are. It is the greatest role of Student Whisperers to understand this. In each decision on every path, we choose between the voice of Fear and the Call of our better Spiral. Student Whisperers follow the right blazes and teach their mentees to do the same.

Mentors help us on The Path. Great Student Whisperers help us on the Spiral, as well. They help us see our current work and lives in the context of something much bigger, and they help us muster the courage to make wise decisions accordingly. Student Whisperers help us see more in ourselves, in our lives, in our purpose—because they help us put aside the fear and follow the Spiral upward.

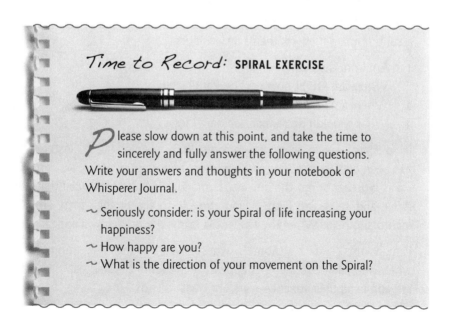

Time to Record: SPIRAL EXERCISE

*P*lease slow down at this point, and take the time to sincerely and fully answer the following questions. Write your answers and thoughts in your notebook or Whisperer Journal.

~ Seriously consider: is your Spiral of life increasing your happiness?
~ How happy are you?
~ What is the direction of your movement on the Spiral?

Are you happier now than ten years ago? Three years? One?

~ Where is your happiness Spiral headed? Where will it take you in a month? In a year? In a decade?

~ The Path has 7 predictable Tests. Overcome them and you will succeed. The Spiral is admittedly more layered, but it can also be very simple. Ask yourself: What is The Call of your Spiral?

~ What are your roadblocks to a life of greater happiness?

~ What mentors do you need to truly and effectively spiral upwards?

~ What actions do you need to take to truly spiral ahead?

~ What else should you do?

Conclusion

Student Whisperers consistently mentor at an inspired level. They know how to invite in the spark of inspiration whenever it is needed, because they know how to deeply understand themselves and their students, through conceptualizing, questioning and choosing. The great questions they ask themselves include:

1. Am I on The Path?
2. Where am I right now on The Path?
3. Where am I now on the Spiral of my life?
4. What should I do to increase happiness?

If your answers to these feel lacking, look to epiphanies. Einstein has been quoted as saying that the most important question we can ask is whether or not the universe is friendly. We are convinced that it is—and so is The Path. If you struggle to accept this, there are mentors to help. When the student is ready, the teacher will appear.

Perhaps the greatest attribute of the Universe is this very thing— when we need help, mentors appear. Such mentors—spiritual, mortal, and in all their varieties—are our truest friends.

Aristotle wondered if there is anything greater than friendship. After studying soul mentors, parent mentors, The Path, the Spiral, marriage, children, gurus, epiphanies and all the other types of mentors, for us the question is resolved. Perhaps the great guru Yogananda said it most eloquently: "The best way to be successful in this adventure of life is to be your own friend."[43]

Be your own friend. The Path is there for you. You can consciously manage the voices that Whisper in your mind, and as you do this your ability to Whisper to those you mentor will improve. You can assess your life and make the choices that will spiral you toward increasing happiness. You can reach out and mentor others, helping them do the same.

When you are ready, the mentors will appear.

Look around. Mentors are everywhere. You are ready.

Appendix I

Student Whispering Questions

- What kind of mentor am I for this mentee right now?
- What Phase of Learning is my mentee in right now?[44]
- Where is my mentee on The Path?
- What Walls or Roadblocks is my mentee facing?
- What is the next step for my mentee on The Path?
- What is the Inner Critic telling my mentee?
- What is the Inner Judge telling my mentee?
- What is the Inner Victim telling my mentee?
- What is the Inner Rebel telling my mentee?
- Does my mentee seem to be listening to some other negative voice, and if so what is that voice telling her?
- What is the Real Her telling my mentee?
- What is the Inspirer telling my mentee?
- Where is my mentee on the Manager/Artist balance?
- Where do I tend to be as a mentor on the Manager/Artist balance?
- What kind of mentor does my mentee need me to be right now on the Manager/Artist balance?
- What changes do I need to make to effectively be the mentor my mentee needs right now on the Manager/Artist balance?
- Where is my mentee on the Healer/Warrior balance?
- Where do I tend to be as a mentor on the Healer/Warrior balance?
- What kind of mentor does my mentee need me to be right now on the Healer/Warrior balance?
- What changes do I need to make to effectively be the mentor my mentee needs right now on the Healer/Warrior balance?
- What Whispering Quadrant does my mentee need right now, and what does that tell me?
- What Whispering Quadrant am I in right now, and how do I need to progress in order to be the best mentor I can?

- What are my mentee's greatest dreams?
- What are my mentee's biggest fears?
- What are my mentee's big angers?
- What four things does my mentee most need of me in the next few months?
- What five things does my mentee need me to *be*?
- If my mentee had an extra hour each day, how would I recommend he use it?
- What is the single most important thing I should do right now (or in the days, weeks or months just ahead)?
- What are my mentee's archetypes?
- What do my mentee's archetypes tell me about how to mentor?
- Where am I on the Spiral of life?

Appendix II

A Student Whisperer's Guide

DAILY

- Apply the Mentor's Creed

WEEKLY

- Voice of the Real Me exercise (plans for each mentee)
- Inspirer Voice exercise (plans for each mentee)

MONTHLY

- Manager/Artist exercise (for each mentee)
- Healer/Warrior exercise (for each mentee)
- Key Questions exercise (for each mentee)
- Re-read the Student Whisperer's Creed (apply to each mentee)

SIX-MONTH INVENTORY

- Clarify Which Step on The Path (for each mentee)
- Archetypes exercise (for each mentee)
- Nine Lessons exercise (for each mentee)

Appendix III

The Student Whisperer's Creed

1. Great mentors believe in freedom—in the world and in one's personal education.

2. Great mentors believe in individualizing the process and content of each student's learning.

3. Great mentors believe that each student has a unique and vital mission in life.

4. Great mentors believe that each student has untapped genius, with the seeds of what is needed for his/her personal mission(s).

5. Great mentors believe that most missions benefit from a superb, broad, deep, leadership education in the classics.

6. Great mentors believe that students learn more and better when they are inspired and intrinsically motivated than when they are compelled by requirements.

7. Great mentors believe that one of the most powerful means of inspiration is example.

8. Great mentors set an example of rigorous, passionate study of the classics.

9. Great mentors exemplify seeking truth and searching out principles in many worldviews, ideas, sources and perspectives, and comparing them with the principles taught in their core book.

10. Great mentors exemplify pushing themselves outside of their own comfort zone and consistently expanding their breadth and depth of knowledge and skills.

11. Great mentors set an example and encourage students to learn from all mentors—authors, teachers, innovators, artists, thinkers, scientists, classmates, spiritual insights, and any other enlightening source.

12. Great mentors foster a culture of friendship and cooperation in and out of the classroom. Mentors genuinely like their students, and they know their students will teach them and friends/classmates much of what is learned.

13. Great mentors use many tools to inspire and create an environment of learning, including group discussion, readings, writing, lecture, simulations, field experience, personal coaching, refinement of talents and skills, visiting speakers, assignments, small group tutorials, projects, etc. They feel successful when students leave their meetings (or classrooms) and passionately study with self-starting enthusiasm and rigorous tenacity.

14. Great mentors seek and revere quality, and therefore do not orient themselves by rote conformity or other arbitrary measures. They know that simple, inspired study is the surest path to excellence in learning.

15. Great mentors acknowledge the working of higher principles and inspiration, and operate in harmony with them in a process that literally changes the world—building leaders for all walks of life who will greatly impact the future of family, prosperity and freedom.

16. To all these, great mentors add their own personal style, gifts, interests, specialties and areas of passion and enthusiasm. They truly pass on a little bit of their best selves to every student they serve.

Endnotes

1 Whereas the term "mentor" derives from a proper name in a Greek story about a man, Mentor, who was a father figure and teacher to Telemachus, and the "-or" ending does not refer to one who takes a certain action (as in "spectat-or," "jur-or," "don-or," "dictat-or"), the term "mentee" is a back formation.

2 See the original movie "Karate Kid," where the martial arts master Mr. Miyagi has his protégée practice basic fundamentals through repetition by waxing a car, sanding a fence, etc.

3 Rick has since recovered completely.

4 Spoken by Lady Macbeth in Shakespeare's *Macbeth*, Act 1 Scene 7.

5 See Descartes, *Replies 7, AT 7:481*.

6 See Descartes, Prin. *1.13, AT 8a: 9-10*.

7 See Nichomachus, *Introduction to Arithmetic*, ch. 2.

8 See Dewey, *Experience and Education*, ch. 1.

9 See Hobbes, *Leviathan*, Introduction.

10 See Dewey, *Experience and Education*, ch. 1.

11 See Suzuki, *Nurtured by Love: The Classic Approach to Talent Education*.

12 Ibid.

13 Ibid.

14 Ibid.

15 See Allan Bloom, *The Closing of the American Mind*.

16 Ibid.

17 Theodore Roosevelt speech, National Convention of the Progressive Party, Chicago, IL, August 6, 1912.

18 See Demosthenes, *The Third Philippic*.

19 Patrick Henry speech, "Give Me Liberty or Give Me Death," March 23, 1775.

20 See Demosthenes, *The Third Philippic*.

21 See Aneladee Milne and Tiffany Earl, *The New Commonwealth School*.

22 See Marcus Buckingham: *First, Break All the Rules*; *Now, Discover Your Strengths*; and others.

23 Based on two statistics: According to capenet.org (Council for American Private Education), there were 6,049,000 students enrolled in private schools as of 2009, representing 11% of the school-aged population. According to nheri.org (National Home Education Research Institute), Brian Ray has estimated that as of Spring 2008, there were over 2,000,000 school-aged children being home schooled. At more than 8,000,000 students in non-compulsory programs, this constitutes 15% of the pre-college student population.

24 See Maria Montessori, *The Absorbent Mind*.

25 See Tolkien, *The Lord of the Rings*.

26 See Dennis R. Deaton, *Ownership Spirit: The One Grand Key That Changes Everything Else*.

27 **Note from the authors:** Religious sentiment is one of the most powerfully animating and unifying of forces—both for good and for ill (sometimes within the same community or culture). It is unfortunate that some people of the most deeply held convictions about peace, charity, freedom, family, etc., seem to have little ability to connect with anyone but those who already share their specific religious views—from Judeo-Christian to Ethical Humanist. We fear this limits their influence for good; and in most cases we don't see that the actual tenets of their faith require this sort of isolationism, but rather idealize and promote just the opposite.

As authors and educators, we are sometimes asked to comment on the "ambiguous" tone of our writings and lectures when we refer to "God," "Good" and "the Universe" interchangeably. Over the years, we have realized that the principles of Leadership Education ("Thomas Jefferson Education," or "TJEd") were resonating among people all over the world from distinct backgrounds. There are TJEd practitioners in England, China, Indonesia, New Zealand, Korea, Madagascar, Australia, Uganda, Qatar, Jordan, Puerto Rico, Guatemala, Mexico, and of course, the USA and Canada, etc. We personally know of many individuals and families who are LDS, evangelical Christian, Catholic, Buddhist, Hindu, Jewish, Muslim, Ethical Humanist, Atheist, etc.

One of the basic tenets of Leadership Education is to safeguard the sacred will of the individual, and encourage and empower the individual to act congruently with his or her conscience. TJEd does not seek to admonish parents, families, teachers or students on what "right" is for an individual—either in education or religion, or any other arena. Parents have the God-given privilege to guide their children on this path, and we would never want for any parent to delegate to us, as the promoters of an educational philosophy, that sacred role.

Our religious lives are the center of everything for us and our religious convictions inform and animate everything we do. At the same time, we have sought for our respective professional endeavors not to be a pulpit from which to persuade others to see things "one" way, but rather a light to help each person come to understand better his or her highest path.

We dearly hope that such inclusive language is not a stumbling block for those of devout religious convictions—just as we hope that people of different religions, or no dependence on religion at all, can likewise find meaning and inspiration as they ponder on the principles that we endeavor to teach. It is absolutely not a reflection of any wavering or lack of interest on our part, but rather a humble invitation for people of any creed (ourselves included) to draw closer, step by step, to the process of aligning their lives and choices with the greatest power in the universe. This is not an expression of moral ambiguity for us, but rather an expression of deep faith.

We appreciate one woman's comment about it being a great jumping-off point for the discussion of world religions. In our opinion, there is a time for us to help our children and especially our adult mentees to develop a more inclusive vocabulary and communication style. We are deeply optimistic about the potential for good as people of pure faith and strong convictions cooperate in achieving common goals. To that end, we hope that our writing style is not only inclusive of people of any worthy moral creed, but is also helpful in building rapport between people of conscience everywhere.

28 See Lewis, *Prince Caspian.*

29 See Porter, *Pollyanna.*

30 See Gardner, *Multiple Intelligences.*

31 For more information on the Phases, and renegotiation of lost Phases, see Oliver and Rachel DeMille, *Leadership Education: The Phases of*

Learning and Rachel DeMille, "A Thomas Jefferson Education in our Home: Educating through the Phases of Learning." Thanks to Aneladee Milne for suggesting the concept of the phases and her work defining the phases.

32 Ibid.

33 From the original movie "Karate Kid," where the martial arts master Mr. Miyagi has his protégée practice basic fundamentals through repetition by waxing a car, sanding a fence, etc.

34 We highly recommend the work of relationship/parenting mentor Nicholeen Peck for mentoring in setting up an environment of love, discipline and order that empowers the troubled child or youth to make good choices and take responsibility for their happiness and behavior. See Peck, *Parenting: A House United*, and www.teachingselfgovernment.com.

35 See Jung, *Man and his Symbols*.

36 For more extensive lists of archetypes, see the writings of Carl Jung, Joseph Campbell, and Caroline Myss.

37 See op. cit., "Karate Kid."

38 The 7 Keys of Great Teaching:
    1. Classics, not Textbooks
    2. Mentors, not Professors
    3. Inspire, not Require
    4. Structure Time, not Content
    5. Quality, not Conformity
    6. Simplicity, not Complexity
    7. You, not Them

    For more on the 7 Keys, see http://tjed.org/about-tjed/7-keys/.

39 The 5 Environments of Mentoring include: Tutorial, Group Discussion, Lecture, Testing and Coaching. For more information see Oliver DeMille, *A Thomas Jefferson Education: Teaching a Generation of Leaders for the Twenty-first Century*, pp. 74-78.

40 See Lewis, *The Weight of Glory*.

41 From pp. 251 of *Leadership Education: The Phases of Learning* by Oliver and Rachel DeMille: "*Mission Phase is a metamorphosis of becoming that marks a new level of commitment to the primary allegiance, a new clarity and consecration to mission, a more refined ability to affect*

change in the world and a greater ability to impact the people within the sphere of influence. The catharsis of this adult transition transports the individual to a time when his purpose is to achieve the personal mission and impact for which his Educational Phases have prepared him. The drive to 'prepare for greatness' shifts to a drive to deliver. In short, the foundational and educational phases brought to fruition demand that an individual inspire greatness in others and move the cause of liberty."

42 See Albert Einstein, *The World as I See It.*

43 See Paramahansa Yogananda, *Living Fearlessly: Bringing Out Your Inner Soul Strength.*

44 For more on the Phases of Learning, see DeMille, *Leadership Education: The Phases of Learning* or visit http://tjed.org/about-tjed.

About the Authors

Oliver DeMille is the author of *A Thomas Jefferson Education, The Coming Aristocracy, FreedomShift,* and other books on education and freedom. He is a popular keynote speaker for business, educational and civic events, and he is the founder of George Wythe University. He has mentored the great books and leadership education for twenty years, and writes a blog for the Center for Social Leadership. Oliver and his wife Rachel co-authored the book *Leadership Education,* and they are the parents of eight children. These books and many other resources are available at TJEd.org.

Connect with Oliver on Twitter, LinkedIn, Facebook and YouTube. Visit him on the web and subscribe to his daily emails at http://oliverdemille.com.

Tiffany Rhoades Earl is the author of *SayGoBeDo, Mentor's Guide, Parent Mentoring,* and *The Thomas Jefferson Planner,* as well as other books and audios on mentoring, education, and impact. She is the co-founder of *Leadership Education Mentoring Institute* (LEMI), which develops Commonwealth Schools, promotes families, and mentors others along The Path. Tiffany and her husband Rick (her partner in LEMI) are the parents of five children.

Tiffany's works, including resources on key topics taught in this book, are available at www.lemimentortraining.com.

LEMI

~ Builds Community
~ Trains Parent Mentors and Leadership Mentors to:
~ Mentor youth and adults through Scholar Phase and along The Path

If you enjoyed hearing from Tiffany Earl, you may also benefit from the mentoring and resources available through Leadership Education Mentoring Institute:

Building Community

- Create a New Commonwealth School in your area:
  NCS Builder
- Teach other families and adults: The Liber Community Series

Leadership Mentors

- "The Secret To Wealth: Mastering the 6 Creative Powers" mp3cd series.
- "The Power Structure of Freedom" mp3cd series
- The Mentor's Guide: LEMI Philosophy and Methodology audio and book
- Say Go Be Do book or audio download
- "Seasons" What is your number one, two, and three? Systems for success audio.
- "Forms and The 21st Century" audio download
- LEMI CLASSICS Top ten audio lessons on the Art of Mentoring
- Live Mentoring Series by Tiffany Earl and her team at LEMI

Parent Mentoring

- Parent Mentoring audio seminar: 7 Musts for Effective Parenting
- LEMI CLASSICS Top Ten Picks by Parents

Scholar Projects

- Leadership classes in your community!

Visit LEMI online at www.lemimentortraining.com

A THOMAS JEFFERSON EDUCATION
AN EDUCATION TO MATCH OUR MISSION

What parent hasn't thought:

My kids deserve better than this; ...but this is all I know

Parents and teachers often get so concerned with the "what" to teach that we neglect the "how" and the "why." Yet these make all the difference between success and failure. Understanding them also creates happier, more empowered children.

TJEd gives you the "how" and the "why" to make the "what" more powerful, more memorable, more relevant to your children. As you apply the 7 Keys of Great Teaching and the 4 Phases of Learning, your kids will love to learn, and you will be empowered to inspire them to greatness.

Don't just do the conveyor belt at home. Your kids need...

An Education to Match Their Mission.

Visit www.TJEd.org today and get your free gifts

1. The Future of American Education: 8 Trends Every Parent Should Understand by Oliver DeMille (83 page article in pdf format)
2. List of Recommended Classics (15 page pdf with lists for Family Reading, Youth, Adults, Biblical Highlights, Math Classics and more!)
3. What is TJEd? (37 page pdf covering The 3 Types of Education, The Phases of Learning, The 7 Keys of Great Teaching, etc.)
4. A Thomas Jefferson Education in our Home by Rachel DeMille (34 page article in pdf format; many have said this is their favorite TJEd article of all!)
5. Let's Learn Times Tables by Rachel DeMille (11 page pdf with step-by-step suggestions for how to painlessly commit the multiplication tables 1 – 12 to memory!)

Explore TJEd.org to find these other resources to help you get off the conveyor belt and on the Path of Leadership Education:

- Daily Inspire! Emails
- Free audio downloads and sample excerpts from the TJEd Library
- TJEd.org blog
- TJEd Online Store (with books, audios, CDs and Gift Certificates)
- Find us on Facebook, Twitter and YouTube

Get your FREE
Student Whisperer Journal...

Enhance your experience with *The Student Whisperer* by downloading your free Student Whisperer Journal on the Student Whisperer website.

- Enjoy free audio and printable resources
- Browse our other offerings to help you in your mentoring
- Get free, personalized assistance to engage with your place on the Path

**Visit us today and download
your Student Whisperer Journal at:**

http://Student-Whisperer.com.

Book design and illustration by Daniel Ruesch
www.danielruesch.net